Nabokov's Cinematic Afterlife

# Nabokov's Cinematic Afterlife

EWA MAZIERSKA

McFarland & Company, Inc., Publishers
*Jefferson, North Carolina, and London*

LIBRARY OF CONGRESS CATALOGUING-IN-PUBLICATION DATA

Mazierska, Ewa.
 Nabokov's cinematic afterlife / Ewa Mazierska.
    p.    cm.
 Includes bibliographical references and index.

 ISBN 978-0-7864-4543-1
 softcover : 50# alkaline paper ∞

 1. Nabokov, Vladimir Vladimirovich, 1899–1977 — Film adaptations.  2. Motion pictures and literature.  I. Title.
 PG3476.N3Z7375    2011
 791.43'75 — dc22                                            2010041977

British Library cataloguing data are available

©2011 Ewa Mazierska. All rights reserved

*No part of this book may be reproduced or transmitted in any form or by any means, electronic or mechanical, including photocopying or recording, or by any information storage and retrieval system, without permission in writing from the publisher.*

Front Cover: John Moulder-Brown as Frank, David Niven as Dreyer and Gina Lollobrigida as Martha in the 1972 *King, Queen, Knave,* directed by Jerzy Skolimowski

Manufactured in the United States of America

*McFarland & Company, Inc., Publishers*
 *Box 611, Jefferson, North Carolina 28640*
 *www.mcfarlandpub.com*

# Acknowledgments

This book would not be possible without the help of many colleagues and friends, to whom I wish to express my gratitude. Agnès Edel-Roy, Petra Hanáková, Lars Kristensen, Robert Murphy, Will Norman, Elżbieta Ostrowska, Jonathan Owen, Derek Schilling and Michael Witt read the whole or parts of this manuscript, and provided insightful comments. Eva Näripea helped me familiarize myself with Estonian cinema and obtained a wealth of information about one of the films discussed in the book, *Affair of Honor* by Valentin Kuik. Adam Wyżyński, from the Polish Film Archive, provided me with much of the secondary material used in this book. Jeff Edmunds (from *Zembla* website), Agnès Edel-Roy and Lars Kristensen were also helpful in locating some of the material which was difficult to find. I am also indebted to Felix Maschmann for sending me a copy of *Mademoiselle O*, and to Valentin Kuik and Jerzy Skolimowski for providing me with valuable information about the production of their films, and for granting me permission to use stills from them.

Finally, I am grateful to the School of Journalism, Media and Communication at the University of Central Lancashire for financing my trip to St. Petersburg in June 2009, which allowed me to participate in the Fourth International Nabokov Conference, meet Nabokov scholars and visit many places connected with Nabokov's life.

A preliminary version of Chapter 4 was published in *Journal of Adaptation in Film and Performance,* Vol. 3, No. 1. I thank the journal editors (Richard Hand and Katja Krebs) and the publisher (Intellect) for permission to reproduce the essay.

# Table of Contents

*Acknowledgments*     v
*Abbreviations*     ix
*Introduction: Nabokov's Afterlife in Cinema*     1

1. Humbert Between Dignity and Romanticism: *Lolita* by Stanley Kubrick (1962) and Adrian Lyne (1997)     13
2. Going Blind in Swinging London: *Laughter in the Dark* by Tony Richardson (1969)     51
3. Nabokov, or the Logic of Late Capitalism: *King, Queen, Knave* by Jerzy Skolimowski (1972)     70
4. Escape into a Different Person, Escape into a Different Reality: *Despair* by Rainer Werner Fassbinder (1978)     87
5. Remembrance of Things Unspoken: *Mademoiselle O* by Jérôme Foulon (1994)     104
6. Duel in Contemporary Estonia: *An Affair of Honor* by Valentin Kuik (1999)     125
7. Nabokov as a Gentle Feminist: *The Luzhin Defence* by Marleen Gorris (2000)     143
8. From B-Movie Script to Greek Tragedy: "The Assistant Producer" by Vladimir Nabokov, and *Triple Agent* by Eric Rohmer (2004)     163
9. Vladimir Nabokov and Jean-Luc Godard     181

*Appendix: Films Discussed in the Book*     211
*Chapter Notes*     215
*Works Cited*     219
*Index*     229

# Abbreviations

| | |
|---|---|
| AH | *An Affair of Honor* |
| AP | *The Assistant Producer* |
| BS | *Bend Sinister* |
| Def | *The Luzhin Defense* |
| Des | *Despair* |
| Ench | *The Enchanter* |
| Gift | *The Gift* |
| Laugh | *Laughter in the Dark* |
| LL | *Lectures on Literature* |
| LRL | *Lectures on Russian Literature* |
| KQK | *King, Queen, Knave* |
| Lo | *Lolita* |
| LoS | *Lolita: A Screenplay* |
| PoT | *Problems of Translation: "Onegin" in English* |
| SO | *Strong Opinions* |
| NWL | *Dear Bunny, Dear Volodia. The Nabokov-Wilson Letters* |
| SM | *Speak, Memory: An Autobiography Revisited* |

# Introduction
## Nabokov's Afterlife in Cinema

"An author's fondest dream is to turn the reader into a spectator; is this ever attained?"—Vladimir Nabokov, *Despair*

"A tortured author and a deceived reader, this is the inevitable outcome of arty paraphrase."—Vladimir Nabokov, *Strong Opinions*

"If one of the greatest stylists of modern literature, a man bilingual from earliest childhood, cannot translate his own poetry, then who can?"—D. Barton Johnson, "Contrasting Phonoaesthetics, or, Why Nabokov Gave Up Translating Poetry as Poetry"

"I always advise the copying of a model. It is impossible to copy exactly; new blood is always infused, and it is by that we can judge the poet."—Jean Cocteau, Francis Steegmuller, *Cocteau: A Biography*

This book is devoted to film adaptations of Nabokov's prose and the links between Nabokov's books and contemporary cinema. The premise of this study is that they are worth researching because they give us new insights into specific books and films, and a wider area of the interstice between literature and cinema. However, before I move to exploring them in detail, it is worth asking why filmmakers have been interested in Nabokov's prose.

## The Pleasures and Dangers of Adapting Nabokov

There are more than ten films based on Nabokov's books,[1] making him one of the most screened twentieth century writers. One reason for this interest of cinema in his works is the sheer power of Nabokov's name, especially in the 1960s and 1970s, when a large proportion of films based on his books were made and several projects of high-budget films were discussed, including an adaptation of *Ada*.[2] In this context it is understandable that *Lolita*, being the most popular work by Nabokov, was the first book to make it to the screen and that the resulting film became the biggest box office hit of all Nabokov adaptations. Secondly, Nabokov's books include two elements which are very attractive for the average cinemagoer: quirky and forbidden romance, and death. It is no coincidence that those of Nabokov's works which contain them in the highest proportion—*Lolita, Laughter in the Dark* and *King, Queen, Knave*—were filmed first. This does not exhaust all the reasons why they made it to the screen, but they certainly facilitated this road. Thirdly, Nabokov's books are renowned for their "cinematic qualities," such as the use of frames, stage directions and descriptions suggesting specific camera positions and movements. They also contain film imagery, focus on the problems of sight, apply narrative techniques that can be compared to non-continuity editing, and feature characters for whom cinema is at least as important as reality—who are even, as Julian Moynahan puts it, "driven to madness and death through their devotion to false images" (Moynahan 1971a: 13). Again, the novels which were screened first, *Lolita, Laughter in the Dark* and *King, Queen, Knave,* can be described as particularly cinematic. Finally, I suggest that Nabokov's books are of interest to cinema because of their adaptability to different times and places. This potential to travel results from their different settings and the complicated national and cultural background of the characters, and the fact that they were written in three different languages. Hence, they might appeal to filmmakers of different nationalities. They are also adaptable to different settings and times because of Nabokov's conscious attempt in some of his works, such as, again, *Laughter in the Dark, King, Queen, Knave* and *Ada,* to erase their historical contexts, furnishing them with a fable-like quality. The transnational aspect of Nabokov's works is confirmed by the fact that they attracted directors of many nationalities who find crossing national boundaries relatively easy. Among them we find an American, two Englishmen, an Austrian, a German, a Pole, a Dutchwoman, an Estonian and a Frenchman. The transnational character of Nabokov's prose is also corroborated by the national composition of the cast and crew of the respective films, and the complexities of their financing. To these reasons we can also add qualities of specific works which might appeal to specific filmmakers, such as their exploration of a divided self, surrealist imagery or an exploration of totalitarian rule.

However, the same reasons which attracted some filmmakers to Nabokov's works put others off. For example, Nabokov's reputation of being one of the greatest writers of the twentieth century brought, for many filmmakers, the danger of being overshadowed by the literary genius. Thomas Leitch attributes an anxiety of this kind to Alfred Hitchcock, writing that "in order to establish himself as an auteur, Hitchcock had to wrest authorship of his films away from another plausible candidate: the author of the original property" (Leitch 2005: 110). I am mentioning Hitchcock on this occasion not only because he perfected the art of adapting literary works without losing the authority and status of an author/auteur, but also because he is the filmmaker most often compared to Nabokov, despite the fact that he never adapted any of his works (for example, Stringer-Hye 2002; Davidson 2007; Straumann 2008). I will risk the statement that Hitchcock's avoidance of Nabokov's books helps us to see in him Nabokov's double. If he ever filmed a book by Nabokov, he would be reduced to the position of a mere adapter, and most likely one who did not to live up to the reputation of the original (as is the case with virtually all filmmakers discussed in this book). A similar avoidance strategy to Hitchcock's was employed by another unquestionable auteur, Jean-Luc Godard, whom I will compare with Nabokov in the last chapter of this book. In an early part of his career Godard also tapped obscure sources, even books he did not like, including the second-rate imitations of *Lolita*. Only when his position as an auteur became unchallenged, and, as he himself put it, he realized that on whatever project he embarked he would end up making his own film, did he adapt such well-known works as *King Lear* and *Carmen*. Even those filmmakers who are not concerned about being eclipsed by the author of the adapted book might regard the job of adapting a masterpiece superfluous on account of its perfection. Such an idea was put forward by François Truffaut in his interview with Hitchcock, when he stated, "Theoretically, a masterpiece is something that has already found its perfection of form, its definite form" (Truffaut 1985: 72). This view was echoed by Stanley Kubrick, who confessed about his adaptations of *Lolita*: "If it had been written by a lesser author, it might have been a better film" (LoBrutto 1997: 225).

Another factor which might act as an obstacle to filming Nabokov is the perceived closeness of his prose to cinema. Such a perception, on the one hand, potentially reduces the desirability of adapting his books for the screen because if Nabokov was able to turn the reader into a spectator, why repeat what he already achieved? Even if the filmmaker rejects this claim, s/he encounters a problem in transferring the cinematic aspect from book to screen. Such an operation is far from easy because the "cinematic qualities" of literature or other artworks are different from the "cinematic qualities" of cinema. For example, the mode of narration of a novel, suggesting a cinematic editing technique, when transposed to film, might come across as literary. This is because, as E. H. Gombrich and Nelson Goodman argue, the faithful adaptation is one in which there is a match between different elements used in different contexts to create the same or similar esthetic effect, rather than one in which the artists working in different media use the same elements (Gombrich and Goodman, quoted in Andrew 1992: 424–5). This failure in adapting an apparently cinematic work to screen is excellently illustrated by the case of René Magritte, who, on account of his interest in film, can be described as the "Nabokov of plastic arts." Robert Short observes "the loss of potency occurring with the transfer of Magrittian figures from the canvas to the screen. While they might tantalizingly imply movement, they just as determinedly resist it" (Short 1997: 107). If, against the odds, the adapter succeeds in adapting cinematic literature to screen, most likely his/her success will be regarded as easily achieved. If s/he fails, s/he might be criticized for the perceived lack of fidelity. As I will demonstrate in due course, films based on Nabokov's prose excellently illuminate the problem of transferring the cinematic element from literature to cinema. In practically all cases, when such a cinematic work was screened, especially *King, Queen, Knave* and *Laughter in the Dark*, we observe its drastic reduction. Paradoxically, the richest in cinematic references of all Nabokov adaptations is the film by Valentin Kuik, based on the short story "An Affair of Honor," where the cinematic references are more difficult to spot.

When talking about obstacles to screening Nabokov I shall also mention that although his books are adaptable to different locations, times and cultures, they were not welcome in all locations and times. This refers especially to the country where he was born, Russia. During communist rule, his books were forbidden and heavily criticized. Naturally, it meant that there was no possibility to film them. Censorship is also partly to blame for the lack of any Polish, Hungarian or Czech films based on Nabokov, although the Polish director Jerzy Skolimowski shot *King, Queen, Knave* in West Germany. I believe that the perception that Nabokov is not a "truly Russian writer" is a factor in the fact that no Russian director made a film based on his work, despite the particular Russian fondness for masterpieces of their own literature.

## *Critical Neglect*

The relationship between Nabokov's work and cinema is a subject of numerous studies and comments, but the focus of this type of scholarship until recently has been on the cinematic influences on Nabokov's books (for example, Appel 1974; Stuart 1978; Chatman 1978: 69–70; Wyllie 2003; Wyllie 2005) rather than on the way cinema makes use of Nabokov, except for the discussions of the two adaptations of *Lolita* (for example, Corliss 1994; 1998; Jenkins 1997; Stam 2005; 2007; Naremore 2007). Equally, the relationship between Nabokov's prose and developments in cinema that occurred after the writer ceased going to the movies, including European New Waves and postmodern cinema, remains practically untouched. Even in a book devoted specifically to the parallels between Nabokov's prose and other media, *Nabokov at the Limits* (Zunshine 1999), the relationship with film is missing.

In the light of a significant number of films based on Nabokov's prose, and the high profile of directors who made them, the lack of interest in Nabokov's afterlife in cinema is surprising. However, on reflection it is understandable. One reason for this neglect is the international and transnational character of the adaptations of Nabokov's works, as exemplified by the different nationalities of their directors. Although transnational cinema constitutes a growing sub-field of film studies, it is still a minority interest among film historians, who predominantly use a national framework. A national approach is no less prevalent in the studies of film adaptation. The majority of existing sources in English concern national rather than transnational cinema or, at best, the cinema of two countries using the same language (e.g., UK and USA, with examples being studies of adaptations of Jane Austen or Charles Dickens). Secondly, critical attention is focused on adaptations which constitute a cycle. By contrast, adaptations of Nabokov's works come across as the opposite of a cycle — a collection of random films made by a collection of random filmmakers not always for the right reasons. It thus feels difficult to draw a coherent picture of them and to justify placing them in one book. The third factor might be Nabokov's reputation as a difficult writer who should not be approached without a significant background in literary studies, which is less the case in the studies of films based on works by Charles Dickens, Jane Austen, E. M. Forster or Shakespeare. Not only are these authors somewhat easier to grasp; but, largely because they were adapted many times, the "originals" with which to compare the films are not necessary the literary texts but "mediated" texts, such as specific critical readings of them or previous film adaptations. In the case of Nabokov, with the exception of *Lolita*, it is more difficult to identify texts standing in the way between the literary source and the adaptations.

However, I regard the difficulty of obtaining the films as the most important detractor in studying films based on Nabokov's works. The majority of the films have not been released on DVD, and some are unavailable even in the archives of the countries where they were made. On one occasion I was made to believe that the film was lost forever. This unfortunate situation is to a large extent a correlative of the period when some of them were shot, when VHS tape or DVD did not exist, as well as the fact that a large proportion of them were made for television. This was also the reason why writing this book involved some detective work, which eventually paid off. I managed to find all but one film from the list mentioned on IMDB as Nabokov adaptations, as well as many that lend themselves to the treatment in the context of his books. This study offers a close analysis of the vast majority of these adaptations and of some films which bear significant similarity to Nabokov's oeuvre.

## *Intertextuality and Fidelity*

In common with recent studies of adaptation [for example, Sheen 2000; Stam 2000; Elliott 2003; 2004; Aragay 2005],[3] including my own work on Polanski and Skolimowski's films (Mazierska 2007: 138–62; 2010: 107–46), informed by the theories of Barthes, Bakhtin and Foucault, in this book I will refrain from treating the books as originals and the films based on them as their copies, but will regard them as two potentially equal pieces of art and important cultural phenomena, each unique but at the same time not entirely original and entangled in a web of intertextual relations. From this perspective the old "original" and the old "adaptation" are both regarded as adaptations to numerous aspects of the environment in which they find themselves. According to this view, the author of an adapted book is the originator of a discourse, not the creator of a work that remains insensitive to the context in which it is located (Sheen 2000). This also means that the work of adaptation does not finish with the production of the film, but continues through its distribution and reception.

My aim is to identify and discuss some of the relations into which these two contingent works, the book and the film, enter. The most important, however, is the link between the book by Nabokov and the film based on it. My study will thus incorporate some aspects of the old-fashioned "fidelity investigation." However, I will not question whether the film is faithful to the book *tout court*, but will compare only their specific aspects and interpretations. Moreover, I reject fidelity as a criterion of assessing the artistic value or even the overall success of a screen adaptation. I will not condemn the directors or scriptwriters for "betrayal," namely deviating from the alleged "letter" or "spirit" of the "original" (written in quotation marks because I accept that no work is absolutely original, and the "letters" and "spirits" of the book mutate as they travel from culture to culture), or praise them for their efforts to be faithful to the novel. Instead, I will attempt to establish the possible reasons why certain aspects of the book were adhered to and others were dropped, and what was inserted in their place and with what result.

To fulfil this goal I will look at the context of the film's production: how it adapted to its target audience, the country (countries) where it was shot and set, the cinematic fashions of the day, the moral tone of its times, the genre in which it was located, and so on. I will also discuss the specificity of the director's style and ideology, and situate the adaptation in the context of his or her films, both those preceding the discussed adaptation and following it. I will also look, in some measure, at Nabokov's books as the products of adaptation to the environment in which he wrote them, and to his projected readers. I will consider them not only as works of art, the products of his genius, but also as cultural facts in a dynamic relationship with changing audiences. To the greatest extent, this will refer to *Lolita*, the book by Nabokov which inspired the most varied readings and around which a certain myth was created, which overshadowed the "original."

I will also investigate possible connections between different film adaptations of Nabokov, in order to establish whether the earlier adaptations influenced the later ones, or at least if the later resemble the earlier, and hence whether we can justifiably talk about cycles of his adaptations. I would also like to establish whether there are any national or transnational variations in the filmmakers' attitudes towards Nabokov's prose. To facilitate my investigation, I will break with chronology and discuss the two adaptations of *Lolita* in one chapter, along with other films inspired by the book or lending themselves to interpretation in the context of Nabokov's masterpiece.

Because in this book I adopt an approach which privileges intertextuality over fidelity, I decided to drop some films which are "official" adaptations of Nabokov's works and instead include films which are not their adaptations but show some meaningful connections with them. To one such work, *Triple Agent* by Eric Rohmer, I will devote a whole chapter. For the same reason, one chapter will be dedicated entirely to a comparison between Nabokov and Jean-Luc Godard, on account of the similarities between their lives, works and views.

Although in this book I privilege the search for intertextual connections over the study of fidelity, some concepts from the "fidelity school" of adaptation studies proved useful in my analysis. For example, the categories of transposition, commentary and analogy, used in the influential study by Geoffrey Wagner, *The Novel and the Cinema* [1975], helped me orient myself to the tasks awaiting adapters. Following Wagner, I believe that adapters transpose, comment on and seek analogies for the literary work, although, unlike Wagner, who divides adaptations into these three separate categories, I regard the three functions are closely connected: each adaptation is simultaneously a transposition, a commentary and an analogy. For example, by the very act of transposing/transporting the characters and narratives into a new space, the adapter comments on the source book.

While I agree that literature and film are different media, I believe that this does not preclude their comparison — if they would elude comparisons, a study of adaptation would make little sense. The comparison might refer to the fact that both are narrative media: they tell stories and present characters; they also usually speak in a particular ethnic language or languages and attempt to render visually people, places and events. Many books are also mixed media due to their containing illustrations (Elliott 2004). They are also artifacts and therefore can be judged according to various aesthetic criteria, such as originality. Furthermore, they convey ideological perspectives. The majority of books and films also belong to specific genres or schools, and therefore can be compared according to the place they occupy within the history of these genres or schools.

Of course, this study will be largely influenced by my interpretations of books and films, which are equally contingent and shaped by a multitude of factors, including the studies with which I familiarized myself and those which I had no opportunity to read. The reader will find in the bibliography a full list of the works I quoted and consulted. However, I shall admit that I was most influenced by those authors who argued that there is more to Nabokov's prose than metaliterary pursuits — who see in this author somebody deeply interested in reality ("reality" or "realities") and willing to reflect this interest in his works. For me, the interesting question about Nabokov is not whether he is a realist or not, but what type, layer or aspect of reality he attempted to reflect in his books, or what realities his readers found in them.

I hope that the results of my investigation, apart from offering a specific case study of adaptations of Nabokov's prose, might also be of wider use for Nabokov scholars and film historians. The benefit for the former might lie in providing information about certain aspects of the afterlife of Nabokov's works. This is because each adaptation can be seen as a way of interpreting his book, which reflects both the specific interest and taste of its authors and the way these authors think Nabokov should be interpreted to suit the interests and tastes of the public, to which the film is addressed. Hence, adaptations can be regarded as, however provisional, tests of the attractiveness and adaptability of Nabokov's books to varied environments. They can also be seen as a test of the attractiveness of specific ways of interpreting Nabokov — for example, as realist or anti-realist writer, Russian, American or transnational author, misogynist or feminist — and as an addition to the pool of existing interpretations of Nabokov's prose. The possible benefit to film historians I would see as locating adaptations within, among others, the contexts of national versus transnational cinema, and art-house versus popular/genre cinema.

## NABOKOV AND THE ART OF READING, ADAPTING AND TRANSLATING

Nabokov was not only a fiction writer, but a distinguished historian and theoretician of literature, as well as a scriptwriter. Therefore, I feel obliged to present his views on film adaptation before moving on to those of the filmmakers. However, this is by no means a straightforward task, because Nabokov did not discuss this issue in a systematic way. Attributing to him any theory must be a matter of reconstruction and speculation, which I will base on his theory and practice of reading, adapting/translating his own works and other authors, and of "literary translating" *Eugene Onegin*, as well as his remarks on his sceenplay for *Lolita* and comments on two films based on his books — Stanley Kubrick's *Lolita* and Tony Richardson's *Laughter in the Dark*.

Nabokov presents his views on the correct reading on literature in his essay, "Good Readers and Good Writers," which opens his *Lectures on Literature*, where he advocates approaching a book with an open mind and reading it in tune with the author:

> There is nothing wrong about the moonshine of generalization when it comes *after* the sunny trifles of the book have been lovingly collected. If one begins with a ready-made generalization, one begins at the wrong end and travels away from the book before one has started to understand it. Nothing is more boring or more unfair to the author than starting to read, say, *Madame Bovary*, with the preconceived notion that it is a denunciation of the bourgeoisie. We should always remember that the work of art is invariably the creation of a new world, so that the first thing we should do is to study that new world as closely as possible, approaching it as something brand new, having no obvious connection with the worlds we already know. When this new world has been closely studied, then and only then let us examine its links with other worlds, other branches of knowledge [LL: 1].
> 
> What should be established, I think, is an artistic harmonious balance between the reader's mind and the author's mind.... The reader must know when and where to curb his imagination and this he does by trying to get clear the specific world the author places at his disposal. We must see things and hear things, we must visualize the rooms, the clothes, the manners of an author's people [ibid.: 4].

This opinion is reinforced in *Strong Opinions*, where, to the interviewer's question about the pleasures of writing, the writer replies:

> They correspond exactly to the pleasures of reading, the bliss, the felicity of a phrase is shared by writer and reader: by the satisfied writer and the grateful reader, or — which is the same thing — by the artist grateful to the unknown force in his mind that has suggested a combination of images and by the artistic reader whom this combination satisfies [SO: 40].

Nabokov's "good reader," despite investing much time and effort in comprehending or "seeing" the book, is thus essentially a passive consumer: a receiver, not a creator of a new work out of the material he finds in the book.[4]

Such expectations of the reader are also conveyed by Nabokov quoting a quiz with ten definitions of a reader, from which the students had to choose four that would combine to make a good reader. The correct answer is that a good reader has to have imagination, memory, a dictionary and some artistic sense. Meaningfully, being a budding author is not included by Nabokov as a feature conducive to good reading. From its placing among such definitions as "The reader should belong to a book club" and "The reader should concentrate on the social-economic angle" we can even conjecture that being a budding author is, in Nabokov's view, an obstacle in reading a book in the right way. If this is the case, then a filmmaker with creative ambitions of his own would, according to Nabokov, have little chance to transmit the meaning of the book to the screen.

From the fragments quoted we can also deduce that for Nabokov a book has a definite and constant meaning. Such a view is also conveyed in his two volumes of lectures, where we often find the opinion that a specific masterpiece is not about this, but about that. For example, when discussing Proust's *Swann's Way*, translated by Nabokov as *The Walk by Swann's Place*, he claims:

> One thing should be firmly impressed upon your minds: the work is not an autobiography; the narrator is not Proust the person, and the characters never existed except in the author's mind. Let us not, therefore, go into the author's life. It is of no importance in the present case and would only cloud the issue, especially as the narrator and the author do resemble each other in various ways and move in much the same environment [LL: 208].

Such an essentialist approach to works of literature is also confirmed by Nabokov's theory of "literary translation," which he developed during his work on the translation of Pushkin's *Evgeny Onegin*. According to this concept, it is possible to translate exactly a work of literature from one language to another, as conveyed by such words:

> The person who desires to turn a literary masterpiece into another language, has only one duty to perform, and this is to reproduce with absolute exactitude the whole text, and nothing but the text. The term "literal translation" is tautological since anything but that is not truly a translation but an imitation, an adaptation or a parody [PoT: 504].

Of course, in Nabokov's eyes his translation of *Onegin* was definite: correct and resistant to the erosion of time.

On the other hand, recent studies emphasize Nabokov's allegiance to the contingency and openness of meaning, as exemplified by the collection of essays, edited by Will Norman and Duncan White, meaningfully entitled *Transitional Nabokov* (Norman and White 2009; see also Green 1996). Stephen H. Blackwell, in one of the essays included in the collection, proposes to attribute to Nabokov a "fugitive sense"—a conviction that science and literature are a succession of paradigms, not an accumulation of truth (Blackwell 2009). Other authors suggest that Nabokov's views on interpretation changed during his life—from "totalitarian" to a more liberal attitude to the art of reading and interpreting (Karshan 2009).

Even if Nabokov's ideal is absolute fidelity to the author in reading, interpreting and translating—namely, reconstructing his unique world in a different language or medium—he was aware that it is not always possible. Hence, he differentiated between translation and adaptation. He himself undertook several types of adaptations: adapting works of different authors to Russian, re-translating himself from Russian into English and English into Russian, and writing a screenplay from his own book to be used in film. Jane Grayson, who analyzed Nabokov's translations from Russian into English, noted that on each occasion "Nabokov is concerned not only to rework, but to conserve his original. The conscientious translator coexists with the creative artist" (Grayson 1977: 167). A similar conclusion is reached by authors studying his translations into Russian (for example, Connolly 1995c). Grayson also notes that Nabokov's approach to preserving the original in translation varies. Sometimes he is more concerned with keeping the literal meaning in the new medium, sometimes with achieving a similar stylistic effect. As a translator/adapter of his works, he acts as a kind of intermediary between the original work and the new environment in which the adapted work is to appear (Grayson: 182–219). Contrary to his own aloof approach to the issue of environment, I believe that he was very well aware of the specificity of his audiences, and although he did not pander to their tastes, he certainly took them into account. Many signs of this we find in his correspondence (NWL), as well as his forewords and afterwords to his works.

I see a close analogy between Nabokov's literary adaptations and the cinematic adaptations of his works. Both attempt to rework and preserve the original, and what is preserved varies from film to film. Sometimes it is a literal meaning, sometimes a stylistic effect, sometimes the setting, and on other occasions the characters. Judging from his brief remarks about the films based on his books, Nabokov was most happy when the filmmaker found his own but equally accomplished way to convey the meaning present in his novel, and most unhappy when his own devices were substituted with some of a lower quality, which at the same time subverted the original meaning. An example of the first is his praise of "the scene with the water-ski girl, gulping and giggling" in *Laughter in the Dark*, which Nabokov describes as "exceptionally successful" (SO: 137) in the otherwise bad film, in his view; of the second was his sense of embarrassment at seeing the collapsible bed in

Kubrick's *Lolita*. If my reconstruction of Nabokov's views is correct, then we can find a distinct similarity between his views and those of authors such as the previously quoted E. H. Gombrich and Nelson Goodman, who see a faithful and successful adaptation in a match between different elements used in different contexts to create the same or similar aesthetic effect. In common with Nabokov, I also find those adaptations faithful to literary masterpieces according to Gombrich and Nelson Goodman's criteria to be successful. However, it is not the only type of successful adaptation of Nabokov I envisage; others might include films which come across as unfaithful but are highly accomplished as films, or films which are mediocre but offer an unexpected insight into an adapted book or a wider aspect of Nabokov's prose.

In this study I am less interested in assessing the artistic value of the films and more in discussing them as signs of the afterlife of Nabokov's books. Therefore I celebrate and enjoy all films based on his books, as well as those adaptations which allow the viewer to think about Nabokov when watching them, including those which are allegedly poor or unfaithful. This is because each adaptation takes the book on a journey to a place about which the author never dreamt or feared. Conversely, without such journeys, Nabokov's books will wither and die, even — or perhaps especially — if they become classics locked in their definitive interpretations.

# 1

# Humbert Between Dignity and Romanticism
## Lolita *by Stanley Kubrick (1962) and Adrian Lyne (1997)*

"Literature is Love. Now we can continue."—Vladimir Nabokov, *Despair*

"You can always count on a murderer for a fancy prose style."—Vladimir Nabokov, *Lolita*

"today is the day we make choices:
you or the foster home
you or the jail"—Kim Morrisey, *stepfather*

Published for the first time by Olympia Press in Paris in 1955, and by G. P. Putnam's Sons in the United States in 1958, *Lolita* is one of Nabokov's most artistically accomplished books and the most commercially successful book of his career—his unquestionable bestseller. *Lolita* is also a worldwide phenomenon, as captured by the title of Ellen Pifer's essay, "The *Lolita* Phenomenon from Paris to Tehran" (Pifer 2005), which refers to the title of Azar Nafisi's *Reading Lolita in Tehran* (Nafisi 2003). This means that the ways of reading, interpreting, re-imagining and recreating it now attract as much attention, if not more, than the source of these various discourses: the book Nabokov published over fifty years ago. The two films based on *Lolita*, as well as other movies that only allude to it, were both affected by this phenomenon and played a role in creating it. Writing about films titled *Lolita* thus palpably demonstrates the inadequacy of the fidelity model in the discussion of adaptations. At the same time, this model cannot be ignored because discourses around the films are haunted by the problem of fidelity. The question of fidelity or its lack will also be discussed in this study, but not to establish how much the adapters diverged from the original version, but rather to find out what the filmmakers were faithful to and with what effect. For this reason I will also try to present some competing readings of *Lolita*— by critics of different generations, by Nabokov the scriptwriter, the authors of two screen *Lolitas* and their critics, and by the authors of the films that lend themselves to interpretation in the context of this novel.

## *Ways of Reading* Lolita

The immense popularity of *Lolita*, as already indicated in the Introduction, was the reason why it was the first book by Nabokov that made it to the screen. Apart from the two cinematic *Lolitas*, there was also a musical version by Alan Jay Lerner and John Barry (1971), and a play by Edward Albee, which opened in New York in March 1981 (Pifer 1995: 306). In addition, such prominent authors as Harold Pinter and David Mamet expressed interest in adapting it (Stam 2005: 235). While it fascinated adapters, *Lolita* simultaneously posed a challenge to them, with its scandalous theme, considerable length and cult status. The first characteristic puts the potential adapters on a collision course with censors; the second with "average" readers; the third with "good readers," as defined by Nabokov — those who carry a distinct image of the book in their mind and are reluctant to give it up, even for two hours of sitting in the cinema theater.

In other senses, however, it is easier to screen *Lolita* than many other Nabokov works. The competing readings of the novel could be seen as a liberating force for the filmmaker: proof that there are many *Lolitas* to choose from and an alibi against criticism that something important was omitted or twisted on the way from book to screen. This was indeed the case when the films were assessed; their narrative coherence or possessing a distinct style were valued higher by the critics than faithfulness to Nabokov's vision. Furthermore, losing his language and overall style on the way from book to screen could be seen as less of a problem than in the case of adapting his other books. This is not because its language is weak (it is excellent) or that it is poor in literary allusions (it is very rich in them)[1], but because there is more to this book than exquisite language, as proven by its popular appeal and the concern expressed by prominent representatives of the general public, including politicians, that it could corrupt its readers (Rampton 1984: 102–3). The book is deliberately commonplace in romantic structure through including motifs of quest, hunger for the unattainable, attainment, journey, loss, pursuit and revenge (Long 1981: 138–9). "Not for *Lolita* the complications even of the triangular love-plot: here the pattern is the straight line, in accordance with whose unrelenting extension Charlotte Haze loves Humbert, who loves Lolita, who loves Quilty, who seems to love no one at all" (Sharpe 1991: 57). In summary, there is enough content valued by creators of popular cinema to attract those with little ambition to account for the subtleties of Nabokov's style. Of course, the aesthetic ideal will be to do in the film what Nabokov did in the book: "to apply a high style to a low life" (ibid.: 75).

The story in *Lolita* is Humbert Humbert's story; in first-person narration he offers us his view of himself, as well as of other characters. His reports and assessments are always partial because they are his, as opposed to that of a neutral observer, and because he is driven by his unhealthy attraction to young girls, which he is not shy to describe as perversion and madness. This affliction affects not only his assessment of himself and Lolita, but of everything he experiences. Other people exist only in relation to his position, as conveyed by the name he gives to Charlotte Haze's neighbor, "Miss Opposite." However, although within the main body of his work Nabokov provides us no external vantage point from which to assess Humbert's character, he makes us aware that "there are themes and revelations of which Humbert is not fully in control" (Bader 1972: 57). We learn this early on in the novel, where Humbert's description of his first marriage to Valeria suggests that he knew very little of his wife and was manipulated by her. At the same time, Nabokov also suggests that Humbert attempts to manipulate his readers by representing himself in a positive light, as an artist (or an artist *manqué*) and romantic lover, as opposed to an ordinary pervert and bad reader (ibid.: 58). The result is that *Lolita,* which is "a case study in child abuse, also manages against all the odds to be a passionate and poignant love story" (Boyd 1993: 227). Humbert is "tauntingly immoral, deeply unpleasant and exploitative; but his memoir engages our better selves in its unfathomable complexity and devious subterfuge" (Moore 2002: 97). Or, at least, the book does this for a large proportion of its readers.

An important line dividing the readers of *Lolita* is between those who give in to Humbert's manipulative talents and perceive him as a romantic lover and those who focus on the "reality" of his life and see in him a rapist and fantasist. This division overlaps with another — between those who admire the novel for its exquisite style and those who regard its style as a means to tell something important about (external) reality. The romantic interpretation is typically coupled with the metaliterary or aesthetic reading — the anti-romantic with the realistic one. These readings can be mapped onto the history of the book's critical and popular reception. The romantic and metaliterary readings (for example, Trilling 1958; Proffer 1968a; Appel

1971; Josipovici 1971) prevailed during the first two decades or so following the book's publication in the United States and can be seen as an attempt to defend it against the accusations of pornography. They were undertaken chiefly by erudite male literary historians, some of them undoubtedly affected by New Criticism and therefore more sensitive to Humbert's erudition and eloquence, and less to Lolita's suffering. The closer we come to the present, the more often we encounter the realistic and anti-romantic approach. This can be explained by the fact that today nobody seriously denies the novel the status of a masterpiece; therefore, it is more acceptable to look behind its exquisite style towards what the book says about people and their cultures. Since the 1980s, the growing "army" of feminist literary and cultural historians have embarked on a fight to save *Lolita* from the callous hands of haughty male critics (for example Brand 1987; Kauffman 1989; Pifer 2003; Devlin 2005: 156–61; Collins 2009: 189–93). On some occasions they are joined by the representatives of other content-oriented critics, especially those who attempt to locate *Lolita* in history. Ellen Pifer compares Humbert to Axel Rex from *Laughter in the Dark* (Pifer 1980: 158–71), one of the most obnoxious characters in Nabokov's prose, who lends himself to the treatment in the context of Nazi ideology. Her comparison contrasts with that of Julian Moynahan, who a decade earlier linked Humbert with a more positive and pitiable Albinus (Moynahan 1971a: 25–32). Anna Brodsky, who discusses *Lolita* openly in the context of the Holocaust, claims that "Humbert's destruction of Doloros Haze's childhood bears the trace of Nazi terror" (Brodsky 2002: 53). Her words are echoed by Susan Mizruchi, who maintains that "While the crimes [of Humbert] are of an altogether different dimension and magnitude, there are crucial continuities between some of Humbert's most cherished beliefs and Nazi ideology, as well as even more striking continuities between Nazi and Humbertian methods of defense" (Mizruchi 2003: 640).

I believe that in relation to these female critics the opinion that Humbert's version "entrances the reader against his will," making him an "accomplice" in Humbert's crimes (de la Durantaye 2007: 1–17), is no longer true. Brodsky, for example, gives the impression of not being seduced by Humbert's rhetoric even for a second; from the first sentence she sees in Humbert a total scoundrel. There are also some male readers, such as Robert T. Levine (Levine 1979) and the novelist Martin Amis, who share such an interpretation of Humbert. Amis does not just fail to be seduced by Humbert's narrative, but regards him as a monster and treats his attempt to write his story as his worst perversion: "Humbert is surpassingly cruel in using Lolita for the play of his wit and the play of his prose" (Amis 1992: 110). Humbert's use of Lolita for art is what reminds me of a certain type of Nazi, as immortalized, for example, in Tadeusz Borowski's prose or in Andrzej Munk's *Pasażerka* (*Passenger*, 1963): somebody who does not simply torture or kill his prey, but does it with an accompaniment of a violin quartet and an assistance of a camera."

The approach foregrounding the metaliterary character of *Lolita* is most famously exemplified by Alfred Appel, who, in his numerous works on *Lolita*, including the celebrated *The Annotated Lolita*, only peppers his discussion of the book's intertextuality with some casual, off-hand remarks about its eponymous character and her lover. A feminist author, Linda Kauffman, singles out and dissects one such remark (which also caught the attention of Rachel Devlin and myself when I first read Appel's essay) with cruel precision in her essay:

> Humbert's terrible demands notwithstanding, Lolita is as insensitive as children are to their actual parents; sexuality aside, she demands anxious parental placation in a too typically American way, and affords Nabokov an ideal opportunity to comment on the Teen and Sub-Teen Tyranny [Appel 1995: xIviii; Kauffman 1989: 134; Devlin 2005: 215].

Kauffman criticizes Appel for his disregard of the issue of child abuse, palpably present in the novel, and his double standard in assessing male and female characters of the novel, as well as its readers: "When it comes to women, such critics seem to forget that their main point is that the novel is *not* realistic!" (Kauffman 1989: 134). Appel can also be criticized for not "reading" Lolita's attitude to the surrounding culture carefully. For him, she epitomizes a spoilt, consumption-oriented America, while, as Rachel Bowlby (Bowlby 2003) and Emily Collins observe, it is Humbert rather than Lolita who betrays a fetishistic attachment to objects:

> Humbert makes his living from quintessentially fetishized goods, and though he sneers at the Prinet print above his bed, it has indirectly supported him in its role as a perfume advertisement. During his "quiet poetical afternoon of fastidious shopping," Humbert's main preparation for the rape he intends, the clothes he inspects become "phantom little Lolitas" before he "round[s] up the deal" by buying nightclothes [Collins 2009: 191].

Lolita, on the other hand, is the opposite of a fetishist: she discards objects once she has finished with them (ibid.: 190).

Appel's attitude to Lolita, in addition to the previously mentioned factors, can be explained by belonging to a generation which was frightened of teenagers (he was born in 1934). At the same time, his antipathy to Lolita demonstrates that Nabokov, who was over thirty years older than his celebrated critic, was much less affected by modern sociological trends and more in tune with the trends which would come twenty or so years later[2].

Nabokov himself, as Lucy Maddox observes, envisaged both a realistic and a metaliterary reading of his book by including John Ray's Foreword and his own Afterword, titled "On a book entitled *Lolita*." The first advocated seeing the book as a psychological and sociological case study; the second as material for a purely aesthetic enjoyment (Maddox 1983: 66–85). However, these two additions to the main body of text fulfill different functions. Ray's Foreword is there to ridicule psychologists and sociologists of literature, even if furnished with academic titles. Nabokov's Afterword is meant to direct the reader towards the "right" way of approaching it, which Appel follows somewhat too eagerly for contemporary tastes. At the same time, I have little doubt that Nabokov did not want the reader to see in Humbert a romantic lover. For example, in his Foreword to *Despair* he wrote, "Both [Humbert and Hermann] are neurotic scoundrels" (Des: 11); in *Strong Opinions* he describes Humbert as a "hateful person" (SO: 26). Conversely, he has only warm words for Lolita, such as "There is a queer, tender charm about that mythical nymphet" (SO.: 21; see also Boyd 1991: 336–37).

The readings offered by Appel and his kin on the one hand, and by feminist critics on the other, also point to a number of basic options for adapting the novel for the screen. The filmmaker can try to make a realistic or unrealistic film of it (for example, in a form of parody or an "intertextual collage.") He or she can give in to Humbert's "dominant vision" and depict him as a romantic lover, even a passive victim of the nymphet's sexual power, and a poet whose subtlety distinguishes him from the social mainstream. Conversely, Humbert can be depicted as a 'neurotic scoundrel' who not only rapes, manipulates and enslaves a child, but almost until the end of his life hides his actions behind a barrage of ornamental language. However, in order to convey convincingly onscreen the idea that Humbert is a romantic lover it is necessary to add some years to the object of his attraction, because for the vast majority of viewers a child aged between nine and twelve years cannot be the willing lover of an older man, much less a cynical manipulator. In a wider sense, a filmmaker opting for such a reading of *Lolita* is forced to reduce the gap between the lovers to make their relationship socially acceptable. The opposite, anti-romantic approach would consist of unearthing a true version of events from the weight of Humbert's self-justifying discourse, and see in him a ruthless predator and a liar. It would also require allowing Lolita to say what she thinks about Humbert. Such a hypothetical project might be compared to some attempts by feminist writers to give Lolita a voice — for example, that of Kim Morrisey, who wrote *Poems for Men Who Dream of Lolita,* and Pia

Pera's *Lo's Diary* (Paglia 1995: 157) and, perhaps, to the unfilmed screenplay written by Harold Pinter (Stam 2005: 235)[3].

Another option concerning representing the main characters amounts to preserving both a romantic and anti-romantic reading by conveying the protagonist's vision and at the same time allowing the reader to realize that there is a gap between the narrator's discourse and intersubjective reality. Such a method, although demanding significant inventiveness from the filmmaker, was applied in other films before the first cinematic *Lolita* had its premiere. For example, *The Innocents* (1961) by Jack Clayton sustains the epistemological ambiguity of its literary original, *The Turn of the Screw* by Henry James, and can either be read as the story of a governess' madness or of the possession of children in her care by some evil spirits. With the passage of time, telling competing or complementary versions of the same events without compelling the viewer to choose one of them became the staple diet of postmodern cinema. However, as the title of this chapter suggests, the adapters of *Lolita*, by and large, opted for a reading privileging and exhorting Humbert's version. Again, I shall repeat that this vision is subjective, as poignantly reflected in Humbert's definition of a "nymphet," the crucial term in his private dictionary:

> Between the age limits of nine and fourteen there occur maidens who, to certain bewitched travellers, twice or many times older than they, reveal their true nature which is not human, but nymphic (that is, demoniac); and those chosen creatures I propose to designate as "nymphets" [Lo: 1955: 18].

This description suggests that the girl is a "nymphet" only in the eye of the beholder, who from the perspective of our culture we will call a pedophile. For the vast majority of observers, the nymphet is only a child or a girl on the threshold of puberty with no demonic powers whatsoever.[4] There is a second, somewhat less explored, ambiguity pertaining to a nymphet. The girl is a nymphet when she is a product of imagination, not of physical possession. When possessed, especially sexually, she loses her demonic powers, and her overall allure disappears. Tony Sharpe notes that Lolita "is never less a 'nymphet' than when they [Lolita and Humbert] live together, whether in motel after motel or in their perilous cohabitation at Beardsley; never is he less the poet, more the pervert" (Sharpe 1991: 63). Humbert's problems with the "real" Lolita excellently demonstrate the wider issue of "romantic love." Friedrich Kittler observes that Romanticism construed woman as the passive and silent recipient of male attention and affection, as a narcissistic support for the formation of male identity. For romantic men, a woman had to remain an enigma: she was most perfectly loved from a distance, when observed through a window, admired in letters, even married to another man. When possessed, she lost her allure (Kittler 1990: 124–73). Not surprisingly, Diana Butler compares a "nymphet" to a butterfly, as both nymphets and butterflies are essentially unattainable, "combining matter and an appearance of spirituality, but eluding the grasp of man" (Butler 1960: 60).[5]

The multiple identities of Lolita are signified by multiple versions of her name: Dolores, Lolita, Lo, Dolly — with Dolores referring to the "official" girl; Lolita, as perceived by Humbert and Dolly, as seen through her own eyes and those of her friends. They have also quite different connotations, which are at play in Nabokov's novel. In Spanish, where "Dolores" is most popular, it is short for *La Virgen María de los Dolores* (*Virgin Mary of Sorrows*). "Lolita" can also be regarded as diminutive of "Lola," which, as Camille Paglia observes, is traditionally a great name — as in Lola Montez — for a courtesan figure (Paglia 1995: 147). Humbert pronounces Lolita in the Spanish not American style 'Low-leed-uh' (on different connotations of "Lolita," see SO: 25), which points out that "he appropriates Lolita on his own terms" (Boyd 1993: 229) or, as Humbert himself puts it, that he "solipsizes her." These different names given to Lolita also parallel the sequence of "nymphets" Humbert encounters in his life, beginning with his first love, Annabel Leigh, and their ultimate dispensability following their maturing into womanhood or death (as in the case of Annabel). For Humbert, no woman is thus truly unique; each can be replaced by another woman or her imaginary substitute, and each eventually is. Nabokov's nympholept even dreams about Lolita giving birth to a new version of Lolita, and her, in due course, producing an even newer one, so he has enough nymphets to satisfy his desires till the end of his life.[6]

America is also an important aspect of Humbert's vision. He construes this country in a similar way to how he construes Lolita: as kitschy and passive. An example is his description of a town in Appalachia:

> The town was dead. Nobody strolled and laughed at the sidewalks as relaxing burghers would in sweet, mellow, rotting Europe. I was alone to enjoy the innocent night and my terrible thoughts. A wire receptacle on the curb was very particular about acceptable contents: Sweepings. Paper. No garbage. Sherry-red letters of light marked a Camera Shop. A large thermometer with the name of a laxative quietly dwelt on the front of a drugstore. Ribinov's Jewelry Company had a display of artificial diamonds reflected in a red mirror. A lighted green clock swam in the linenish depth of Jiffy Jeff Laundry [Lo: 274].

As Dana Brand observes, "The quite deadness of the town is a readiness for Humbert's imaginative impregnation. He takes advantage of its silence just as he wanted to take advantage of a sleeping, drugged Lolita" (Brand 1987: 16). Again, the reader/adapter has a choice of trusting or distrusting Humbert's vision of America, showing it as an unmediated reality or presenting it in quotation marks; or even substituting Humbert's vision entirely with one reconstructed from the gaps in his discourse.

The different readings of *Lolita* also affect possible representations of Quilty in the film. For Humbert, he is a deranged and cynical man who steals from him, and neglects and abandons his lover. It is, however, possible to see him as Lolita's true love and her liberator, or, at least, the lesser evil of the two she has to live with. While some critics grant Quilty an existence independent from Humbert, others see in him only a product of Humbert's deranged imagination — Mr. Hyde to his Dr. Jekyll (Sharpe 1991: 65), the repository of his self-loathing and self-disgust. Such interpretation, of course, further de-romanticizes Humbert.

A realistic reading of *Lolita* by a potential adapter does not require him to give up on the cinematic references with which the book is littered. On the contrary, they are an important aspect of the novel's realism, pertaining to the fact that the characters tend to look at the world through the prism of the films they watched and, in a wider sense, through popular culture. In *Lolita*, in common with Nabokov's earlier novels, such as *King, Queen, Knave* and *Laughter in the Dark*, Nabokov represents a society saturated with media, becoming in this way a predecessor of such theoreticians of postmodernity as Jean Baudrillard and Fredric Jameson. In the case of Humbert, his mediated perceptions testify also to his deeper epistemological deficiency: an inability to see the world afresh and to adjust himself to the world.

## *Surrealistic* Lolita: Lolita: A Screenplay

The first author to deal with the question "how to make a film of *Lolita?*" was Nabokov himself, who was invited to write the script for a film to be directed by Stanley Kubrick. His main purpose was to "cinematize" his novel (Appel 1974: 231–32), which had two dimensions. One consisted of finding visual equivalents to some unfilmable passages of the book or describing how certain fragments should be filmed. The second amounted to adapting the personages and events to the demands of the director, producer and audiences of the time. There are, of course, different ways to visualize the novel, attesting to scriptwriters' varying imaginations. Nabokov wanted the film based on his novel to diverge from mainstream, narrative cinema by including unrealistic vignettes: dreams and imaginary sequences, and very complex scenes from the perspective of mise-en-scène and camerawork. Had they been filmed, writes Robert Stam, "These vignettes would have formed part of a completely different film, featuring an anti-illusionist aesthetic more reminiscent of Fellini or Woody Allen than of the early Kubrick" (Stam 2005: 228). Nabokov's visual imagination lends itself also to a treatment by Jerzy Skolimowski, who in due course would direct *King, Queen, Knave*, where he also brings to life characters' dreams. Another filmmaker whose sensitivity appears to be close to that of Nabokov the scriptwriter is Jean-Luc Godard. The inclusion of cinematic apparatus in the diegesis, and making the characters address the camera, as proposed by Nabokov, bring to mind Godard's films from the 1960s, such as *Pierrot le fou* (1965) and *La Chinoise* (1967). Such techniques demand from the viewer a certain sophistication associated more with European art-house cinema than Hollywood. Other decisions, however, which consist of cleansing his "original" of some too difficult or ambiguous metaphors, suggest that Nabokov expected his viewers would be less sophisticated than his readers. Take, for example, the scene in the Enchanted Hunters, where one of the hotel guests, Dr. Braddock, explains the meaning of the mural: "The hunter thinks he has hypnotized the little nymph but it is she who puts him into a trance" (LoS: 107). Perhaps the viewer Nabokov had in mind for his movie would be a film erudite but not necessarily literary erudite, again of the type attracted to the cinema of Skolimowski and Godard.

The insertion of unrealistic scenes by Nabokov not only adds to the visual content of the text but plays an important ideological function, allowing the viewer to access the inner life of the main character and see him as pompous or insane. An example is a scene where he imagines himself as a knight, or another in which he transforms into Hamlet and Edgar Allan Poe. Paradoxically, thanks to accessing Humbert's inner life, we recognize in him a man who does not look for any intellectual or aesthetic pleasures of a higher kind in literature and art, but limits himself to "collecting" literary nymphets. A similar function of stripping Humbert of dignity plays out in scenes from Humbert's life before he moved to the Hazes, especially his fit of insanity when giving a lecture about nymphets in literature. From the very beginning then, everything which Humbert says or does in this version is rendered unreliable. Consequently, he stands little chance of charming the viewers, even if he succeeds in attracting Charlotte, Lolita and others whom he meets on his way. The previous life of Nabokov's nympholept is not only shown but also commented on by Dr. Ray, the psychiatrist and first reader of Humbert's testimony. Ray encapsulates those features of scientists which Nabokov himself deeply disliked, such as striving for general rules, self-importance and lack of a sense of humor; therefore, his representation of the pedophile is not entirely convincing. Nevertheless, his power to assess Humbert further undermines the protagonist's charisma and renders the nympholept's accounts dubious.

In *Lolita: A Screenplay*, Lolita speaks with her own voice and comes across as more mature than the girl described by Humbert in the original

*Lolita*. Clare Quilty's role is immensely increased in comparison with the novel. However, as these changes survived the road from screenplay to film, and some were even introduced at the request of Kubrick and Harris, I will discuss their significance in the next part of my essay.

Nabokov's was a script for a long film — too long for Kubrick's and producer James B. Harris' standards, and the Hollywood norms. Undoubtedly, this was one of the reasons why only scraps of it were used in the final version. The real authors of the script finally used by Kubrick were Harris and Kubrick himself.

## *Posh* Lolita *of Stanley Kubrick*

> My first reaction to the picture was a mixture of aggravation, regret, and reluctant pleasure.... Most of the sequences were not really better than those I had so carefully composed for Kubrick, and I keenly regretted the waste of my time admiring Kubrick's fortitude in enduring for six months the evolution and infliction of a useless product.
>
> — Vladimir Nabokov, Foreword to *Lolita: A Screenplay*

*Lolita* was filmed twice, and on each occasion the result was an American film. This can be explained by its American setting, bestselling status, and belonging to the road genre — all features attractive to an American audience. At the same time, its various European traces are reflected in the "ethnically unpure" character of the films (for example, the choice of European actors for the role of Humbert). The two films were made in 1962 and 1997, by Stanley Kubrick and Adrian Lyne respectively. Their very names, for current viewers at least, as well as the periods when the films were made, suggest very different approaches to the task. Stanley Kubrick has a reputation as an arthouse and maverick director, perhaps the greatest stylist and most independent American director of his generation. However, although he is heralded as a Hollywood outsider (which was confirmed by his relocation to Britain), in "sexual politics" he was a Hollywood director through and through. His films are always male-centered, with women being either absent completely from the narrative or treated only as vehicles of male self-discovery. As Richard Corliss puts it, "Kubrick's is a man's world, a metaphorical boot camp" (Corliss 1994: 24). Due to his independence, craftsmanship and misogyny, Kubrick can be seen as a successor to Alfred Hitchcock. Another thing these two directors have in common was their ability to eclipse the authors of the books they adapted, as well as anyone else involved in making the film. However, as Thomas Leitch argues, Hitchcock "preferred to finesse around the authors he eventually eclipsed beneath the success of his generic branding. Stanley Kubrick, by contrast, earned his auteur status the old-fashioned way: by taking on authors directly in open warfare" (Leitch 2005: 111).

As Leitch and other authors argue, at the beginning of the 1960s, Kubrick was a successful genre director associated with war and crime films. In the later part of his career he also retained interest in genre conventions. His films *A Clockwork Orange* (1971), *Barry Lyndon* (1975), *The Shining* (1980), *Full Metal Jacket* (1987) or *Eyes Wide Shut* (1999) are all genre films, and the genres Kubrick employs run in parallel to those utilized by Nabokov (erotic thriller, literary biography, dystopia, spy thriller). However, it is thanks to his films of the 1960s — *Spartacus* (1960), *Lolita* (1962) and *Dr. Strangelove; or, How I Learned to Stop Worrying and Love the Bomb* (1964) that Kubrick transformed himself from matteur-en-scène to an auteur who uses genre conventions to demonstrate his originality.

*Lolita* was thus a vehicle of the transformation, and the disrespect with which Kubrick treated Nabokov's script was one aspect of it. This disrespect was part of Kubrick's larger strategy for the treatment of literary sources, which consisted of two basic ideas. According to the first one, the perfect novel from which to make a movie is not the novel of action but one concerned with the inner life of the characters. The adapter should attempt to render the psychology of these characters, not an external action of the book — this can be invented to suit the psychological dimension of the book. This means that he is allowed to invent new scenes or dialogues in the name of fidelity to the book's spirit (Koszarski 1977: 306). Secondly, the director does not need to convey the book's style but should find the style which would suit the film (ibid.: 307). Not surprisingly, in a different context Kubrick confessed that he "enjoyed dealing with a slightly surrealistic situation and presenting it in a realistic manner" (Kubrick, quoted in Jenkins 1997: 25). Kubrick's attitude to adaptation amounts to allowing the adapter to do practically everything he wants with the source material to achieve an effect which pleases the director rather than the writer. As previously mentioned, in the end, Nabokov's script was discarded in favor of a version written by Kubrick and Harris, although the author of the novel was credited as the sole author of the script. In this way Kubrick's *Lolita* began a pattern of adapting Nabokov's books in which the scriptwriter's version is eventually ditched by the director in favor of his own interpretation. This would also be the case with Skolimowski's *King, Queen, Knave* and Fassbinder's *Despair*.

The question can be asked why, in the light of Kubrick's views, Nabokov was approached to write the script. The main reason was Kubrick's rejection of the first version of the script, written by the novelist Calder Willingham

(Corliss 1994: 18). Nabokov's name on the script also acted as an alibi against possible accusations by the critics of "butchering the masterpiece" and decreased the risk of the writer himself complaining about the result of adapting his novel. Indeed, Nabokov's comments about the film give the impression that he was unhappy with the movie, but felt prevented from expressing his views. Finally, making a film so different from the novel and the script, while bearing many marks of Kubrick's personality, demonstrated that the author of the film entitled *Lolita* is indeed Kubrick, not Nabokov.

The film was shot in England on account of the funds that the financing company had available in Britain (Walker 1972: 31) and the lower the risk of harassment from pro-censorship pressure groups in comparison with America (Walker 1966: 158). Shooting *Lolita* in England, as well as making it a black and white film, also fitted Kubrick's idea of making it look more "respectable" and palatable for the censors. In the early 1960s sexual content in films was much more heavily censored and self-censored than in the 1990s. This fact, as almost everyone who writes about this film notes, greatly affected the way the director represented the central relationship (Walker 1966: 158–60; Appel

Sue Lyon as Lolita, and James Mason as Humbert in *Lolita* (1962), directed by Stanley Kubrick.

1974: 228–29; Corliss 1994: 8–9; Jenkins 1997: 32–3; Naremore 2007: 100–101). Alfred Appel puts it most amusingly: "Kubrick's *Lolita* is akin to a film of *Moby Dick* that would omit all harpoons, if not the whale itself, and the director's candor is understandably restrained" (Appel 1974: 229). Indeed, Kubrick did everything he could to close the gap and thus normalize the relationship between Humbert and Lolita. There is no sex in his film, and the eponymous character appears much older than the twelve-year-old Lolita at the beginning of Nabokov's story. Sue Lyon, who plays Lolita, looks even older than the fifteen to sixteen years she was during *Lolita*'s shooting. Take, for example, the sequence of the high-school dance, where, in a tight dress with a corset-like top that emphasizes her fully-developed breasts, Lyon comes across as a woman in her twenties. According to James Naremore, this scene was a direct response to the censors' demand to "add years" to Lolita (Naremore 2007: 100). Yet, the fact that Kubrick and Harris decided to make *Lolita* suggests that they were reasonably comfortable with the censors' demands. Most likely, these demands did not destroy their overall concept of the film, as suggested by Harris' claim that "being explicit was never of any interest to us" (Harris, quoted in Naremore 2007: 104).

Enforced by censors or not, Lolita's maturation on her road from book to film prevented Kubrick's film from becoming a story of an older man's attraction to a child, changing it into a tale of his infatuation with a young woman, which is much less outrageous. Due to the intervention of the censors, who requested deletion from the script an episode showing a series of images of nymphet-type adolescents (schoolgirls, store girls, cinema usherettes) while the film's protagonist presents to the viewer his "theory of nymphets" (Walker 1966: 160), Humbert's erotic obsession stopped being an attraction to a type, becoming an affection for a unique person – Dolores Haze. This individualization of Humbert's object of affection dignified his actions.

Kubrick not only added years to Lolita, he also made her appear and behave in a way which conveys her self-confidence and a natural good taste, even if tainted by her humble class background and limited education. Both Humbert in the book and Humbert in the film attribute to her an "eerie vulgarity," which is practically an oxymoron, as "vulgarity" (from vulgus – people or common folk) connotes ordinariness, while "eerie" means being out of the ordinary, supernatural, awesome. Such expression betrays Humbert's perception of Lolita and America, whom Lolita epitomizes for him, as "horribly hybridized" (Haegert 2003: 141–44). The cinematic Lolita, however, is definitely closer to the "eerie" than "vulgar" side of "eerie vulgarity." In this way, Lyon's Lolita is reminiscent of characters played by Grace Kelly in Alfred Hitchcock's films; she could be taken for Grace Kelly's younger sister. There is also some affinity between her and Marilyn Monroe's character in Laurence Olivier's *The Prince and the Showgirl* (1957), regarded as a Hollywood version of Shaw's *Pygmalion*, although Lyon's character reveals greater potential to become a sophisticated European-style lady than Monroe's Elsie Marina.[7] These features, which allow Lolita to pass, even if only under appropriate tutelage, as an upper-class person, constitute for Humbert in Kubrick's film an attraction at least as great as her young age. Thanks to them, he can mold her into his own image.

In her un-kitschy vulgarity, Lolita constitutes a spitting image of her mother, who is vulgar because she cannot accept the way she is and strives to become something better: a sophisticated European lady. Charlotte's unfulfilled intellectual and cultural pretensions — as testified by her collection of reproductions of Impressionist paintings, poor French, and a dream to have a French maid — put Humbert off her at least as much as her age and appearance. One can assume that such mockery of American lack of success in becoming European, which fills, proportionally, a large part of the film, was gladly received by European viewers at the time, especially art-house regulars, and it preserved some of its appeal for the film's audience to the present day. However, the fact that a middle-aged man in the film stands for European sophistication, while a middle-aged woman encapsulates American vulgarity, is a testimony to Kubrick's rather than Nabokov's misogyny and anti–Americanism. Nabokov does not assert Charlotte's vulgarity, only states that Humbert perceives her as vulgar. As Humbert's perceptions tend to be wrong, we can infer that his opinion about Charlotte also does not adhere to reality. Nabokov also suggests that Humbert, despite his intellectualism and worldliness, as demonstrated by the quality of his style and numerous literary allusions, is limited in his interests and taste. He rambles through the history in search of nymphets. Thus Humbert in the book is not very different from Charlotte, who also has a very selective and pragmatic attitude toward art. Charlotte's connecting Dr. Schweitzer with Dr. Zhivago parallels the way Humbert moves through the history of literature to find his favorite motif. The only difference is that Humbert uses art to reassure himself in his sexual choices, Charlotte to move up the social ladder.

Kubrick closes the gap between Lolita and Humbert not only by making Lolita older than in Nabokov's novel, but also, paradoxically, by making Humbert older too. James Mason, who plays this character, was born in 1909, so he was over fifty when cast as Humbert; the "original" Humbert was only thirty-seven. Mason appears even older than his real age due to his manner of acting, which harks back to British cinema of the 1940s, as opposed to the style employed by actors in British New Wave films, such as Richard Burton or Albert Finney, which was rougher and more aggressive. Kubrick often makes Mason walk in a silk dressing gown and slippers, which undermines Humbert's alleged virility and, again, contrasts with the style of dress of younger actors, who had a penchant for tight underwear, accentuating their muscles. According to Stam, the "understated, stern, paternal, Mason throughout most of the film seems more the harried father than the dirty old man" (Stam 2005: 231). Indeed, Humbert in the film is more interested in Lolita's academic education than her sex education. He enjoys passing on to his pupil (if possible, nonchalantly) some scraps of his knowledge and observe her reaction. He recites Poe to her, takes her to concerts and museums, and, when his step-daughter is in the hospital, he brings her a collection of romantic poems and *A Portrait of the Artist as a Young Man*. Most of the time he appears to be moderately amused by and moderately bored with Lolita, not unlike Professor Higgins with Eliza Doolittle in Shaw's *Pygmalion*. Mason's Humbert is also too in love with himself to madly love or desire another person. Therefore, when Lolita eventually runs away from him, it is not because she cannot stand his sexual bondage, but because she is fed up with his tutelage, his overpowering presence, his aloofness (as was, on many occasions, the more patient Eliza). Of course, Nabokov's Humbert is also extremely self-centered, but he needs to consume another person to feed his passions.

In his desire to educate Lolita, Humbert is not dissimilar to Charlotte, who also tries to shape Lolita in her own image by instilling in her daughter good manners and Christian values. However, Kubrick looks at the two types of education with a different eye: Humbert's tutelage is embraced, Charlotte's ridiculed. Even more preposterous appears Charlotte's attempt to teach Humbert how to dance the cha cha. The dancing teacher comes across as inept, and her education borders on physical assault, as Humbert only gives in when Charlotte drags him from his comfortable chair. By contrast, Humbert's teaching Charlotte to play chess comes across as a lesson in both substance and style; unlike the dancers, the chess players are depicted as dignified. Thus we deduce that if Humbert fails to learn to dance, it is because of his teacher's fault, while if Charlotte fails to learn chess, this is because of her hopeless ineptitude. Such rendering of these two types of education can be regarded, again, as encapsulating Kubrick's attitude toward the relationship between men and women, the old and the young, Europe and America. Women, according to this director, have much to learn from men, America from Europe, the young from the old, but not vice versa.

The confrontations between Humbert and Charlotte, as well as with other people whom he encounters, produce a sense of absurdity. It is Humbert who consciously leads to absurd situations, as when he replies, "Cherry pies," to Charlotte's question about what persuaded him to take lodging in her house. This is because he derives great pleasure from provoking and observing the gap between his self-knowledge and other people's perceptions of him. Largely for this reason, as Pauline Kael observes, he conveys a "sly, almost dirty sense of farce" (Kael 1992: 361). Nabokov's Humbert is also into creating the absurd (for example, when he cheats a psychiatrist by inventing stories from his past). However, there is a difference between Nabokov's and Kubrick's approach to "Humbert the absurdist." Kubrick shares Humbert's absurdist outlook on life; he laughs with him at the naïve and duped Americans. Nabokov, on the other hand, demonstrates that the sense of superiority Humbert gets from cheating other people is only a part of his deranged vision; the reality of these situations is different. Or even if he is sometimes able to cheat someone, more often he is made a fool of and punished for his actions. He is left by his wife and humiliated by her lover, left by Lolita and humiliated by Quilty, goes to prison and dies of a heart attack. Even the loss of his beloved Annabel can be read as punishment for his future sins. The moments when he thinks that good fortune is smiling on him turn out ultimately to be unlucky. When Lolita suggests that they begin travelling again, it is not a sign of her love for him, but of her growing desperation to escape. Any good luck Humbert enjoys, like the lucky coin his predecessor finds in *The Enchanter,* turns out to be counterfeit. Ultimately, Nabokov's Humbert cannot be happy; people like him are "beyond happiness." Nabokov's *Lolita* thus does not convey a sense of absurd, but of a match between human actions and their results, crime and punishment. By contrast, Humbert in the film is happy most of the time because absurdity reigns in Kubrick's universe.

A major change between the novel and Kubrick's film pertains to the nature and role played by Clare Quilty. Unlike in the novel, where Quilty lurks in the shadows or even is a shadow, in the film he comes across as very material and plays a crucial role in the narrative, entering the stage soon after Humbert. He appears at a college dance to which Charlotte takes Humbert, and it is revealed that he is her old flame. Similarly to Humbert, Quilty attracted Charlotte because of his intellect and she invited both men to the book club she chaired. Humbert epitomizes the old, high, literary and European culture; Quilty the new popular media and American culture. They can be compared respectively to Nabokov and Kubrick (Naremore 2007: 112). Humbert is like Nabokov in being a recluse and a compulsive collector of observations, almost unable to pass anything without immortalizing it in his diary. He also shares Nabokov's literary taste (for example, his love of Joyce). At the same time, he is not entirely immune to the pleasures of popular art, as suggested by his (albeit false) claim that he goes to Hollywood to work as a "consultant" on an "existential" film.[8]

Quilty resembles Kubrick in using the camera as his main artistic tool. We see him taking a picture of Lolita, and we learn from her last confession that Quilty wanted to use her in some kind of "arty" film, a request which she denied. In accordance with the stereotype of media people, Quilty is an extrovert who seeks popularity, as demonstrated by friendly chats with various people he meets on his way (such as the hotel porter) and posing for a cigarette advert. The idea that Quilty is Kubrick's alter ego is strengthened by Peter Sellers' references to *Spartacus* and the fact that he went on to play in Kubrick's later film, *Dr. Strangelove,* and is probably more associated with Kubrick's cinema than any other actor.[9] Although Humbert and Quilty in Kubrick's film represent different cultural traditions, their sense of being masters of their art allows them to treat women with disdain. For them women are a "lower species," whose sole attraction lies in their ability to arouse them sexually or act as their acolytes.

Although some features of Quilty in film were taken from Nabokov's screenplay, no doubt Quilty is Kubrick's most original addition, to the extent that the author of the script of Adrian Lyne's version of *Lolita*, Stephen Schiff, says that Kubrick made a film that might better have been titled *Quilty* (Schiff, quoted in Stringer-Hye 1996). The whole film is a story of searching for the "true Quilty," not unlike in *Citizen Kane* (1941), which centered on a search for the "true Kane." Opinions are divided as to whether this addition was successful. While Pauline Kael, Alfred Appel, and Schiff (Appel 1974: 239; Kael 1965: 205; Stringer-Hye 1996) claim that Quilty remains the most energetic part of Kubrick's movie, Ellen Pifer criticizes the way he is represented for hollowing out Humbert in the film (Pifer 1995: 314). I agree with Pifer and find Quilty in Kubrick's film to be like a joke that has run its course, his antics outdated and repetitive. Moreover, as one viewer commented on the IMDB website, he "comes from a different film": bringing a different mode of acting and aura, which in due course were associated with his most famous creations, that of Inspector Clouseau in Blake Edwards's *Pink Panther* movies and *Being There* (1979) by Hal Ashby. In *Lolita,* Sellers' sensibility clashes with other aspects of the film, such as the acting of other actors, visual style and music.

Increasing the screen presence and narrative function of Quilty led to the sidelining and belittling of Lolita — she is reduced to an object in the game of the two powerful men, Humbert and Quilty, with no agency of her own. Another way in which Kubrick marginalizes her is by omitting her from the final credits, which inform the viewer about Humbert's death. In this way he renders Lolita's story unimportant, deprives her life of tragic dimension, and plays down Humbert's responsibility for setting in motion the chain of events which culminate in her premature death.

Kubrick's film focuses on the first part of the novel, finishing with Charlotte's death. This part can be described as a "comedy of manners." The last part, depicting Humbert and Lolita's final journey, is the most abbreviated. In the book, the journey fulfils two functions: it shows America, albeit through Humbert's eyes, and provides Humbert a rite of passage; he realizes then that Lolita was exceptional not only as a nymphet, but as a human being. The mastery with which Nabokov represents the road is an important factor in *Lolita*'s status as an American book and a cult book, which it shares with Jack Kerouac's *On the Road* (Stringer-Hye 2002: 153). By contrast, in the film only a small fragment of travel survived, and the car-driving sequences lack energy, due to the use of matte shot effects, achieved by masking out part of an image using a matte and superimposing another image so that it combines with the rest of the original. As Robert Stam observes, although "made three years after Godard's jazzy and polyrhythmic *À bout de souffle* and Resnais' modernist *Hiroshima mon amour*, it deploys a relatively conventional pre–New Wavish style" (Stam 2005: 233). Kubrick's film shows no connection to some of the later cult American road movies, such as *Easy Rider* (1969), directed by Dennis Hopper, and *Five Easy Pieces* (1970), by Bob Rafelson. By reducing the road episodes, Kubrick also gives the impression that the characters do not change throughout the film, either externally or internally. The way Kubrick filmed the couple's journeys was partly a consequence of shooting the film in Britain, which, as Richard Corliss argues, was a reflection of Kubrick's personality: "Kubrick, bred in the Bronx, fled the U.S. for England and stayed there, an emperor hermit" (Corliss 1998: 37). However, it was also in tune with representing Humbert on film as somebody who does not need to change, who is justly content with himself.

The conservative style, deployed in the travel sequences, is augmented by a number of other aesthetic choices. One of them is Kubrick's drawing heavily on film noir (which was the style of 1940s and 1950s cinema, rather than of the 1960s) by using the play of shadow and light, mise-en-scène of gothic mansions, and shooting in black and white. Even the choice of James Mason, whose greatest role was probably in *Odd Man Out* (1947) by Carol Reed, adds noir connotations to the story. Film noir is also evoked by non-visual means, such as the circular narrative structure, with the same murder presented at the beginning and the end of the film, as in *Mildred Pierce* (1945) by Michael Curtiz; and the references to Edgar Allan Poe, which were extensively used in films such as *Laura* (1944) by Otto Preminger and, post–Kubrick, the neo-noir films of David Lynch. However, Kubrick is selective in his drawing on film noir, as he omits an important element: a femme fatale.

The question can be asked whether this style is suggested by the book. The answer, again, depends on the reading, not least because Nabokov's *Lolita* is visually very rich, evoking a number of different visual styles and pictorial traditions. There are certainly traces of noir and gothic there. Moreover, using the style associated with the 1940s and 1950s reflects the America Nabokov knew first hand and understood.[10] By contrast, the American 1960s, with its anti–Vietnam demonstrations, civil rights protests, and psychedelic and sexual revolutions, was completely alien to him (Johnson 2002: 147). Yet, on the other hand, *Lolita* the book is "shot in color," with detailed descriptions of the shades of pink of Lolita's clothes and the effect of weather on the color of nature, as in "El Greco horizon." Judging by Nabokov's screenplay, the writer saw the film in color too, as suggested by terms such as "gay cotton."

A conservative style is also added by the romantic score of Nelson Riddle. Robert Stam observes that the "static, pre-modernist, rather syrupy muzak-style love theme does not change or progress either rhythmically or melodically" (Stam 2005: 231). The use of (verbal) language plays a similar role. Many dialogues and monologues, including some long ones, were transferred verbatim from the book to the film. However, unlike in Nabokov's original, they often feel too crafted, too rich in witty observations, *double entendres* and literary allusions, and too revealing of the overall nature of the personages to sound natural. The cumulative consequence of using Nabokov's language adds to the sense of listening to literature.

The conservative style fulfils an important narrative and ideological purpose: it reduces the incompatibility between Humbert and Lolita, making both of them look decent and upper class, and suggesting that they are only playing lovers rather than being in love. The use of comedy, at the expense of tragedy, also serves such a function. There is enough comedy in Nabokov's novel to afford the comical adaptation. Yet, the comical dimension of the film is not so much a result of Kubrick's transportation of the comic features of Nabokov's book to the film as imposing on the literary "original" the director's own sense of humor. One element of it is slapstick; Pauline Kael even describes *Lolita* as "the first new American comedy since those great days in the forties when Preston Sturges recreated comedy with verbal slapstick" (Kael 1965: 205). The oft-quoted example is the collapsible bed in the hotel which Humbert attempts to unfold with the help of the hotel boy, about which Nabokov was particularly unhappy (LoS: xiii). Another source is Sellers himself. He brings to Quilty his unique persona of an apparently absent-minded, disoriented, mumbling, yet ultimately successful man. Sellers' self-indulgence in "verbal slapstick," whose roots are "stand-up comedy, radio parody and the *Goon Show*" (Stam 2005: 230), are all references absent in the book and most likely alien to Nabokov fans. Another source of humor is Charlotte Haze: her vulgarity and inability to see Humbert's indifference towards her. Charlotte is also ridiculed by Humbert in the book for the same reasons. Yet, it is a matter of opinion if and to what extent Nabokov shares his protagonist's attitude toward Charlotte. In my view, Humbert's inability to see in Charlotte anything genuine and precious, apart from being a weak copy of her daughter, reflects his own limited outlook on life rather than her. While instilling the film with his own sense of humor, Kubrick fails to account for the main source of comedy in Nabokov's book — namely, the disparity between Humbert's perceptions and reality, especially the gap between the way he sees himself and the way he really is. However, in order to convey this type of comedy, the director would have to demote Humbert from his position of stern professor and romantic lover to that of a mentally and morally blind, self-centered buffoon. And this, as I suggested, would result in a very different film.

Most likely for the same reason — namely, to preserve Humbert's dignity — Kubrick omitted from his adaptation the motif of Humbert the writer. We see him writing something in his diary, even trying to convince Charlotte that his description of their life together does not represent the way he sees it but serves as a sketch for his future novel. However, we never witness the process of transforming Humbert's life into his prose. In order to do so, Kubrick would have to point to the gap between the real and literary Humbert by showing how low Humbert's life is. Kubrick's Humbert is not in wont of art because he does not need atonement or transcendence: he is comfortable with himself the way he is. Therefore it seems inconsistent to me on the one hand to accept Kubrick's reading of Humbert as a dignified man and, on the other, criticize the director for missing or attenuating what many readers see as the ultimate subject of Nabokov's novel — namely, "the transcendent value of art itself" (Naremore 2007: 116).

If we look at the reviews of Kubrick's *Lolita*, we will notice the prevalence of adjectives pointing to its timidity and mediocrity: balanced, even-handed, elegant, restrained, stylish, cold (for example Croce 1962; Sarris 1962; Kael 1965). Style or stylishness is the most frequent compliment; lack of wicked edge, of anything scandalous or emotional, is the most common criticism, as in a review by Andrew Sarris: "We face the problem without the passion, the badness without the beauty, the agony without the ecstasy" (Sarris 1962: 11). By making an inoffensive film, Kubrick offered an adaptation faithful to a certain reading of Nabokov's book that emphasizes its erudite character and plays down its overt content, as encapsulated by Appel's writings. Conversely, the director made a film unfaithful to both the legend and Nabokov's idea of visualizing *Lolita*.

Kubrick's *Lolita* not only reflected a certain way of reading the book, but also affected its status, helping to move it from a position of scandalous work to that of classic: something an educated person should read — not for any illicit pleasures, but because it is great art. We can appreciate the significance of Kubrick's film in "dignifying" *Lolita* if we imagine what would happen if instead of this director somebody like Walerian Borowczyk or Tinto Brass had decided to film it.

As stated previously, Kubrick was not intimidated by the greatness of books or the names of their authors, and he refused to be assessed by any fidelity criteria. Yet, in due course he admitted that on this occasion his film did not live up to the reputation of its "original." The director put the blame, conveniently, on the book, claiming, "If it had been written by a lesser author, it might have been a better film" (LoBrutto 1997: 225). Unfortunately, it is impossible to prove. What is, however, clear to me is that Nabokov's *Lolita* and Kubrick's *Lolita* point, figuratively, in opposite directions. Nabokov's *Lolita* was ahead of its time, both as a work of art and as a sociological statement. It used a high style to represent a low life, style which still puzzles and

Sue Lyon as Lolita in *Lolita* (1962), directed by Stanley Kubrick.

enchants its readers. It also looked ahead toward the time when children would be more believed than adults, and abusing children would be treated as a serious offence. Kubrick, on the other hand, looks back at the golden years of Hollywood and European cinema, using an elegant and outmoded style. Equally, in common with the prevailing opinions about children and teenagers, he shows no interest in the psychology of Lolita or the specificity of her generation; he communicates through his film with like-minded people for whom observing the intellectual duel between two sophisticated middle-aged men, and the vulgarity and mental ineptitude of a middle-aged woman, is in-finitely more interesting than the accompanying anguish of an abused girl. Largely for this reason, however, Kubrick's *Lolita* quickly became an object of nostalgia, as testified by the warmer tone of reviews and critical studies of it by those closer to the present day (Burns 1984: 246). Another factor in creating a nostalgic detachment is the fact that the film became immortalized in a small number of carefully chosen and endlessly repeated stills, the most famous showing Lolita in the heart-shaped glasses and her foot being pedicured by Humbert. These two images have little connection with the rest of the narrative, and the second even disagrees with the overall representation of Humbert as a dignified teacher of Lolita. The way of remembering Kubrick's *Lolita* as a handful of images brings to mind Umberto Eco's definition of a "cult film" as a film that tends to be remembered as a collection of fragments, not as an organic whole (Eco 1988). I am not arguing that Kubrick's *Lolita* is a typical cult film in the sense of being narratively disjointed or ideologically incoherent, as is *Casablanca* (1942) by Michael Curtiz, which Eco uses as his main example of cult film. However, in my view, through the careful publicity and "acts

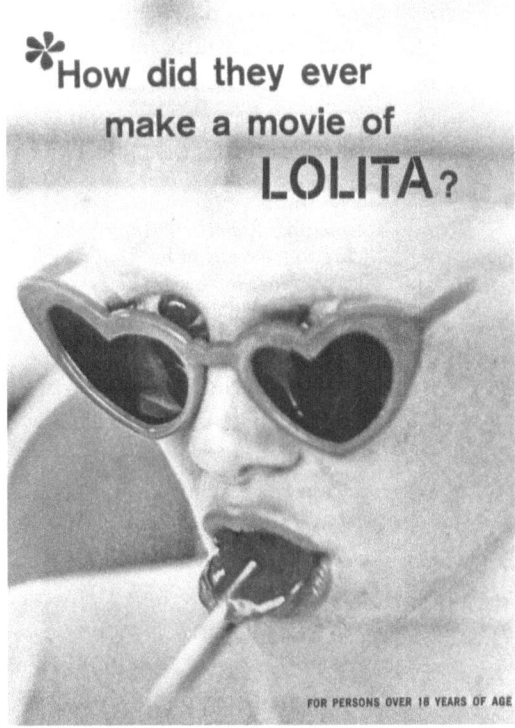

Poster for *Lolita* (1962).

of commemoration" of the film through recycling these images and retelling the story of making *Lolita*, its semi-cult effect was facilitated.

The greatest outburst of nostalgia for Kubrick's *Lolita* could be observed at the time of the premiere of the second adaptation of *Lolita*. A seminal example is a review of Adrian Lyne's film by Alan A. Stone in *The Boston Review*, where we find statements such as "Today Kubrick's *Lolita* is considered something of a milestone in modern film making" and "James Mason *was* the Humbert Humbert of the novel" (Stone 1998). This nostalgia is fortified by the fact that the majority of the cast and crew are dead, including Kubrick. The film itself thus became a legend and a yardstick by which to measure almost all subsequent adaptations of Nabokov's books, and especially Adrian Lyne's version of *Lolita*.

## *Ethnographic* Lolita *of Adrian Lyne*

The artistic reputation of Adrian Lyne, the director of the second screen version of *Lolita*, is very different from that of Kubrick. As a perfect Hollywood insider (despite being British by birth), Lyne tends to be praised for technical competence but criticized for lack of originality and "soul," due to cynically adjusting to the audience's expectations. A typical assessment of Lyne's work is offered by Richard Corliss, himself an author of the book, devoted to Kubrick's *Lolita*:

> Adrian Lyne, like Ridley and Tony Scott, is an honors grad of the Brit commercial schools, and to me many of his films play like two-hour adverts for passion. ("Lyne's Hot Sauce! You love it, you need it, you'll buy it"). There is something clinical about Lyne's facility for Rolfing the audience in *Flashdance*, *9½ Weeks*, and *Indecent Proposal* [Corliss 1998: 37].

In a similar vein, Devin McKinney writes, "Lyne has been identified with a lack of aesthetic ethics — a technician's love of the effective effect, reliance on shock" (McKinney 1999: 49). I believe that the relatively low-art reputation of Lyne affected the way his *Lolita* was promoted by playing down his input into its creation and playing up that of its main star, Jeremy Irons, and the author of the script, Stephen Schiff, who was a well-known journalist working for *Vanity Fair* and *The New Yorker*. For example, judging by the long interview Irons gave to the influential *Sight and Sound*, in connection with the British premiere of Lyne's *Lolita* (James 1998), one could infer that it was Irons rather than Lyne who made the film.

I must admit that Lyne's aesthetics, so derided by Corliss and McKinney, worked on me in my teens and twenties. I was especially enchanted — or, as

Corliss would say, lured and duped — by Lyne's treatment of eroticism in *9½ Weeks* (1986) and *Fatal Attraction* (1987) because women in these films did not come across as mere pawns in male affairs but as independent agents. Lyne might not be a feminist or even a director particularly sensitive to women's problems, but at least he does not overlook women. His specialism is depicting women who yearn for sexual fulfillment and do everything to achieve this goal. Certainly they would not shrink from destroying men and their families if this is the price to pay for their sexual bliss. In this sense, Lyne can be seen as a successor to the creators of film noir. Not surprisingly, the period of his greatest activity and successes, the 1980s, coincides with the revival of this genre.

Lyne's task in adapting *Lolita* was in some ways easier than Kubrick's because the shortcomings of his predecessor's film (albeit treated by critics and historians with the politeness granted to masters) demonstrated what should be avoided in future. In other ways, however, following Kubrick was difficult. The main problem the director encountered was how to deal with Kubrick's high-art reputation (albeit achieved mostly post–*Lolita*), which led many potential viewers to the opinion that Kubrick's version must be better than his, or that if the director of *2001: A Space Odyssey* and *A Clockwork Orange*, armed with Nabokov's script, failed to account for the novel's greatness, any lesser director would fail too.

In common with Kubrick's *Lolita*, Lyne's *Lolita* is a child of its time. It reflects the interest invested in the book by feminist critics, and the consciousness that children, lest teenagers, are no longer innocent (Winn 1983: 3–7). More than that, however, it betrays the long legacy of reading *Lolita* as a romantic novel or even, as Lionel Trilling pronounced, as a book about "the last lover" (Trilling 1958). Lyne's *Lolita* is also emblematic of a certain trend in adaptation in the 1990s, characterized by a desire to "return to the original," as marked by making films with titles such as *Bram Stoker's Dracula* and *Mary Shelley's Frankenstein*. Whether these films are indeed closer to the "originals" than the versions which do not pronounce overtly their status as adaptations, is a matter which exceeds the scope of this essay. What is beyond doubt, however, is that such titles convey the belief in faithfulness to the "original" as an important duty of the adapter. Accordingly, the scriptwriter, Stephen Schiff, defended the new version as being much closer to Nabokov's novel than Kubrick's film — indeed, as close as the movie can be (Stringer-Hye 1996).

In some ways he was right. Lyne, armed with Schiff's script, follows the narrative of the novel much closer than Kubrick. He also attempts to recreate the cultural space in which Nabokov's *Lolita* is set. Dominique Swain, who plays Lolita, although still not looking like a twelve-year-old or even fourteen-year-old girl, at least appears closer to a pre-teenager than to Grace Kelly in *Rear Window*. Her chest is flatter, her hair is darker and does not look as if it were styled by a hairdresser, and her wardrobe belongs to a child. Swain's Lolita is also more ordinarily vulgar (as opposed to exuding an "eerie vulgarity"); her vulgarity is a consequence of her age and upbringing, coming from provincial America and being a daughter of a woman who has intellectual pretensions but no means to fulfill them.

Richard Corliss observes that Swain "exudes a precocious inner caprice, but she's a bit too plain to radiate the pupal star quality that any nympholept should be able to spot in Lolita" (Corliss 1998: 38). I see Swain's ordinariness and her lack of obvious sex appeal as her asset, as it confirms Nabokov's idea that a nymphet is the subjective construct of a pedophile, not a temptress with which every man would fall in love. This point is reinforced in a short scene in which Humbert looks through the window and sees two girls playing tennis: Lolita and her friend. Although the other girl appears to be the more sexy and pretty of the two players, it is clear that Humbert is more attracted to Lolita, regarding her unblossomed womanhood as her greatest charm. Swain's Lolita also comes across as impenetrable.[11] On various occasions the viewer is not sure whether she is serious or joking, or says something because she believes it or because she wants to provoke Humbert. Her words often sound as if they were quotations, as if she was aware that she is playing the mythical Lolita rather than being the "original." Take, for example, the scene in the car where she reproaches Humbert for stealing her virginity or when she tells Humbert that he is limiting her civil rights. When he asks her where she learned this language, one is tempted to answer on her behalf that she learned it from *Lolita* and its numerous offshoots. The effect of playing Lolita's representation, is augmented by slowing down her movements and situating her on frames. Casting Jeremy Irons in the role of Humbert augments this postmodern effect, as he already played a man in a film about romantic love directed toward an elusive woman — in *The French Lieutenant's Woman* (1981) by Karel Reisz. However, this "echo effect" might result from my over-exposure to *Lolita* products rather than the consequence of Lyne's conscious attempt to create a postmodern version of the novel.

In contrast to Kubrick, who attempted to close the gap between Humbert and Lolita by representing Lolita as, at least having the potential to pass as an upper-class person, Lyne brings his characters closer to each other by making Humbert more ordinary and willing to cleanse himself of his European heritage. Unlike Mason's Humbert, who regards himself as one of a kind and stays aloof from anything American, Jeremy Irons' Humbert is

1. *Humbert Between Dignity and Romanticism* 39

Dominique Swain as Lolita, and Jeremy Irons as Humbert in *Lolita* (1997), directed by Adrian Lyne.

less snobbish. He does not sneer at Charlotte's literary taste or choice of interior design, most likely because he is too ashamed of his own conduct to boast about his worldliness. Moreover, rather than educating Lolita by instilling in her a love of high art, he tries to learn from her. This is because he is more touched by the trashy world of his stepdaughter than the literary treasures of the old world — precisely because his is the old, dusty, even immaterial world, while Lolita epitomizes everything young, new and concrete, like the pieces of chewing gum stuck to his car that cannot easily be brushed away.[12] For Humbert in Lyne's film, Lolita and America is also a vehicle to become somebody else, a semi–American perhaps, and a simpler, less tormented version of himself. Such representation of Humbert concurs with the readings of Nabokov's novel as a story of the Americanization of Humbert, mirroring Nabokov's own enchantment with America (Haegert 2003). The difference in representing this aspect of the novel can be attributed to the different cultural tastes of Kubrick and Lyne — the first being "European American," the second, "English American" (at home in America and with everything American).

On a number of occasions in voice-over, Irons' Humbert admits to abusing Lolita, even destroying her youth and her life. In this sense he is unlike

Mason's Humbert, who until the very end has no sense of guilt towards his stepdaughter, and in his actions is propelled solely by hatred of his rival. Yet, ultimately, Lyne sides with Humbert by rendering Lolita's destruction problematic. The director creates this impression by showing Lolita as the one who is more scheming and erotically active in her relationship with Humbert than he. When Charlotte is still alive, their triangular arrangement is for Lolita an opportunity to create an alliance with Humbert and upstage her mother. We see it, for example, in the garden scene, when, sitting between Humbert and Charlotte, she denies her mother direct access to Humbert and exchanges caresses with him via her retainer, which she takes out of her mouth and puts into Humbert's glass. The animosity between Lolita and Charlotte in Lyne's film, more than in Kubrick's version, exceeds the average conflict of generations, becoming an open hostility.

Lyne also shows that Lolita gets much pleasure from sex with Humbert, even if a side effect of that are some bruises for which she reproaches her lover. On the whole, it feels like Lyne's Lolita wants to have the privileges of both the adult and child's life: enjoy sex like an adult woman and at the same time be pitied like an orphan and an abused child. The focus on Lolita's sexuality also suggests that the reason why she abandons Humbert and escapes to Quilty is not his violence but her boredom. Not having a rival in her mother renders her relationship with Humbert mundane. A symbol of her need for extra stimulation is the pneumatic, coin-operated bed she uses in hotels where she stays with Humbert. Hence, we never see Lolita as an "innocent" child uninterested in sexual matters and defenseless in her dealings with Humbert. Therefore, the last confession of Humbert, precipitated by his hearing the voices of some children, which Lyne transfers verbatim from the book—"I stood listening to that musical vibration from my lofty slope, to those flashes of separate cries with a kind of demure murmur for background, and then I knew that the hopelessly poignant thing was not Lolita's absence from my side, but the absence of her voice from that concord" (Lo: 299)—which in the book attests to his realization that he stole Lolita's childhood, in the film sounds not poignant but hollow. We feel that he did not take her from the chorus of children's voices because her voice was never there, or, perhaps, the chorus sounded differently from the way he imagined it. Yet, despite the lack of convincing correspondence between Humbert's utterances taken from the book and the world as conjured by Lyne, the viewer can appreciate the beauty of *Lolita*'s language much more than in the Kubrick version. I will risk the statement that Lyne's film gives a new, even more literary meaning to the words "fidelity to the letter" used in relation to adaptation.

Lyne also shows that even if Humbert indeed in some measure ruined Lolita (for example, by depriving her of her mother), he ruined himself even more. Such a conclusion is in large measure a consequence of casting Irons, an actor who specializes in the roles of men tormented by sexual yearning and who shows an immense ability to humanize even the most obnoxious characters. His role in *Lolita*, in this sense, evokes his creations in *Swann in Love* (1984) by Volker Schlöndorff, *Damage* (1992) by Louis Malle, *Stealing Beauty* (1995) by Bernardo Bertolucci, or even *Moonlighting* (1982) by Jerzy Skolimowski. In order to afford Humbert the viewer's sympathy, Lyne provides him with his pre–American history (which Kubrick erased from his film entirely) — his early love for Annabel. This episode, unlike Humbert's marriage to Valeria, which exposes him as a cruel and obnoxious character, dignifies his nympholepsy by suggesting that at the root of his sexual perversion lie his romantic yearning and nostalgia. Other episodes also augment the perception that Humbert feeds on nostalgia, always trying to retrieve something from the past. When he sees Lolita for the first time and smiles at her, the smile comes across as a sign of recognition — a memory of his lost love. He also carries with him a ribbon from Annabel's underwear, and before entering Haze's house he takes something from his sock, as if to assure himself that he did not lose anything. His manner of walking, which lacks energy, and an almost lethargic behavior in the house of the Hazes, suggest that he is lagging behind. Even Humbert's diary is not a means to comment on the present day or achieve something in future, but to commemorate the past. Again, casting Irons enhances the sense of Humbert's nostalgia, as the actor's look, voice and smile predestine him to playing nostalgic characters.

I mentioned previously that Mason gives the impression of being a tired and exasperated father. Irons' Humbert also comes across as a fatherly figure, but in a "new man" style. We see him engaging in domestic chores — cleaning the house, ironing Lolita's clothes and attending meetings with her teachers — while Mason's character only said that he cleaned and cooked; while their equivalent in Nabokov's book used a maid and limited himself to making the beds to conceal any sign of his illicit activities. Such a representation makes Irons' character more sympathetic by showing his relationship with Lolita as more balanced than in the novel: Lolita services Humbert with sex, but he is at her service too. In his effort at being Lolita's father, Humbert in Lyne's film also comes close to the protagonist of *The Enchanter,* who says: "I know that I would be a most loving father in the common sense of the word, and to this day cannot decide whether this is a natural complement or a demonic contradiction" (Ench: 23). Humbert's attitude toward Lolita, as displayed in Lyne's film, points to the conundrum experienced acutely in the last decades, as eloquently put by Camille Paglia:

> We want to draw the father into the family unit closer and closer. Fathers now freely push strollers in a way that would have been embarrassing for them in the 1950s. But now, how close is too close? Just what are the boundary lines of acceptable physical behavior between fathers and children? [Paglia 1995: 158].

Ending the film with the dates of the deaths of Humbert and Lolita, which are in close proximity, underscores that they shared a common fate to the end: although separated, they remained united. Thus, by and large, Lyne continues the tradition of exonerating Humbert; but unlike Kubrick, he does not do it by furnishing him with an old-gentlemanly dignity, but by romanticizing him. For some critics this was a much greater sin on the part of the film's author than the film's alleged sexual explicitness.

Cinematic means, such as painterly, impressionistic lighting, careful framing, slow motion underscoring the unique moments Humbert shares with Lolita, and the nostalgic music of Ennio Morricone, are mobilized to represent Nabokov's pedophile as a romantic lover. This is also helped by a camera that applies Humbert's perspective. Lyne's protagonist, of course, uses his eyes to look at Lolita, but his gaze is not conventionally voyeuristic but nostalgic. He never looks at her "erotic" parts, but rather at objects he associates with their shared past and her uniqueness, such as her bobby pin (Stam 2007: 125). Humbert appears to be touched by everything she does — indeed, as a father enchanted by his child.

Although the styles of Kubrick and Lyne's films are very different, they are similar in the sense that both hark back to earlier traditions. While Kubrick drew on film noir, Lyne follows in the footsteps of European art-house films of the 1960s and 1970s — to the contempt of the critics, who see in him a fake European auteur (McKinney 1999: 49). The most likely model for Lyne's *Lolita* appears to be *Elvira Madigan* (1967) by Bo Widerberg, which also tells a story of impossible love using an impressionistic style. It is also worth mentioning that by following in the footsteps of Impressionists (the painters and their cinematic followers), Lyne, probably unconsciously, dignifies the choice of Charlotte Haze in Kubrick's *Lolita*, who was very proud of her collection of Impressionist reproductions. There is also a touch of noir in Lyne's version, thanks to the representation of Lolita as a femme fatale and a penchant for certain visual motifs often used in this genre, such as fans hanging from the ceiling, whose frenetic movements convey the inner anguish of the protagonist (we find them frequently in the films of the Coen brothers).

Quilty in Lyne's version, played by Ben Langella, is closer to the novel in the sense of being "cut to size": he does not steal the show from Irons'

Humbert, appearing less frequently and adhering to the script, both figuratively and literally, saying some of the most memorable words Quilty uttered in the novel, including the verbal exchange between Humbert and Quilty in the Enchanted Hunters, full of ambiguities and puns, and beginning with: "Where the devil did you get her?" (Lo: 125). The episode in the hotel is, in my opinion, one of the most successful in Lyne's film, both as a scene in its own right and as a rendition of the situation described by Nabokov.

Unlike Sellers' Quilty in Kubrick's film, whose attraction for Lolita was his worldliness, Langella's Quilty's main allure is his sexual experience. He comes across as a man who knows how to handle adventurous girls and make sure his dealings with them are not interrupted by unwelcome intrusions. Accordingly, unlike Quilty in Kubrick's version, who attempted to distract Humbert in their last confrontation by offering him a game of tennis, Langella's Quilty tries to put Humbert off from killing him by proposing that he see his collection of erotica.

Another difference between the two cinematic versions of *Lolita* concerns the representation of Humbert and Lolita's travels, which fill a large part of Lyne's film. No doubt they would please Nabokov, who said that if he had any influence on the production of films based on his novel, he would stress the different motels in which Humbert and Lolita were staying (SO: 21). The importance of journeys in Lyne's *Lolita* is manifold, just as is their lack in the Kubrick version. Firstly, as Stephen Schiff argues, thanks to them the viewer has a chance to see Humbert and Lolita's ordinary life: Humbert's everyday struggle with Lolita and his immense attachment to his nymphet, both of which were excluded from Kubrick's version (Schiff, quoted in Stringer-Hye 1996). Secondly, Humbert and Lolita's journeys point to their life together being outside the normal order of things, to their rejection of cultural norms and isolation from mainstream society, which is a prerogative of characters in American road movies. Lyne's Humbert is aware that in order to keep Lolita he "needs to keep driving," prolonging their vacation as long as possible. Travelling is for Humbert also a means to cheat time and freeze Lolita in her nymphet's personality. At the same time, as creators of road cinema are well aware, travelling is a powerful means of changing human identity. We observe such change both in the book and in the film, where Lolita gets bored with Humbert, and Humbert is made aware of the gap between his and Lolita's desires. In its focus on the couple's travels and the care in reconstructing the cultural landscapes they traverse, complete with the pop music popular in the 1950s, Lyne's version is very faithful to the ethnographic dimension of *Lolita*. Indeed, it would be difficult to upstage Lyne in this respect.

Unlike Kubrick's version, which is not really interested in showing erotic attraction between Humbert and Lolita, and can be used as a textbook of the ways to avoid censorship, Lyne in his film shows the couple making love, although in a rather discreet way (again associated with European art-house cinema). An important part of the life and afterlife of Lyne's *Lolita* concerns the fact that the director had difficulty finding an American distributor. This was related to the increased sensitivity about pedophilia in the U.S. and an expectation of a new, tighter anti-child-pornography legislation. As a result, *Lolita* premiered on the cable TV Showtime channel — to the humiliation of the film's director, scriptwriter and actors. Not surprisingly, taking into account Lyne's somewhat cheesy reputation, in due course he was also accused by many critics of translating Nabokov's novel into soft porn (Dick 1998: 52; Stone 1998; Stam 2005: 237–9; Naremore 2007: 104). Many critics even used the allegedly pornographic character of Lyne's film to defend Kubrick's adaptation (Stone 1998; Naremore 2007: 104).

I believe that the accusation of producing pornography most likely would not have appeared or would have been muted, if, paradoxically, Lyne tried less hard to be faithful to Nabokov. The similarity between the plots of the two works, the careful reconstruction of roads and motels, give the impression that the film is too much a copy to convey the originality of its original; it is thus pornographic according to Nabokov's definition of this term, where

Dominique Swain in *Lolita* (1997).

pornography is tantamount to a lack of originality, a "copulation of clichés." Lyne's film thus perfectly shows that while the filmmakers might still be criticized for being unfaithful to famous novels, they are even more at risk of being condemned if they attempt to be faithful to them.

For the vast majority of reviewers, Lyne's film was an opportunity to revisit Kubrick's movie, typically pronouncing its superiority (for example, Corliss 1998; Seeßlen 1998; Stone 2008). Although, as I argued, on the whole Lyne's film is very different from Kubrick's version, I believe that Lyne himself facilitated such nostalgic excursions by developing some motifs which ensured Kubrick's film's longevity, especially the motif of Lolita's glasses and her feet with painted toenails. Unlike Kubrick, however, who freezes them in static stills, Lyne puts them into motion. Maybe for this reason they are less memorable and less iconic.

## Lolita's Granddaughters and Grandmothers

The last part of this chapter I decided to devote to films inspired by Nabokov's masterpiece or that showing affinity with his work. *American Beauty* (1999), directed by Sam Mendes, and *Guinevere* (1999), directed by Audrey Wells, were compared with *Lolita* on account of depicting men in love with teenage girls, and being made shortly after Lyne's film (Hentzi 2001: 46; Stam 2005: 242). The better known and much more artistically accomplished *American Beauty* can be described as *Lolita* for the generation of children, or even grandchildren, of the first Lolita. The film depicts a middle-aged and rather affluent couple, Lester and Carolyn, who live in a suburban house with their teenage daughter, Jane. Their marital relationship is in crisis. The wife, who works as real estate agent, cannot tolerate her husband's laid-back attitude, which culminates in his quitting a well-paid albeit boring job in the media. The husband, on the other hand, is exasperated by his wife's constant nagging and her obsession with money and status. The crisis is deepened by each of them finding a new love interest — Carolyn in a fellow real estate agent who is even more ambitious than she; Lester in a friend of his daughter, Angela. Hence, in the structure of interpersonal relations within the film, Lester is given the role of Humbert, Angela of Lolita and Carolyn of Charlotte. The similarity between Lester and Humbert pertains to the narrator recounting the story when it is completed — from the grave. In Mendes' film Lester comes across as a sympathetic character, almost a heroic figure (Jackson 2000: 40). This is because Lester is sincere in his words and his deeds, unlike the other adult people around him, such as his wife who attempts to "project the image of success," as her lover puts it, while deep down feeling unhappy, or the homophobic, gun-obsessed neighbor who is in fact a closet homosexual. Unlike Humbert, who deludes others and himself until it is too late, Lester is able to see things clearly; his perception coincides with the director's vision. Finally and most importantly, he exercises his erotic obsession with Angela mostly in his imagination, and when the girl offers him sex, he resists his desire when he learns that she is still a virgin. Hence, he puts the girl's welfare above his own pleasure. As for Angela, in common with her literary predecessor, she appears to be more sexually experienced and "modern" than she really is. Deep down she yearns not for sex but for affection. She reciprocates Lester's feelings, seeing in him the precious qualities that appear to be so rare in the American "suburban class." In one respect, *American Beauty* reconciles Kubrick's and Lyne's versions by showing young and adult people mutually fascinated by their respective worlds and wanting to learn from each other. As one reviewer notes, the film vividly "deals with the ways that teenagers and adults imagine each other's lives" (Hentzi 2001: 46). Lolita and Humbert in the novel also imagined each other's worlds, but in this case the world of the teenage girl and the adult man remain separated — to the benefit of all concerned. Due to the fact that Lester literally dreams about Angela (unlike Humbert, whose relationship with Lolita is physical), the scenes showing the girl are stylized and even "poetic," although this poeticism is of American pedigree, verging on self-aware kitsch. On a number of occasions Angela appears covered in red rose petals. The petals have a double connotation: of innocence and eroticism. Even in his dreams Lester remains separated from his beloved, limiting himself to admiring her only-partly-exposed body. Such a coy attitude renders Lester as probably the most positive Humbert of all time.

Somehow on the opposite side of the spectrum, I will list *Twin Peaks: Fire Walk with Me* (1992) by David Lynch, which is a prequel to his celebrated television series *Twin Peaks* (1990), although made after the series. *Twin Peaks: Fire Walk with Me* is a story of a sixteen- or seventeen-year-old "American beauty," Laura Palmer, who falls victim to her father's incestuous feelings for her and is eventually killed by him. Unlike Kubrick and Lyne, who privilege the male perspective, Lynch identifies with Laura and even affords her a diary, in which she describes her sexual life and her dreams. Although he shows the girl as sexually active, even promiscuous, this does not make her any less a victim of pedophilia and incest. On the contrary, her sex with boys her age and obnoxious men who pay for her erotic services, often abusing her, underscores the pathology of her liaison with her father. The father, like Humbert, is a respected citizen, but it does not exonerate him or obscure his sins; rather, it renders them even more monstrous. Like Humbert, he also drugs his wife so he can creep to his daughter's bed, and most likely drugs Laura as well, until she herself discovers the pleasures of alcohol and cocaine. The small town where the film is set perfectly adheres to the description given by Nabokov. It is a sleepy, almost dead town dominated by places of transition: the diner, the gas station and the motel. Images dominate its landscape; people hardly look at each other because they always look at the television screen or Laura's photograph. Not surprisingly, the screen images literally take on lives of their own; the doors in the picture hanging on the wall transport Laura to a different reality. Lynch's film is so loaded with cinematic references and so aestheticized that the actual plot at times comes across as almost meaningless. It is also worth adding that in the *Twin Peaks* series cherry pies feature prominently. In summary, *Twin Peaks: Fire Walk with Me* can be described as a cross between Alfred Appel's reading of *Lolita* as a metafictional work and Nabokov's own rendition of *Lolita* as surrealistic film; plus it adheres to the contemporary image of pedophiles as utter monsters.

I also regard as interesting relatives of *Lolita* Roman Polanski's *Tess* (1979) and some films by Jean-Luc Godard. As I will devote a separate chapter to the relationship between Godard and Nabokov, I will limit myself here to a brief discussion of the Nabokov-Polanski connection. To begin with, like Nabokov, Polanski can be described as a master of form, which is revealed in his search for an ideal form for each new subject he chooses. Yet, for the bulk of viewers Polanski is linked to Nabokov, and *Lolita* especially, not because of his film style but his lifestyle. More than any other living filmmaker, he is famous for his dealings with "nymphets" in his private life, following his alleged rape of a thirteen-year-old girl and subsequent flight from the U.S. at the end of the 1970s, where he faced a lengthy prison sentence. This crime haunts him in his older age. While I write these words, he is under house arrest in Switzerland, awaiting extradition to the U.S. to be tried on the old charges, despite the fact that his victim publicly forgave him. This prolonged episode is a vivid testimony to the fact that while Western art has no problems condoning older men having sex with "nymphets," Western law takes a different view.

Apparently because of his first-hand knowledge of the subject described in *Lolita,* Polanski was once offered to adapt Nabokov's bestseller, but, unsurprisingly, he refused due to his tarnished reputation. Yet, my argument here is that Polanski's *Tess*, despite being based on the work of a different author (Thomas Hardy), being set in a different place and time (the fictitious English county of Wessex during the Victorian period), and even having as a lead character a much older girl, encourages comparison with Nabokov's masterpiece. The similarity pertains to the fact that Polanski puts at the center of his film the sexual relationship of a young and vulnerable woman with an older and powerful man, Tess's "cousin," Alec. Although Hardy's novel and Polanski's film are set in times when women were expected to marry and bear children earlier than in the culture depicted by Nabokov, and forcing a woman to have sex against her will was regarded as less of a crime than in 1950s America, the director represents Alec's subjugation of Tess as a greater moral sin than Humbert's forcing himself on Lolita in any of the screen versions of

Nastassja Kinski as Tess in *Tess* (1979), directed by Roman Polanski.

Nabokov's novel. Polanski's heroine, in common with Nabokov's Lolita, is an immature woman at the beginning of her life journey who knows little about her sexuality and even her own emotions, and is unable to predict the consequences of her actions. Alec's first sexual encounter with Tess, like Humbert's with Lolita, is rendered ambiguous; it is literally clouded in fog, which allows interpreting it as either seduction or as rape. Her later life with Alec is also not dissimilar to Lolita's life with Humbert, as she is pampered by her guardian/oppressor with gifts and appears to enjoy his generosity. However, after some time, despite Alec's begging her not to do so, and being pregnant by him, Tess leaves her lover and returns home. She later confesses that Alec took advantage of her immaturity and destroyed her life. Polanski endorses Tess' view that even if Alec loved her, he had no right to express his love in the way he did, which is a conclusion Kubrick and Lyne avoided in relation to Humbert. At the end of the film Tess kills Alec, who in the meantime 'recaptured' her, again taking advantage of her vulnerability, this time caused by her poverty. While granting Tess the right to punish the man who took advantage of her, Polanski does not give in to the temptation of idealizing Alec, despite the fact that, judging by his actions, he is a much more noble person than Hubert: he loves Tess as a unique individual and would do everything to make her happy, including letting her go and live her own life. The ultimate testimony of playing down Alec's importance is the fact that his death is represented not as a tragedy in itself, but only as a means to illuminate Tess' tragedy.

Hence, paradoxically, although Polanski in his private life, as revealed in his autobiography, *Roman*, tried to defend his nympholepsy by arguing that his teenage partner was, in fact, a mature woman who enjoyed sex with him, his film does not condone pedophiles or any man taking advantage of a woman's class, poverty, lack of sexual experience or any other reason which renders her vulnerable.[13] On the contrary, if there is a lesson to be learned from Polanski's film, it can be read as: "If in doubt whether your love or desire will be beneficial to its object, avoid expressing it to her." Great sexual desire, or even love, as we infer from *Tess*, is not sufficient reason to encroach on the desired person's life, which is also, as I indicated, a message that was clearly conveyed by Nabokov in *Lolita* and outside the novel.

## Conclusion

In conclusion, it is possible to make a film of *Lolita*; only the result will be partial and, in the opinion of the bulk of critics, unsatisfactory, either due to its perceived lack of fidelity and sexual timidity, as in the case of Kubrick's adaptation, or due to its explicitness and lack of originality, as in the case of Lyne. I believe that these two films, so poignantly revealing the risks of adapting Nabokov's masterpiece, will act as a warning to any possible adapters of Nabokov's book. At the same time, the traces of *Lolita* are appropriated by new generations of American directors and noticed by critics discussing them, testifying to the fact that the theme of a middle-aged man in love with a female child shows no sign of abating, and that this motif is strongly associated with *Lolita*, although probably less with Nabokov's novel as with its name, which functions today as a free-wheeling signifier penetrating new spheres of culture, especially the Internet. It can be said that Lolita, who was once a star, became a celebrity: somebody who is famous because she is famous. Nabokov was very aware of the power of his creation, claiming that Lolita is famous, not him; but he probably did not predict how much her fame would outshine his.

# 2

# Going Blind in Swinging London
## Laughter in the Dark
### by Tony Richardson (1969)

> Once upon a time there lived in Berlin, Germany, a man called Albinus. He was rich, respectable, happy; one day he abandoned his wife for the sake of a youthful mistress; he loved, was not loved; and his life ended in disaster. — Vladimir Nabokov, *Laughter in the Dark*

> I wandered through various public rooms, glory below, gloom above: for the look of lust always is gloomy; lust is never quite sure — even when the velvety victim is locked up in one's dungeon — that some rival devil or influential god may still not abolish one's prepared triumph. — Vladimir Nabokov, *Lolita*

*Laughter in the Dark*, set in Berlin in the 1920s and published in 1938, is a translated and substantially modified version of Nabokov's *Camera Obscura* (1936), his English translation of the Russian *Kamera obskura*, published for the first time in 1933. The different incarnations of the novel is one reason, although not the most important one, that the book, in common with *Lolita*, invites different interpretations. In one type, best exemplified by the works of Dabney Stuart, the book is perceived as an attempt at parody, although extremely sophisticated, because Nabokov's parody is cross-generic; the object parodied is film, not literature (Stuart 1971; 1978). The subtitle of one of the essays Stuart devotes to *Laughter in the Dark* speaks for itself: "The Novel as Film." Stuart emphasizes his point by claiming that "the mode of the telling of the story is more important than the salient events of the story" (Stuart 1971: 75). Alfred Appel, the critic most likely to over-aesthetize Nabokov, does not argue that the book is pure parody, but complains that "Nabokov's own attitude toward its popular ingredients was not sufficiently highlighted by irony or parody" (Appel 1974: 263).

The second approach, which in Nabokov's book sees a simple "slice of life," as far as I can judge from the literature which was available to me, was not fully realized. The closest reading to it is probably offered by Leona Toker, who, in her essay accounts for both the metaliterary and realistic dimension of the novel (Toker 1989).[1] Again, comparing the dates of the publishing of the respective analyses is revealing: Stuart's works, like Appel's and Proffer's studies of *Lolita*, reflect the importance of New Criticism and the efforts of Nabokov scholars to demonstrate his greatness by presenting him as a subtle aesthete, a genius at creating literary and cinematic puzzles.

The second possible reading concerns the importance of its themes and characters. It is thus possible to see the book as concerning mostly love or art, predominantly men or predominantly women. Not surprisingly, male critics focus on male characters and art, female on love and women. In some studies female characters are practically overlooked or are seen solely as vehicles to reveal the nature of Albinus and Rex. I believe that, more than *Lolita*, *Laughter in the Dark* lends itself to aesthetic and masculine interpretation, although the feminists and the representatives of the Holocaust studies (as well as Marxist literary historians) focused on social class would find here plenty of interesting material to draw on.

As the title of the original version suggests, cinema is its prominent element. The main couple, Margot and Albinus, meet for the first time in a small cinema theater, where Margot works as an usherette. Her ambition is to be a movie star, and she attempts to fulfill her dream by approaching producers, taking lessons acting and, after meeting Albinus, persuading him to invest in a movie in which she can play one of the main roles. Albinus is an art critic who dreams about creating animated cartoons based on "some well-known picture, preferably of the Dutch School, perfectly reproduced on the screen in vivid colors and then brought to life" (Laugh: 5–6). Axel Rex, Margot's lover, is an illustrator whom Albinus wants to realize his dream of setting the works of old masters in motion. The occupations and the ideas of these characters pertain to the period after the First World War, when cinema attempted to assert its position as an art form by imitating more developed disciplines or forging alliances with them in the production of *Gesamtkunstwerk*—a total work of art. Film during this period was regarded as a semi-communal experience; in the movie theater films were watched together, but also separately, because in the darkness there was less scope for exchanging impressions with fellow viewers than when watching a theatrical performance (Metz 1985: 546–57). Nabokov also evokes early cinema through the contrast between shadow and light, making the black-clad Margot the negative of her lover, whose name connotes whiteness and whose wife is pale (Stuart 1971: 77).

Nabokov's characters abandon their static existence for the frenetic pleasures of life that imitate film (ibid.: 76–7). This is especially true of Albinus, who has a "slowish mind," is clumsy and speaks with hesitation. His life with his wife Elisabeth is inert and passive because she is delicate, phlegmatic and docile. Margot disrupts his existence like an earthquake. Margot is herself nervous, mobile, impatient and full of energy, but prior to meeting her rich lover she is like a caged animal; he sets her free and allows her to spread her wings. The same is true of Axel, who is also very mobile but whose travels are often enforced and futile. Thanks to Albinus and Margot, Axel's directionless life is transformed into a coherent narrative.

For the main characters, sight takes primacy over other senses, as well as over the power of rational thinking. Albinus describes sight as the "prince of senses" and, revealing his typical bad judgment, predicts that "talkies would kill cinema." More importantly, he abandons his pale, passive wife for Margot, who entrances him with the expressiveness of her features and the grace of her movements. He appears blind to her intellectual deficiencies, bad manners, and obvious moral faults, such as greed and selfishness. For Albinus, even sex with Margot is less important than simply gazing at her. For Margot, sight matters too, but she is less interested in looking than being looked at. Her delight brings to mind old movie stars for whom their only perfect lover was the camera. In *Laughter in the Dark*, Nabokov also draws attention to the fact that the gaze, as much in cinema as in real life, is never objective or neutral, but is determined by the interests and values of the gazer. They who look are always, in a sense, myopic — they only see what they want to see, remaining blind to everything else in front of their eyes and what might be clear and important to other viewers.[2] Such is the case with Albinus, who is unable to see that Margot betrays him with Axel, although the mutual attraction between her and Axel is obvious to virtually everyone else in the novel. The "prince of senses," the faculty on which we rely most in our learning about the world, is also the sense most prone to mislead its user.

Another reason for *Laughter in the Dark*'s cinematic character is the fact that the author does not conceal its artificial character or the banality of the story. This banality is already announced in the first paragraph of the novel, which I used as an epitaph for this chapter (Laugh: 5). Nabokov also distances the reader by describing the place of action as if it was the setting of a film or a play, most importantly at the end of his novel:

> Stage directions for last silent scene: door — wide open. Table — thrust away from it. Carpet — bulging up at table foot in a frozen wave. Chair — lying close by dead body of man in a purplish brown suit and felt slippers. Automatic pistol not visible. It is under him. Cabinet where the miniatures had been — empty. On the other (small)

table, on which ages ago a porcelain ballet-dancer stood (later transferred to another room), lies a woman's glove, black outside, white inside. By the striped sofa stands a smart suitcase, with a colored label still adhering to it: "Rouginard, Hotel Britannia." The door leading from the hall to the landing is wide open, too [ibid: 187].

This passage, like many others in the book, points to the importance of doors, frames and framing in the book. As Leona Toker and Julian Connolly argue, such imagery often underscores the author's powers of control over his characters: it is he who ultimately provides the frames in which they are placed (Toker 1989: 114; Connolly 1995: 225). Finally, the crucial events in Albinus' life with Margot — namely, a car accident in which he loses his sight, and his attempt to kill Margot — are foretold in the movie that he watches in the cinema where she works. Hence, Albinus and Margot are constructed as characters in a film — a film Nabokov makes for the pleasure of his readers.

And yet the characters' fascination with cinema and their attempts to model themselves on movie characters and stars can be regarded not as a sign that *Laughter in the Dark* is a metafiction but, on the contrary, that it is a realistic novel. This is because in the epoch of "mechanical reproduction," cinema and other media became part of everyday reality and the prism through which people start to look at the surrounding world. By illuminating the vulgar conventionality of his characters, Nabokov foreshadows the approach that such leading creators of modern and postmodern cinema as Jean-Luc Godard, Pedro Almodóvar and Atom Egoyan would take with their characters.

The realistic reading of *Laughter in the Dark*, as David Rampton argues, was encouraged by Nabokov himself, who in one interview said: "I tried to express a world in terms as candid, as near to my vision of the world, as I could. If I was cruel, I suppose it was because I saw the world as cruel in those days" (Nabokov, quoted in Rampton 1984: 21). The fact that *Laughter in the Dark* lends itself to realistic interpretation is one of the likely reasons that, after *Lolita*, it was Nabokov's most popular novel. Its universal appeal can be measured by its being translated into fourteen languages (Appel 1974: 262). In the correspondence between Nabokov and Edmund Wilson we find the information that there was an attempt to adapt it for the stage as early as 1941 (NWL: 60) and that the screen rights were first acquired in 1945 by "a cinematographic firm in Paris" (ibid.: 173). It was Nabokov's second book, after *Lolita*, to be made into a film.

Looked at from a realist perspective, *Laughter in the Dark* confirms the opinion of Julian Moynahan that "Nabokov's great theme, which he shares with the Beethoven of *Fidelio* and the Gluck of *Orfeo* and *Alceste*, is that of married love" (Moynahan 1971b: 251).[3] The writer measures the value of all unions against the standard of a bond of two people of the opposite sex "against the loneliness of exile, the imprisoning world, the irredeemable nature of time, the voidness of eternity" (ibid.). Because married love is for Nabokov a sacred union, in his novels he pitilessly condemns anyone who betrays it, and Albinus is no exception. Nabokov treats him particularly harshly, more so than Martha and Dreyer in *King, Queen, Knave,* or Hermann in *Despair,* because unlike these characters, Albinus is deeply loved by his wife and daughter. By embarking on his affair with Margot, he deprives his wife and daughter of the husband and father they love — and he himself gives up on the treasure of their love, marked by stability, serenity and gentle affection — for the flimsy pleasures provided by his young and unfaithful mistress. He lacks the courage to clarify his position towards the two women. He clearly does not want to give up Margot and return to Elisabeth, but, equally, he does not want to divorce his wife. At one point Albinus even writes to Elisabeth an "ornamental letter" in which he attempts to explain his behavior and make her well-disposed towards him, while at the same time allowing himself to indulge in the extra-marital affair. Margot summarizes him as "a liar, a coward and a fool" (Laugh: 35). At the same time, when comparing himself with other men of his social position (not unlike Humbert in *Lolita,* who compared himself with a fellow pedophile), he considers himself unlucky because the others managed to keep their wives and their mistresses without causing scandal or moral discomfort. Nabokov's respect for marital love might also be the reason why he treats Albinus more severely than his chief antagonist, Axel Rex, who is undoubtedly more cynical and cruel.

> When, as a youth, he had first left Germany (very quickly, in order to avoid the war), he had abandoned his poor half-witted mother, and the day after his departure for Montevideo she had fallen downstairs and injured herself fatally. As a child he poured oil over live mice, set fire to them, and watched them dart about for a few seconds like flaming meteors. And it is best not to inquire into the things he did to cats [Laugh: 91].

Yet Axel is partially excused by the author for his cruel deeds because, in due course, he satisfied himself with imaginative cruelty. Moreover, unlike Albinus, Axel is not a hypocrite, and, as if aware of his potential to harm people, he has no wife or children and avoids any long-term commitments. A Marxist critic, interpreting crime as caused by difficult circumstances, might even argue that Axel and Margot are partially excused for trying to extract money from Albinus, being themselves poor and subjected in their youth to violence from their families and society at large. Axel and Margot thus attempt, acting as individuals, to regain what they deserve to be given as members of the working class. However, Nabokov, an ardent individualist, rejects such reasoning by introducing Margot's brother as a deeply unpleasant character who uses a socialist ideology to excuse his actions as a cruel crook.

At first glance, nothing is easier than to screen the "cinematic novel'; the director only needs to transfer the cinematic aspects from novel to film. However, as I argued in the Introduction, in practice such transmission is far from easy because the cinematic qualities of literature or other works of art are different from the cinematic qualities of cinema. Choosing as the heroine of *Laughter in the Dark* a woman who fails to make the transition from acting in real life to acting in film can even be regarded as Nabokov's warning to any potential adapter of his novel not to imitate it slavishly. The subject matter of *Laughter in the Dark* also poses a challenge: the theme of marital infidelity might be eternal, but attitudes have changed, and Nabokov's damning attitude to adultery is shared by fewer readers now than it would have been seventy years ago.[4]

Tony Richardson, like Stanley Kubrick, had built his career on adapting literary works, including *Look Back in Anger* (1959), *The Loneliness of the Long Distance Runner* (1962) and *Tom Jones* (1963) in Britain. In the mid–1960s Richardson had directed two films with the French star Jeanne Moreau, who fascinated him in the role of Catherine in François Truffaut's *Jules et Jim* (1961) (Pauly 1999: 143): *Mademoiselle* (1966), based on an original screenplay by Jean Genet, and *The Sailor from Gibraltar* (1967), adapted from a Marguerite Duras novel. Thus, Richardson's cinema during this period stands at the crossroads of the three cultures — British, American and French — to which Nabokov was closely linked during his life. One could expect that Richardson would achieve success by appealing to an international audience in the same way that Nabokov did. Another reason why Richardson could be regarded as a good match for Nabokov is that, despite his association with the British New Wave, he had proved himself increasingly willing to venture beyond the borders of realism.

Yet, neither of his international productions were a box office successes, and they either attracted critical or mixed reviews. Sheldon Hall claims that "Richardon's career was severely damaged by the films' hostile reception" (Hall 2006: 512). However, as Robert Murphy observes, the hostility of the British critics to some of these films, especially *Mademoiselle*, which, due to its subject matter, is closest to *Laughter in the Dark*, reflects more their conservatism than the films' quality (Murphy 2009: 326). *Mademoiselle* concerns a small-town schoolmistress, played by Moreau, who becomes obsessed with an Italian woodcutter, only to find that several of the local women are already sampling his sexual favors. "Moreau in the part of the embittered heroine excels in crossing the line from beauty to ugliness and turning herself into a femme so fatale she makes other femme fatales look like wholesome milkmaids" (ibid.: 326). She expresses her sexual frustration by destroying her lover and the whole community, opening sluice gates to cause a flood, setting off fires and poisoning the water supply. The film's subject can be described as the blinding power of the gaze. Looking at the man to whom she is attracted conjures in Mademoiselle a desire to possess the object of her gaze, which leads her to losing any moral sense, becoming blind to the suffering of others. On the other hand, when she is looking at herself in the mirror, Mademoiselle appears not to recognize the person looking back; the mirror becomes a vehicle of her split into the one who acts and the one who looks at her with a punishing gaze. Richardson's framing convincingly expresses the voyeuristic and sadistic viewpoint of Mademoiselle.

Although Richardson was a natural choice to direct *Laughter in the Dark* due to being a transnational director and his interest in the fatale love, fed on voyeurism, the book was not his choice. According to his memoir, the project was brought to him by his friend and agent, Robin Fox (the father of the famous actor James Fox, who had made his debut in *The Loneliness of the Long Distance Runner*). Despite his admiration for Nabokov, Richardson was at first reluctant to tackle *Laughter in the Dark*. But, as he puts in his autobiography, echoing Nabokov's words, he began to see a way in which *Laughter* could be set in the "swinging" contemporary art world, and something of its cynicism and cruelty corresponded to his own mood of emotional depletion (Richardson 1993: 210–11). The script was written by the famous British playwright Edward Bond, who wrote dialogue for the celebrated film by Michelangelo Antonioni, *Blowup* (1966). Richardson and Bond adhered to the overall plot of Nabokov's novel, but by moving the action from Berlin of the 1920s to London of the 1960s, omitting several episodes and changing the relationship of the three main characters, they altered the overall message of the film. Such an approach to Nabokov's work prefigures Fassbinder, who, despite sticking to the letter of *Despair*, created a very different work from the original.

The English setting led to changes in the names of the characters: Albinus' wife, Elisabeth, becomes Pamela; Albinus' daughter, Irma, is Amelia renamed; Albinus is transformed into Sir Edward More; Axel is renamed Hervé and only Margot, a name still common in Britain of the 1960s, remained unchanged. While the changes of the names of Elisabeth and Irma can be explained simply by the need to make them sound more English, the others bear greater significance and are accompanied by other changes. Unlike Albinus, which connotes being pale and naïve, and therefore easily duped, Sir Edward More stands for long, aristocratic traditions, and artistic and intellectual pretensions through similarities with the names of the famous sculptor Henry Moore and statesman and philosopher Sir Thomas More. Unlike Albinus, whom Nabokov describes as a mediocre critic unable to execute anything of value, Sir Edward comes across as capable and independent in his work as an art collector and critic. We see him taking part in a television program, shot in the National Portrait Gallery in London, in which he discusses the Holbein portrait of Henry VIII. He seems to be authoritative and as comfortable in the modern media as the art critic Sir Kenneth Clarke and the celebrity photographer Lord Lichfield. These associations add to the impression that More is rich, wellbred and talented. Richardson, in condensing the plot, cleansed the narrative of episodes that underscore the hypocrisy and selfishness of Nabokov's protagonist, such as when in a letter he proclaims love for his wife without renouncing his mistress.

Virtually all reviewers also pointed to the fact that Williamson's character is younger than Nabokov's Albinus. Philip Strick even wrote that "Williamson is uselessly young" (Strick 1969: 189). The very point that Edward is younger than Albinus is debatable, as Nabokov never reveals the age of his protagonist. The only moment when we get a sense that he is much older than Margot is in the beach scene, when an Englishwoman assumes that he is romping with

Nicol Williamson as Edward, and Anna Karina as Margot in *Laughter in the Dark* (1969), directed by Tony Richardson.

his daughter. Julian Connolly observes that this episode suggests that in Albinus' life Margot replaced his daughter. Hence, his relationship with Margot foreshadows Humbert's relationship with Lolita (Connolly 1995: 220). For this reason, Williamson's relatively young age is not useless but useful — it helps us to see his affair with Margot as different from that presented in Kubrick's film. Similarly, if the cinematic Margot looks older than her literary predecessor, it augments the sense that Edward and Margot are unlike Humbert and Lolita.

Pamela, played by Siân Phillips, lacks the features which in the novel make Elisabeth both distinctive and likeable. She is neither absent-minded nor warm, nor furnished with an extra sensitivity which allows her to "see" the suffering of her husband even at a distance. Instead, she comes across as the conventional wife of a rich man: well-organized, even pedantic and not the type to easily let her husband go. Testimony to her frigidity is her rebuff, "Darling, it is late," when Edward proposes sex. Richardson thus portrays Pamela the way Margot thought about her rival. Such a construction of Pamela helps us to understand and forgive Edward's infidelity.

Richardson also limits the screen time allowed Edward's daughter, who is deprived of any distinctive personality. Most importantly, the moving episode of the girl's death, which results from her mistaking a man singing in the street for her father, and that of the family doctor leaving the sick Irma for a much less ill Margot, are both omitted. In this way, Richardson exonerates Sir Edward from responsibility for his child's death. By such transformation he moves the balance of the story from Edward's relationship with his old family to that with his new family, consisting of Margot and Hervé. The question of Edward's betrayal of his family pales into insignificance in comparison with the problems resulting from his doomed affair with Margot. Edward's life with Margot is depicted by Richardson as a road to hell, with each day spent with his mistress taking him closer to his ultimate demise. The crucial stages on this road are Amelia's death, Edward's blinding and, eventually, his death in the cellar of the house where he lives with Margot and, unknowingly, with Hervé. Edward is accompanied throughout by the camera, which shows in close-up his suffering and anguish, and encourages us to empathize with the doomed protagonist. Thanks to the changes in him and around him, Edward comes across as more worthy of our sympathy than his literary predecessor. If we are to believe Tony Richardson, he wanted him to be more sympathetic still. Richardson complained in his autobiography about Williamson:

> He is a brilliant actor, especially on stage.... The only thing the gods didn't give him is the quality of empathy on camera. On stage it doesn't matter, because his pyrotechnics

are so dazzling and so true that they are more than sufficient. It was, however, a damaging flaw for portraying Sir Edward More in *Laughter*, though I didn't realize it at the time. The character needed someone whom an audience could desperately feel for [Richardson 1993: 210].

Hervé, like Axel Rex, is a part-time forger and part-time artist, but without the talent or personality of his predecessor. By giving Edward's nemesis a French name and casting in the role a Belgian actor, Jean-Claude Drouot, Richardson also suggests that he is an outsider in London. For these reasons he operates at the margins, reduced to observing and hanging about those who have power, money or talent. When the opportunity arises, he offers them his services, which they, however, tend to scorn, as we see in the episode of an auction of paintings where Edward pays no attention to Hervé's desperate attempt to catch his eye. There is no chance that the art collector would, of his own accord, approach this man to help him realize any of his artistic projects. Hervé's only truly "artistic" moment consists of starting a fire at a party in Edward's house, which is regarded by the guests as a highly amusing "happening." Hervé's true assets are his brooding, Mediterranean looks, which attracted Margot to him in the past and allow him to regain her heart. Richardson thus reduces Nabokov's character to a kind of luxurious pimp who uses his attractiveness to his whore to extract money from her best client. Even the harsh way he treats Margot is reminiscent of the way pimps treat prostitutes.

Margot undergoes the greatest transformation on the way from novel to film, despite retaining her original name, due to the casting of a non–British actress Anna Karina, who does not hide her Danish accent, described by one reviewer as "hideous" (Strick 1969: 189). This casting choice can also be attributed to the author and producer's desire to capitalize on Karina's popularity, who at the time was at the peak of her career, following her success in the films of her by-then ex-husband Jean-Luc Godard. Like Hervé, Margot wants to move from the periphery of British society to its center. Her meager status and her dreams are signified by her occupation as a part-time usherette, part-time prostitute. As an usherette, often shot in front of the screen, she is "in the movies," but not as we normally understand the term. As a prostitute or "escort," she has access to more affluent men, but not in a way that is socially recognized. Hervé and Margot's foreignness, marginality and dependence on the good will or naivety of others is an additional factor that brings them together. They understand each other better than anybody else can understand either of them. Their conspiracy to sponge off Edward and have fun at his expense can even be construed as a metaphorical revenge on the world in which they are second-class citizens, lurking in the shadows and overlooked

Jean-Claude Drouot as Hervé, Anna Karina as Margot, and Nicol Williamson as Edward in *Laughter in the Dark* (1969).

by those in positions of power. In this sense their attitude can be compared to Colin's decision to lose a cross-country race in order to upset his patron in *The Loneliness of the Long Distance Runner*. However, Hervé and Margot are less idealistic and naïve than Colin; for them their own wellbeing is more important than defeating an enemy.

Along with the similarities between Margot and Hervé, there also exist meaningful differences. Nabokov represents Margot as a strong and ruthless woman who will do anything and everything to achieve her objectives. Her greatest desires are for Axel and stardom, which she attempts to fulfill by using Albinus as her vehicle. Richardson's Margot, by contrast, does not have any specific professional or personal plans. Unlike her predecessor, she is less of a natural gold digger and does not care about fame or success; she only wants to have fun and excitement. The ultimate delectation for her is sex with Hervé, but she also enjoys life's small pleasures, such as listening to music, shopping and playing in the water. Conversely, when she is prevented from immediate gratification, she grows restless, as shown in an episode in Edward's garden when she cannot find a place for herself while her lover is doing some secretarial work for Edward. This scene brings to mind other Swinging London films, most importantly *Darling* (1965), by John Schlesinger, whose heroine, Diana Scott, also becomes restless every time her journalist partner has work to do and eventually leaves him to have an affair with another man. Such scenes demonstrate that for the woman of Swinging London boredom is the best aphrodisiac; they would do everything not to be kept in the house, enduring mundane life.

The need for immediate bliss differentiates Margot from Hervé, who always thinks ahead and is able to sacrifice today's pleasure for future benefits. Consequently, it is Hervé who has to explain to her that as long as Edward is married to Pamela, Margot is not entitled to any of his possessions, and he urges her to extract more and more money from her aristocratic lover. This requirement also, ultimately, changes Margot into Hervé's slave. From his callous behavior in the villa where they stay with the blind Edward, we can deduce that he finds her attractive only when she is able to support his lavish lifestyle. When she becomes, as he puts it, "too thin," he loses interest in her. By this point Hervé is on his way to abandoning Margot for the second time. By making Margot so dependent on Hervé, Richardson, if not exonerating Margot for her crimes against Edward entirely, "dilutes her villainy" (Strick 1969: 189). He further reduces Margot's guilt by showing her objecting to the excesses of Hervé's cruelty towards Edward and by rendering her killing of Edward as semi-suicide.

Margot's spontaneity and at times even naivety is underscored by Karina's acting. Like that of a child, her mood is always changing: one minute she is sad, the next she is laughing madly. Her ultimate innocence is accentuated by the baggage of her previous roles which she brings to this film, especially *Vivre sa vie* (1962) and *Pierrot le fou* (1965), both directed by Godard. In these films she plays an ultimately tragic heroine: a woman who violates the law and harms others not because she is evil, but due to circumstances over which she has no control — typically because she is an accomplice, even a pawn, in male games.[5] As a star of Godard's early films, Karina also became a symbol of sincerity in acting, of cinema in its purest and noblest form. These aspects of her persona are conveyed by her very name, which resembles "Anna Karenina," the heroine of Tolstoy's novel. Nabokov also evoked Tolstoy's character by including in his book the actress Dorianna Karenina; she is cast as the main star in a film produced by Albinus as a present for Margot, who plays the second leading role in it. In contrast to Nabokov, Richardson did not need Dorianna Karenina because Karina excellently fulfills this role. Using Karina in the role of a budding actress opposite any great star would look incredible.

Because of the changes to Margot, the central conflict in the film (unlike in the novel, where Edward is set equally against Margot and Axel) is between Edward and Hervé. However, until the very end Edward remains blind or indifferent to the fact that he is harmed by Hervé, rather than Margot. Even when he gains proof that his secretary cuckolded him, he shows no desire to punish him and is not curious about what happened to his rival; his whole craving for revenge is directed towards Margot. Thus Richardson's film shows that women have to pay for male lust, greed and blindness. However, Richardson does not question the patriarchal attitudes of the society he represents, treating it as entirely natural.

Sight in this film is represented not in a purely physical sense but as an intellectual faculty — an ability to read and react correctly to physical stimuli. Such an interpretation of sight concurs with Nabokov's "vision of sight" and reflects the film's scriptwriter's (Edward Bond) attitude toward this sense, as conveyed in Antonioni's *Blowup*, on which he collaborated. *Blowup*, in common with *Laughter in the Dark*, reveals a great skepticism towards humans'

Jean-Claude Drouot, Anna Karina, and Nicol Williamson in *Laughter in the Dark*.

ability to see things correctly. It can be viewed as a meaningful coincidence that in both films the most blind turn out to be the characters who use sight as their main professional tool, a photographer in *Blowup* and an art historian in *Laughter in the Dark*. I suggest that both films render the late 1960s as a period showing distrust towards human faculties, paving the way for an even more skeptical postmodernism in cinema. The making of a film such as *Performance* (1970) shortly after *Laughter in the Dark* confirms this trend.

Richardson's London is unmistakably Swinging London, with all its pleasures and dangers, including the use and abuse of drugs (and their connection with psychodelia), snobbishness, acceptance of gays into high society and, of course, promiscuity. These themes are strongly evoked during the party episode at Edward's London home, where among the guests we see David Hockney, and at one moment the screen is split to suggest distorted vision caused by drug taking. At the party, as well as on other public occasions, participants are not ashamed to act erotically — they kiss, grope, and exchange meaningful glances. We are led to believe that it is seeing men and women swapping partners without any dire consequences that gives Edward the courage to seduce Margot. Situating his affair in the context of Swinging London helps exonerate Edward from the sin of infidelity. His problem is thus less sin and more bad luck.[6]

Swinging London is a perfect milieu for the type of story told in Nabokov's *Laughter in the Dark* because the late 1960s was a period of profound cultural transition. On the one hand, ideas about "free love" were in vogue; on the other, beliefs about the importance of marital fidelity and "decency" were still very strong. The "Profumo affair" of 1963, which concerned John Profumo (secretary of state for war) and London call-girl Christine Keeler who was also the lover of a Russian spy, was presented in the press as a case of a rich, older, influential and married man being wooed and cheated by a young, poor and cunning woman — not unlike Sir Edward More being cheated by Margot in Richardson's film. Since the 1960s, the scandalous character of such a liaison, which furnishes Richardson's film with much of its poignancy, has diminished. The public at large ceased to be outraged by older men leaving their spouses for women half their age. Richardson's film is thus a transitional work because, on the one hand, it presents a man who cannot resist his hedonistic appetite for youth and sex, and on the other, it shows that such giving in to one's hedonism is still out of the ordinary.

In his representation of Sir Edward and Margot's affair, Richardson also conforms to the dominant representation of erotic liaisons in the Swinging London film cycle. The relationship between a materially rich, emotionally impoverished middle-aged man and a spontaneous, vulnerable, sexually-willing young woman is a common theme in British cinema of this period. Six films released in 1969 — *Three into Two Won't Go*, directed by Peter Hall; *All the Right Noises*, directed by Gerry O'Hara; *Twinky*, directed by Richard Donner; *One Brief Summer*, directed by John Mackenzie; *Age of Consent*, directed by Michael Powell; and the Norman Wisdom comedy *What's Good for the Goose*, directed by Menahem Golan — have this as their main subject (Murphy 1992: 154–55).

Although Richardson's London is similar to Nabokov's Berlin, it comes across as a gentler universe. London streets are safe, and there is no sign of the casual domestic violence to which Margot was subjected in the novel while living with her parents and brother. Consequently, as long as Edward remains in his milieu, Margot and Hervé cannot do him any serious harm. It is only after they leave for Southern Europe that he loses his protection and becomes an object of Hervé's unremitting cruelty. It is thus logical that Edward loses his life in a villa by the sea, in contrast to the novel, where it happens upon his return to Berlin. This part of the film was shot in Majorca, although more likely we are meant to identify the setting as Italy because we hear Italian spoken. Essentially we are in a "generic" European South, with sun, sand and sea rather than any cultural treasures. At this time, Southern Europe functions as a kind of mini–Orient where people can indulge more freely in their erotic passions.

The change of milieu from Berlin of the 1920s to London of the 1960s adds an extra dimension to Edward's affair. In contrast to the book, where Margot signifies bad taste, of which she gradually purifies herself with the assistance of her rich and well-bred lover, Margot in Richardson's film stands for the "new taste"— that of pop art. She brings blow-up furniture and transparent plastic cushions containing red plastic lips to Edward's house, and, after a moment of hesitation (it hardly fits with his staid interior design), he embraces Margot's style wholeheartedly. These gadgets help to liberate him from his stuffy surroundings in the same way her presence liberates him from the clutches of a static, aristocratic culture and marriage. Equally, Margot's physical appearance, marked by strong make-up, short, colorful dresses and a plastic raincoat, is not in bad taste but in new taste. She comes across as a perfect "Soho bitch," bearing resemblance to such characters as Jane Asher's Susan in Jerzy Skolimowski's *Deep End* (1970) or the two women in *Performance*. Margot's style is also conveyed through music. Whenever she appears we hear 1960s pop; by contrast, Sir Edward is associated with a pastiche of Renaissance music — a discordant and badly played version of Monteverdi's *L'Incornazione di Poppea*, adapted by Raymond Leppard. This kind of music would return in the 1980s in the films of Peter Greenaway (the scores of which were written by Michael Nyman), most importantly in *The Draughtsman's Contract* (1982), where music also accentuates the discordant life of the upper classes, albeit in a different epoch.

By and large, Margot's taste, although jarring within the milieu to which she aspires, comes across as harmonious with her personality. Throughout the film Edward wants to learn from her, even imitate her, rather than teach her his own habits and pass on to her his taste. An excellent example is the scene at a beach where the three main characters sit on movable deckchairs. We see that Margot and Hervé change their positions to look at each other, but are followed by Edward, who also lowers his deckchair to enjoy Margot's company. Upon noticing that Edward is at the same level as her, Margot moves her deckchair higher, and Edward again follows her. This changing of the position of deckchairs continues for some time until Margot bursts out laughing, in this way showing Edward that her attempt to avoid his company was in fact only a game.

As previously mentioned, *Laughter in the Dark* is a very cinematic novel. Richardson preserves some of the cinematic qualities of Nabokov's book but discards those which might appear contrived or prematurely betray the outcome of the plot. The film's central couple, as in the novel, meet in the cinema theater, where the (chiefly male) audience members are laughing. We can hear the sounds of shooting, but we do not see the actual film (which in the book contained a prophecy of Edward's fate). Richardson acts in the opposite way to Rainer Werner Fassbinder, who in *Despair* would include a fragment of the silent movie watched by Hermann, foretelling Hermann's future. The whole section of the book devoted to Albinus producing a film, which lays bare Margot's lack of acting talent, is cut out. Unlike Nabokov, Richardson also avoids means which would suggest that his characters inhabit a fictitious world. For example, he uses frames (windows, doors) more sparingly than Nabokov, and probably only those viewers well acquainted with Nabokov's text would see in them a sign that they are watching metafiction. The only moment when we might get a sense that Margot and Edward are merely puppets in the hands of the director is the scene of the car accident, photographed from above as if by an omnipresent spectator-manipulator.

Although only seven years divides Stanley Kubrick's *Lolita* and *Laughter in the Dark*, it seems that more time had passed. This impression results from the different visual styles employed by the two directors, the types of dialogue they used and their approach to eroticism. Unlike Kubrick, who drew on film noir and German Expressionism, making his film look somewhat "retro" even at the time it was made, Richardson attempted to make his film as contemporary as possible. *Laughter in the Dark* is shot on location in "Swinging London" and uses color boldly to convey the different tastes and lifestyles of the characters. Pamela is grey and pale; Margot is sun-tanned, and wears tight red and blue dresses. Since her entrance into Edward's life, even his garden appears to be transformed, with roses blooming everywhere. It is also worth mentioning that, unlike Nabokov's Margot, who discovers Albinus' true identity by finding a name tag on the inside of his hat, Richardson's Margot learns who he is from the television screen. In a similar vein, Edward learns about his mistress unfaithfulness not from his friend, the writer Udo Conrad, but from a gossipy girlfriend of his ex-secretary. This transformation, praised by the reviewers and even Nabokov himself (Strick 1969: 189; SO: 137), again reflects the time the film was made, with its rise of popular and gossipy media, which gradually replaced high literature as a dominant pastime and a source of knowledge about contemporary life for the majority of the population.

The physical attraction between characters is also conveyed more explicitly than in the Kubrick film, although by contemporary standards, Richardson's film is rather coy. Not surprisingly, Nabokov, who was always anxious to distinguish between his approach to eroticism and that of less gifted authors, was "appalled by the commonplace quality of the sexual passages" (SO: 137). However, he only partly blamed Richardson, acknowledging that the art of simulating sex onscreen or in a theater is much behind the art of imitating other typical human actions, such as eating or getting drunk (ibid.: 137). Richardson might not have created a new language of representing sexual attraction here (as he did with the fetishistic symbolism of *Mademoiselle*), but he clearly differentiates between Edward's manner of lovemaking — slow to the point of inertia and never outside the bed — and Margot and Hervé, who prefer more adventurous places and positions: in a boat, in the sea, on the floor of Hervé's apartment. In this respect, Richardson's Margot is very similar to Martha in Jerzy Skolimowski's *King, Queen, Knave*, who would also be willing and able to make love at any time and place. Both Margot and Martha fit the type of woman who frequently appears in Nabokov's prose, one who is sensual, carnal and uses her brain almost solely to get rid of any obstacles to her sexual bliss. At the same time, by representing such a woman, both films convey the aura of greater, although not total, sexual freedom characteristic of Europe in the late 1960s and 1970s.

In *Laughter in the Dark*, Richardson, as in one of his earlier films, *The Loved One* (1965), intertwines two modes of narration: farcical, which dominates in the first part of the film, finishing with the trio of characters moving to the South; and realistic, which prevails in the second part, finishing with Edward's death. Such a lack of emotional consistency hinders identification with the characters and is liable to disorient the viewer. Yet, for contemporary audiences brought up on films which move from comedy to drama and vice versa much more nonchalantly than those of the 1960s, this feature of *Laughter in the Dark* might add to its charm. In a similar vein, *Laughter in the Dark* illuminates the dilemma of interpreting Nabokov either as a late modernist who still believes in reality or as a postmodernist who replaces the difference between reality and fiction with that of fiction and metafiction.

*Laughter in the Dark* was neither a commercial nor critical success, although the reasons for that are not straightforward. Richardson thought that its poor box office results should be largely attributed to changes in the film business in both Europe and America, which disadvantaged arthouse or offbeat movies (Richardson 1993: 215). Reviews were noncommittal, rarely damning or enthusiastic (Strick 1969; Gow 1969; Kent 1969), with the exception of Paul Schrader in *Film Quarterly*, who was openly hostile (Schrader 1970). These reviews reveal more about contemporary prejudices regarding screen adaptations than they do about the quality of Richardson's film. Schrader's review is symptomatic. He purports to identify two principal weaknesses of this film, which can be summarized as a "cheapening" of Nabokov and a lack of (unified) style. According to Schrader, Nabokov's *Laughter in the Dark* concerns a "failed artist who is so blind he does not realize when his dreams are becoming reality, or when his imagination converges with memory'; Richardson's film is merely a "bizarre melodramatic tale" informed by the "familiar, comprehensible value system" (ibid.: 46). The first criticism results from attributing to the novel one essentialist interpretation at the expense of other possible readings, which is an approach I disagree with. The lack of a coherent style is a concern Schrader shares with most critics. But I find this unfair to Richardson, who risks filling the screen with garish colors and eclectic music, and — as in *The Loved One* — intertwining farce with tragedy. What was thus once viewed as a shortcoming might today be perceived as a sign of being ahead of its time. Nabokov himself commented at length on Richardson's film, criticizing it for its handling of eroticism; but his views were neither confirmed nor challenged by Nabokov scholars. Even Alfred Appel, in his *Nabokov's Dark Cinema*, limits himself to quoting Nabokov's opinion verbatim, without adding a view of his own (Appel 1974: 134–35), either from respect to the master or, more likely, because he had not seen the film.[7]

Unfortunately, *Laughter in the Dark*'s charms are difficult to appreciate because it remains one of the most inaccessible films of Richardson's oeuvre, neither released on DVD nor shown on television.[8] The most persistent searcher can find it in European film archives, patiently waiting to be discovered for those interested if not in Nabokov on screen, then in the early signs of postmodernism in British cinema. At the same time, judging by the gossip, the book still attracts the filmmakers. In the mid–1990s, when Adrian Lyne was shooting *Lolita*, Dmitri Nabokov announced that *Laughter in the Dark* soon would move to the screen for the second time (Dmitri Nabokov 1996: 22). I was also told by a number of sources that the popular Russian director Aleksei Balabanov was planning to adapt it. However, so far these plans have not materialized. Perhaps the failure of its "second coming" is a sign that it is increasingly more difficult to convince the viewers that love can be blind.

# 3

# Nabokov, or the Logic of Late Capitalism
## King, Queen, Knave *by* Jerzy Skolimowski (1972)

> They are fools who offer their seats to big strong women. — Vladimir Nabokov, *King, Queen, Knave*

In the Foreword to the English edition of *King, Queen, Knave*, published in 1967, the Russian original of which Nabokov wrote in the late 1920s and published in 1928 while living in Germany, the author notes:

> One might readily conjecture that a Russian writer in choosing a set of exclusively German characters was creating for himself insurmountable difficulties. I spoke no German, had no German friends, had not read a single German novel either in original, or in translation. But in art, as in nature, a glaring disadvantage may turn out to be a subtle protective device [KQK: 7].

Later in the Foreword, Nabokov explains that the "disadvantageous advantage" of setting his work in an unknown territory was a "fairytale freedom" in creating the characters and milieu, and allowing the author emotional detachment from them. Andrew Field has argued that *King, Queen, Knave* "is, in a way, a realistic portrayal of the Russian émigré's way of *not* seeing the natives of the countries into which he had happened to fall except as celluloid or cardboard figures" (Field 1967: 158). If this is the case, Nabokov's approach might serve as a model for all artists who find themselves in a position similar to his — namely, as recent émigrés unfamiliar with their new environment. I will return to this opinion when moving to the cinematic version of the novel.

But the opinion that there is nothing Germanic in *King, Queen, Knave* is not universally shared. In his essay on this novel, Julian Connolly quotes two critics, M. Tsetlin and Georgy Ivanov, who were of the opposite view. The

### 3. Nabokov, or the Logic of Late Capitalism

first remarked that the novel seems at times to read like a translation from German; the second went so far as to claim that it was meticulously copied from mediocre German models (Connolly 1995: 203). Connolly himself, while largely accepting Nabokov's assessment of his work, adds that "certain revisions made for the English translation seem to highlight a specific concern that is explained by Nabokov's dismay over the depredations committed during the years of Nazi rule" (ibid.). For Leona Toker, the "German" or "anti–German" aspect of the novel is one of the most important; she perceives both versions of the novel as a study of the Nazi in the making: "In 1927 V. Sirin was only intuitively aware of what Vladimir Nabokov would highlight in 1967" (Toker 1989: 64).

The main German aspect of the novel pertains to the portrayal of the eponymous trio of characters: Dreyer, Martha and Franz. They seem to be coarse and lacking in spirituality, which can be regarded as typical of the way German people were viewed in Europe at large during and after the Second World War, not to mention by people like Nabokov, who lived in Germany during Nazi rule. Especially antipathetic is Franz, to whom Nabokov attributes a number of unpleasant traits. One is cruelty to animals. In the book we find such a passage: "Nostalgically he remembered a nasty old lady's nasty old pug … that he had managed to kick smartly on several occasions" (KQK: 31). The second feature which renders Franz repulsive is his intolerance towards those who do not fit his standards of appearance or behavior. We see it in an early scene of his journey to Berlin when he sees a "noseless man" (which might be a reference to *The Nose* by Gogol), which, instead of awakening pity in him, arouses his disgust and a desire to leave the compartment where he is exposed to the sight of this man. Thirdly, this young man is obedient; he acquiesces to the will of stronger personalities, such as Dreyer and Martha, even if there is a huge gap between their demands and his desires. Fourthly, Franz is into sentimental kitsch, as revealed by his admiration of the photographs on the wall of the second-class compartment where he finds himself with Martha and Dreyer: "The photographs on the wall were so romantic — a flock of sheep, a cross on a rock, a waterfall" (ibid.: 14). The overall description fits the stereotype of a Nazi man, who deeply dislikes anybody or anything which is different from him and his kin, is obedient, sentimental and begins his "career" by tormenting cats or dogs and finishes by throwing babies into the fire. It shall be recollected that a sadistic streak, including cruelty towards animals, is also a feature of Axel Rex in Nabokov's subsequent novel, *Laughter in the Dark*. Franz can thus be viewed as Axel and, consequently, Hervé's cousin from Tony Richardson's film. All these fictitious men can be regarded as descendents of a certain Dietrich, whom Nabokov had known in Berlin, a "well-bred, quiet, bespectacled" university student "whose hobby was capital punishment" (SM: 278; Toker 1989: 64).

Martha, who comes across as almost as abhorrent as Franz, bears some similarity to Margot in *Laughter in the Dark* by being meretricious and greedy, and even exceeds her in unpleasantness through being conventional and petty as well. In common with Franz, she is also cruel to animals — she beats Dreyer's dog, Tom, when nobody is looking, although in public she praises him. Eventually she poisons the dog; her escalating cruelty to this defenseless creature parallels her growing desire to get rid of her husband. She is also responsible for the death of a monkey that she received from Dreyer earlier in her life, which dies in a fire. The two deaths of animals, by fire and poison, awake association with the Nazi atrocities in the concentration camps.

Dreyer is linked to Albinus due to his being self-centered and metaphorically blind, so much so that he is unable to see other people properly. However, of the three characters introduced by Nabokov, Dreyer comes across as most sympathetic — or at least not entirely off-putting. He might not be idealistic, but at least he does not mean any harm and at times is willing to aid fellow human beings, as shown by his decision to help out his poor relatives, Franz and his mother. Moreover, his affection for Martha is genuine, and there is more to it than mere sexual attraction.

Yet, while in *Laughter in the Dark* the antipathetic characters are balanced by those whom the writer treats with utmost sympathy, Albinus' wife, his daughter and the wife's brother, in *King, Queen, Knave* they dominate the narrative. Consequently, the novel lacks anybody with whom to identify. For some readers and critics, this is a weakness. However, it could also be argued that by deciding to construct his novel in this way, the writer set himself a challenge: to present banal life in high style, and the novel scores high from this perspective. The advantage of the lack of characters to whom one can anchor his or her sympathy facilitates the possibility to see other aspects of the novel: the patterns of events which befall them, the lives of material objects, the Impressionistic effects caused by the changes in lighting or in the position of the observer. Meaningfully, a large part of the criticism devoted to *King, Queen, Knave* focuses on these dimensions (Buhks 1987; Edmunds 1995; Ciancio 1999: 243–44). For these reasons I disagree with the critics who regard *King, Queen, Knave* as Nabokov's minor work, much below *Laughter in the Dark*.

*King, Queen, Knave* yields a strong sense of the absurd in the original sense of the word: "dissonant," "out of harmony" (on the definition of "absurd" see Esslin 1968: 23). The absurdist mood derives mainly from the disparity between characters' self-perceptions and the way others see them. Practically everyone described by Nabokov lives a solipsistic life because his/her self-image does not match that of others. Martha considers Dreyer utterly dull and therefore repulsive. Dreyer, on the other hand, perceives himself as the opposite of Martha's image of him. He sees himself as a kind of artist whose main pleasure in life is manipulating other people, putting them in motion, releasing their energies. A perfect sign of this desire for invention and manipulation is his willingness to invest in the production of automannequins — machines which look and behave like humans. Moreover, he likes financial risk and does not care much about money. Money is for him a means to play games, engage in adventures, make discoveries, amuse himself and release his energy. At the same time, he believes Martha to be frigid and treats her coldness as an insurance policy against her possible unfaithfulness. Yet Martha is not frigid, as evidenced by her passionate affair with Franz, which she initiates and in which she is the active partner. Both Dreyer and Martha are also mistaken in their judgment of Franz. Dreyer does not for a moment consider the possibility of Franz seducing Martha. Martha, on the other hand, not unlike Anna Karenina or Madame Bovary (Clancy 1984: 27), who are also mistaken about their lovers, sees Franz as possessing all the positive qualities that Dreyer lacks and, blinded by her own passions, cannot conceive of Franz ever ceasing to love and obey her. Finally, for most of the narrative, Franz acts as a kind of screen upon which other people's opinions of him are projected. He is clumsy in Dreyer's presence and passionate when visited by Martha. Only gradually does he begin to formulate opinions of his own and distance himself from both Martha (whom he begins to see as an ugly toad) and Dreyer.[1]

Nabokov demonstrates his superiority over the trio of characters by reducing them to pawns in his game (Clancy 1984: 28; Connolly 1995: 213). This is suggested by the very title of the book, which compares them to figures in a pack of cards, and the recurrent motif of automannequins. Most likely their presence encouraged the early critics of the novel to see in *King, Queen, Knave* a story about "automatism, 'the soullessness' of contemporary people" (Foster 1974: 43). The motif of mannequins also awakens associations with fascism and its idea of a "superman." It also can be seen in the context of the Soviet stakhanovite workers, or homo–Sovieticus. Although most likely Nabokov did not have it in mind when writing his novel, these comparisons are in accordance with the writer's ability to "see" the future, especially the ideas put into practice in the totalitarian regimes. By suggesting that the automannequins are sentenced to destruction, Nabokov foreshadows the crumbling of the Nazi and Soviet project of creating a new race of indestructible and perfect men.

The story of Martha, Dreyer and Franz develops in parallel to the construction of a new cinema theater, in proximity to the building where Franz rents his room. At the end of the novel the cinema is about to show a film entitled *King, Queen, Knave*, based on a famous play by Goldemar. The author is fictional, but his name might be seen as a reference to King Goldemar, a king of dwarfs in German folklore. What is significant here is that Goldemar, thanks to being invisible, could see others when they did not want to be seen. In the novel, Goldemar functions as Nabokov's stand-in (Toker 1989: 54). Nabokov also inscribes himself in the narrative under the name of Blavdak Vinomori, who is accompanied by his wife on a butterfly-hunting expedition, where he is spotted by Franz. The beauty and serenity of this foreign couple upsets Franz, as it poignantly contrasts with his own sordid life. Franz senses that Mr. Vinomori knows about his life, which adds to his sense of loss and defeat.

The abundance of literary and cinematic references, and inscribing the novel's author into its very text, encouraged one critic to write, "Perhaps the novel should be read as a form of literary criticism, since the incidents assume the presence of similar incidents in other books, standing between this new fiction and the begging world" (Donoghue 1982: 204). I am not opposing such an interpretation, which brings to mind metafictional reading of *Laughter in the Dark*, as discussed in the previous chapter. However, in common with Leona Toker, I believe that there is enough life in Dreyer, Martha and Franz to allow for a realistic reading of the novel and hence a realistic screen adaptation. The question is whether the filmmaker is able or willing to see it, whether s/he chooses to depict the situation as reality or fiction (or fiction or meta-fiction), or opts for some compromise.

The filmmaker in question turned out to be Jerzy Skolimowski, a renowned Polish director who, for political reasons — namely the censors' attack on his film *Ręce do góry* (*Hands Up!*, 1967 but released in 1981) — left Poland and, in due course, made films in Germany, Italy, Britain and the United States. Skolimowski returned to Poland after the collapse of communism and resumed his directing career in his old country. As a political exile and nomad, Skolimowski of the 1970s resembled Nabokov. During many moments of his career the director even used a similar rhetoric to Nabokov, mourning his emigration as the reason that he lost the natural and nurturing environment of work, the audience who understood him best and a chance to become a first-class Polish director (Yakir 1982; Uszyński 1989; 1990). Skolimowski could practically repeat the words Nabokov used in the introduction to this nove because when he embarked on filming this novel in West Germany, he also spoke no German and knew little about the cultural milieu in which his film was meant to be set. At the same time, as in the case of Nabokov, he was not entirely unfamiliar with this country because his previous film, *Deep End* (1971), was also shot in West Germany. In this film, justly regarded as one of the best in his career, Munich stands for London's Fulham and all the characters speak English.

Being a transnational director who shoots films in many countries, relies on funding coming from different national sources, and uses an international cast and crew, Skolimowski resembled Tony Richardson. Likewise, Skolimowski did not choose to shoot Nabokov's book. The book was offered to him by the producer, together with the promise of a decent fee for the completion of the film. Short of money and desperate, the Pole agreed, despite serious misgivings. As he put in the interviews given to Jerzy Uszyński and to me, although he appreciated Nabokov's genius, he was not in tune with his style. He regarded his books as difficult to screen due to irony, which in his opinion cannot be translated to the screen, but without which the stories he tells become lifeless (Uszyński 1990: 27). Skolimowski was aware that *King, Queen, Knave* could be made either into a realistic film or a parody of a film, and he was happy to adhere to any of these readings. However, he felt that this potential was not realized in the script, despite being written by high-caliber specialists, David Shaw and David Seltzer. (Shaw wrote scripts for numerous television productions; Seltzer would later write a script for *The Omen* (1976) by Richard Donner.) As Skolimowski put it, the screenplay promised neither tragedy nor comedy (ibid.: 28). Seltzer and Shaw based their script on the English version of the book. Yet, taking into account the intensive "de–Nazification" they undertook and which was completed by the director, the impression is that the film is closer to the first version of the novel.

Eventually, Skolimowski opted for parody, to some extent adhering to the recipe Nabokov used in his novel — namely, exhibiting a detachment from the characters and displaying a tendency for "playful inventiveness" towards material objects. However, there are also differences, most importantly concerning the time of action and the characterization of the main triad. Unlike the book, which is set in prewar Germany, which prepares itself for the Nazi takeover, Skolimowski moved the action to contemporary West Germany. In this respect, his film follows in the footsteps of Richardson, who in *Laughter in the Dark* updated and relocated Nabokov's version. Yet, unlike Richardson, who attempted to root the story in the specific atmosphere of Swinging London and to explain the actions of the characters by referring to their class background, Skolimowski hardly bothered to show the connections between the trials and tribulations of his characters and their specific cultural and social milieu. Time and again we get a sense that there is a distance between them and the wider world: they are not interested in it, and the world largely ignores them. At the same time, their behavior reflects two features of an environment in which they operate: a greater, although not total, sexual freedom enjoyed by men and women in Europe of the 1960s and 1970s, and the power of capitalism.

The very fact of updating the text inevitably affected the representation of any possible Nazi traits of the characters. Skolimowski suppressed them even more by changing their nationalities. In his version, Dreyer and Frank (who replaced Nabokov's Franz) are both British, while Martha is Italian. It is suggested that Dreyer, who was a British officer during the Second World War, "saved" Martha from a miserable existence following Italy's defeat. In this way Skolimowski gives Dreyer extra dignity, while suggesting that Martha should be more grateful to him than her literary predecessor. The main roles of Martha and Dreyer were played by international stars — Gina Lollobrigida and David Niven — to increase the international market of the film. John Moulder-Brown, on the other hand, played in Skolimowski's earlier film *Deep End*. Lollobrigida's Martha and the youthful looking (despite being seventeen years her senior) David Niven appear more compatible in age than their counterparts in the novel. At the same time, Martha in the film, being ten years older than her cinematic predecessor (and twenty-six years senior to Moulder-Brown) could pass as Frank's mother without difficulty. Such a positioning of Frank and Martha brings to mind Skolimowski's *Deep End*, where Moulder-Brown's character was almost raped by an older woman who took advantage of him serving her as a public bath attendant. It also harks back to earlier films by this director, such as *Bariera* (*Barrier*, 1966), where younger men are often pitted against older, predatory women.

The author of the film also combined two of Nabokov's characters — the inventor and Frank's landlord Enricht, who play crucial roles in the lives of the trio — into one. In the film they become Professor Ritter, an inventor of "voskin," a material that perfectly imitates human flesh used for the production of auto mannequins; Ritter is also Frank's landlord and neighbor.

These changes do not affect the sense of absurd permeating the lives of Dreyer, Martha and Frank. Despite lacking the novelist's means for communicating the characters' thoughts; and deciding not to use first-person narration (most likely to avoid getting too close to his characters and imposing a "literary" feel to his film), Skolimowski manages to transmit the sense of mistaken perceptions that give the book both its comedy and tragedy. The effect is achieved by accumulating chance encounters and various situations that reveal that the "king," "queen" and "knave" are clueless about each other's actions and opinions. For example, Dreyer is always about to discover Martha and Frank's affair, but fails to do so, largely because, like his literary counterpart, he cannot fathom Martha's having a lover. Everyone in the film is seemingly always in the wrong place at the wrong time, including at the end when, due to a misunderstanding between the three characters, Martha drowns. The ending of the film differs from the ending of the novel, in which Martha dies of pneumonia, but conforms perfectly to the absurdist logic of the book, in which each character is a victim of his or her misguided ideas and actions. The way Skolimowski disposes of Martha reveals the irony of fate that operates in Nabokov's novel even more convincingly than had he preserved the original ending: to die of pneumonia is to die at least partly of natural causes, while in death by drowning, especially in the manner depicted in the film, where three people appear to help one another to stay afloat, human actions play a much larger part.

John Moulder-Brown as Frank, David Niven as Dreyer, and Gina Lollobrigida as Martha in *King, Queen, Knave* (1972), directed by Jerzy Skolimowski.

Another way in which Skolimowski conveys the characters' inability to see correctly is the motif of (real) myopia. It exists in Nabokov's original, but Skolimowski amplifies it by making Frank more disorientated and clumsy than his literary predecessor. Frank in the film is hardly able to see even when he is wearing glasses, not unlike Albinus, who is blind even before his accident. Moreover, it is not only Frank who is blind. Other characters might be described as such: Dreyer, for not seeing the obvious (Martha and Frank's mutual attraction and subsequent affair); the optician, for failing to notice that Martha is not Frank's mother and that she is mortally offended by such an assumption; and Martha, for overestimating Frank's ability to kill Dreyer.

Skolimowski also includes short fragments of Frank's dreams, which underscore the gap between the "real" Frank as a clumsy and sexually inept boy, and his self-perception as a sexy and fashionable male moving among equally alluring people. In Frank's dreams everyone moves in fast motion, as in a silent movie. This reinforces the impression created by Nabokov that Frank, Martha and Dreyer are "cardboard" or "celluloid" figures by suggesting that they look "clichéd," not only from an outside perspective (most importantly, from the viewpoint of their merciless creator — the writer) but also from the inside: they perceive themselves as "celluloid."

Furthermore, the director preserves the absurdist atmosphere of the novel, largely created by Nabokov's filling it with objects which behave as if they have souls. Discussing the original Russian text, Jeff Edmunds observes:

> Objects live, move, and react to their surroundings from the book's outset. A chair reaches out towards the person about to sit (11); shadows of trees rush across the Dreyers' lawn as if running a race (44); a spiritualist's table comes alive (49 — inexplicably removed from the English version); a room and its objects smile (55), and later come alive (96–97) once the human inhabitants have left. Qualifiers normally reserved for animate beings are applied to objects. Like Franz's mysterious landlord, who eyes disapprovingly (118) his new tenant and his lady friend, the couch in the room regards them "neodobritel no" [disapprovingly] (120). In Marta's ultimate delirium, her husband's blue jacket fights for life [Edmunds 1995: 159].

In the cinematic version of *King, Queen, Knave*, objects also have lives of their own or even conspire against people, although these are different objects. Among them we find a plane that leaves before Frank reaches the airport, gates that always open at the wrong time, injuring Frank, and numerous things set in motion when Frank and Martha are making love, diverting their own attention away from lovemaking while attracting the attention of bystanders. As Tom Milne observes, "Sometimes benevolent, but more often malevolent, these objects lend the film a disturbing ambivalence behind its airy façade" (Milne 1973: 250).

David Niven and Gina Lollobrigida in *King, Queen, Knave* (1972).

Most important of them are the automannequins, operated remotely thanks to a complicated system of batteries. Dreyer commissions them from Professor Ritter, the inventor of "voskin." The automannequins, as mentioned above, already existed in Nabokov's novel, so Skolimowski only needed to furnish them, literally and metaphorically, with more body. By setting his film in the period concurrent to its production, the early 1970s, and choosing as the characters non–Germans, he got rid of the Nazi context of the automatons as embodiment of the idea of supermen, replacing it with existentialist connotations. The mannequins in Skolimowski's version of the story embody the characters' detachment from each other and from themselves: their ultimate solipsism. We might infer that for their inventor, a lonely man whose only other occupation is spying on Frank making love to Martha, the automannequins (and even "voskin" itself) are a substitute for sexual contact and perhaps for any human contact at all. The first series of mannequins, as required by Dreyer, are both female and male, but the female versions are more important, and on them the future mass production of the automatons is meant to focus. The link between women and robots is reminiscent of *Metropolis* (1927) by Fritz Lang, which Nabokov might have watched when writing his novel, and with which Skolimowski was most likely familiar.[2]

Initially the automatons are unsuccessful: they collapse and fall apart when switched on and set in motion. However, neither Dreyer nor his American partner, to whom he wants to sell this invention, is put off by the failure. They ask the inventor to resume his work, who, out of the remnants of the old automatons, produces a new, "sexier" model. Falling apart might even be part of the automaton's attraction. As material to be destroyed and reassembled, they serve as perfect objects of the male desire to possess, subjugate and destroy the female, and to do so over and over again.

The automatons not only replace each other and serve as surrogates for some abstract woman whom the inventor and his customers are striving for, but one model actually replaces a real woman: Martha. A mannequin which looks exactly like her is produced shortly after she drowns. Martha's death thus allows the men to preserve the ideal image they have of her in the dummy, or, more exactly, in a series of dummies. The concept of women being perceived as appearing in series is present in Nabokov's books, most famously in *Lolita*, as discussed in Chapter 1. It is also a staple feature of Skolimowski's cinema. For example, in his debut film, *Rysopis* (*Identification Marks: None*, 1964), one actress plays three characters with whom the male protagonist is romantically involved, giving the impression that for this man all women are the same; therefore, one can easily be replaced by another. In their appearance and the function they fulfill within the narrative, Skolimowski's automatons bear a strong resemblance to dolls constructed and photographed in the 1930s by the German associate of surrealists, Hans Bellmer. Made of wood, metal, pieces of plaster and ball joints, Bellmer's *poupées* were manipulated in drastic ways and photographed in sometimes contorted positions. As Hal Foster argues, for Bellmer they produced a volatile mixture of "joy, exaltation and fear," an intense ambivalence that appears fetishistic in nature. Each new version was a "construction *as* dismemberment" that signified both castration (in the disconnection of body parts) and its fetishistic defense (in the multiplication of these parts as "phallic substitutes" (Foster 1993: 102–3). Foster also compares Bellmer's take on the (female) body with that of Breton and Bataille. He quotes Bellmer saying, "The body is like a sentence that invites us to rearrange it" (ibid.: 103), which evokes the Bretonian idea of the shifting of desire. For Skolimowski, the automatons also encapsulate the shifting of (male) desire and the possibility of (female) substitution. Obviously, the rule of substitution deprives a woman of individuality, sentencing her to a fleeting and partial existence. Martha's role as the model for a "perfect automannequin" created by Ritter, and her final replacement by a mannequin, perfectly exemplifies the rule of substitution.

Skolimowski also underscores the production of mannequins as a capitalist endeavor. In one scene we see the batteries and the internal machinery being placed inside a doll's body. However, these details of the manufacturing process, revealed to Dreyer by the scientist demonstrating his invention, are to be kept secret. It is assumed that when the automatons are eventually mass produced and sold all over the world, the details of their construction will be concealed — in accordance with the Marxist account of commodity fetishism operating in capitalism. Dreyer, who regards himself as a successful capitalist and embarks on passing the secrets of his business to Frank, regards concealment as a principal rule of successful trade. In his first lesson to Frank he tells him, "It does not matter what you sell, it only matters how you do it," and insists that Frank conceals from the customers as much as possible of the product he is selling, even hypnotizing them so they do not see the color of the tie, its brand, and, most importantly, do not pay any attention to its price. Two features of automannequins make them especially attractive for late capitalism: their short life-span, mentioned previously, and their usefulness as an element of display, of advertising. The first feature links them with the concept of "throwaway society" — of programmed obsolesce, as theorized by many leading figures of postmodernity, such as Alvin Toffler, Fredric Jameson or Zygmunt Bauman (Toffler 1980; Jameson 1991; Bauman 1992; 1995). The second feature evokes the idea of the "society of spectacle," as associated with Guy Debord (Debord 1994). Debord explains the origin of the society of spectacle in the world's loss of unity, in the growing alienation of human beings; but, equally, he sees the development of spectacle as a factor in the growth in alienation (ibid.: 22–23).

In this context, Martha's importance consists of adding to the value of Dreyer's enterprise by being a kind of "logo." People looking at her are meant to be enchanted by her and trust her husband's business, eagerly buying what he wants to sell them. Such a positioning of women within consumerist capitalism was discussed in European cinema of the 1960s and 1970s, most importantly in the films by Jean-Luc Godard. However, unlike Godard, who criticized treating women as adverts for consumer goods, Skolimowski appears to accept such an approach by showing that Martha is indeed a shallow and materialistic woman who does not deserve a more dignified, spiritual role.[3]

Another means that renders Martha, and in some measure her male companions, as fake and kitschy in their tastes, emotions and behavior is music. Skolimowski uses well-known but badly performed musical motifs. The film opens with what is probably the best known funeral march, Chopin's Piano Sonata No. 2 in B Minor, op. 35, played against an image of Martha and Dreyer returning from the funeral of Dreyer's brother (Frank's father). Not only is the march played too slowly on an organ which is out of tune, but it is also interrupted by strange noises resembling sounds emitted by trains, owls hooting and dogs barking. The sound of the organ is gradually overwhelmed by the orchestra. The exaggerated and eccentric instrumentation suggests that Martha and Dreyer are not really mourning the person whose funeral they are attending; they are merely making a typical "funeral" appearance. Such a "reading" of the music is confirmed by the dialogue when Martha asks her husband how she looks, while applying makeup.

The next motif is played when Frank meets Martha for the first time. She is sitting in the garden, and we hear a banal, "romantic" tune. The music conveys Martha's studied (and therefore ultimately fake) elegance and her desire to live a romance, which is confirmed by the way she looks at Frank. Later, in an episode when the Dreyers have a garden party, the music sounds like a pastiche of Bavarian folk music. Bavarian folk is associated with bad taste, an association also evident at the Dreyers' party, where a piglet, adorned with a ribbon, serves as the main gift to the hosts, and guests amuse themselves with an egg throwing competition. Here music adds to the impression of the Dreyers' indulgence in bad taste, which is not even their natural taste (as he is an Englishman, while she is Italian), but one they have adopted, most likely for commercial reasons: to show their business partners, employees and customers that they are "almost Germans." The party, in line with Debord's formula, is a "spectacle plus alienation." It lacks any spontaneity, but is organized according to a precise scenario. Its participants appear to be very amused when they are watched by others, but in private they show a different side — like Martha, who abandons her husband and chases after Frank. Yet, even with him she lacks spontaneity and, in common with her predecessor in the novel, repeats clichéd words and gestures.

When Martha visits Frank for the first time with the intention of seducing him, we hear three distinctive musical cues, one after the other. First, played too quickly, tuneless string music mimics their growing appetite for sex. This motif is followed by a pastiche of fiery Spanish folk music, with the distinctive sound of castanets announcing that the affair has been consummated. Finally, when Martha and Frank make love for the second time, less hastily, paying more attention to proper facial expressions and body language (which, however, look caricatured), we hear one of the best known pieces of Baroque music: Adagio in G minor by Tomaso Albinoni. It is, however, a butchered version of the Adagio, played on instruments that are completely out of tune by a hopelessly incompetent player. The use of this sequence of musical themes is ironic here, emphasizing that the love affair between Martha and Frank is sordid and clichéd. Such use of music links Skolimowski's *King, Queen, Knave* to Richardson's *Laughter in the Dark*, where the pastiche of Renaissance music also illuminated the discordant lives of the characters.

Skolimowski also includes in *King, Queen, Knave* a fair amount of diegetic music. For example, when Frank visits Martha she first puts on a record of some nondescript music reminiscent of 1960s pop, followed by a record with an aria from an opera. The second tune is played when Dreyer returns home. The contrast between the two types of music reflects a contrast in the tastes of Martha's two lovers, or, perhaps, merely her assumption that being of different generations they cannot possibly like the same type of music. In reality, neither Frank nor Dreyer pays any attention to "their" music. Although the score of *King, Queen, Knave* is very rich, there are no leitmotifs or indeed any cues that might be identified with individual characters. Consequently, we see the titular king, queen and knave as shallow people lacking any true interests or memories.

As previously mentioned, a feature of Nabokov's novel is the abundance of various literary and cinematic references. Such references, in the opinion of the bulk of critics, underscore the parodic, artificial nature of Nabokov's characters and his entire narrative. Yet, the literary and cinematic references can be seen as increasing the novel's realism by choosing as its protagonists people who model themselves on popular culture, which would also be the case in Nabokov's subsequent novel, *Laughter in the Dark*, as well as *Lolita* (see Chapters 2 and 3). Skolimowski, however, in common with Tony Richardson, chooses to ignore the cinematic intertexts. In particular, he does not transfer to the film a scene in which Franz discovers that his landlord's wife in reality is "only a grey wig stuck on a stick and a knitted shawl" (KQK:

175). To include this scene would probably make his film look like a parody of or homage to Hitchcock's *Psycho* (1960) rather than an adaptation of Nabokov. Most likely, the overall reason why he got rid of the novel's "cinematic moments" was the need to tighten the narrative and sustain the viewers' interest in the development of the intrigue. On the other hand, Skolimowski managed to preserve what might be described as the novel's rhythm, which Nora Buhks compares to a waltz, claiming that Nabokov transposes the waltz into a literary work at the level of the schema of the composition as well as the semantic structure. As Buhks observes:

> In daily life, and in comparison to it, dance appears linked to diversion, to play, and to artifice. It is a movement which is effected by means of a series of figures chosen in advance, appearing in a repetitive order.... In *King, Queen, Knave* the playful process becomes one of the dominant processes for the construction of the novel's structure, of the novel's universe, which is ostensibly offered to the reader as playing at life, at a certain level, and as playing at a novel, at another level [Buhks 1987].

Skolimowski mimics the novel's rhythm of a waltz by presenting the characters as if they were dancing, whirling, and simultaneously both enjoying and suffering from dizziness. Their movements are circular, shot from unusual angles and often unrealistically speeded up. The narrative develops through the presentation of a series of couples formed of changing partners, as during a ball. First Martha dances with Dreyer, then with Frank, then Dreyer plays with his young female companions. The director "waltzes" even further than Nabokov by showing that the last couple in this "dance" is made up of Dreyer and Frank, who is about to inherit his uncle's fortune. Such a suggestion is absent from the novel, in which there is no indication that the youngster will inherit anything from his uncle: Dreyer is only a distant relative of Franz and is rather contemptuous of the boy to the very end of the story.

The difference in this case, however, derives not from Skolimowski's search for cinematic equivalents to the literary original, but rather from his different approach to certain issues and themes present in the novel. Skolimowski's entire cinema demonstrates that he is a more misogynistic artist than Nabokov. In the book the author's antipathy is divided almost evenly between Martha and Franz, or even Franz is rendered the most unpleasant character, while Dreyer is depicted somehow more sympathetically. In the film, on the other hand, Frank is the most positive character of the three, and the director's hostility is concentrated on Martha, who becomes the true "dark character" of the story and is punished for the harm she inflicted on the young man. In this sense, her story repeats the fate of Susan in Skolimowski's earlier film, *Deep End*, who also seduced a young and innocent man and died at his hands in a pool. In both films the deaths of the women are rendered accidental.

Such an ending allows for rescuing the young man from the grip of a predatory woman, and at the same time exonerates him from any accusation of murder.

In contrast to Nabokov, who gives little thought to the issue of the relationship between younger and older generations in his books, for Skolimowski this topic, especially the relationship between younger and older men, is very important. He privileges the father-son relationship, as well as other homosocial bonds, over the relationships between men and women. I suggest that in *King, Queen, Knave* the two men subconsciously wish for Martha's death. Her "disappearance from the picture" allows male friendship to blossom, as demonstrated in the scene in which Frank and Dreyer return from Martha's funeral as if they were the best of friends. This scene especially harks back to Skolimowski's *Rysopis* (*Identification Marks: None*, 1964) and *Walkower* (*Walkover*, 1965), in which a young heterosexual man scorns the pleasures offered to him by women and chooses male company and masculine pursuits. To put it crudely, the director uses the material offered by Nabokov's novel to create an Oedipal story *à la* Skolimowski. In this version Frank adopts the position of an Oedipus by sleeping with his uncle's wife, but rather than this leading to a mortal conflict between "father" and "son," it brings them closer. Martha is a vehicle for Frank's maturation, necessary to his uncle to ensure the successful future of his business. Her erotic (and economic) tutelage completes the young man's transition to his position as Dreyer's successor. She plays this role well; at the end of her instruction Frank is indeed transformed into a self-confident young man, ready to free his uncle from the clutches of responsibility. The replacement of Martha by Frank in Dreyer's life is underscored by the use of the circular narrative, in which the end of the film mirrors its beginning. On both occasions we see the guests returning home from a funeral, but in the first episode it is Dreyer and Martha who are in a car, in the second Dreyer and Frank.

John Moulder-Brown and Gina Lollobrigida in *King, Queen, Knave*.

## 3. Nabokov, or the Logic of Late Capitalism

Gina Lollobrigida and John Moulder-Brown in *King, Queen, Knave* (1972).

Skolimowski's film allows us to see what would happen if, to use the metaphor of a card game, the writer were to "shuffle his cards" by changing slightly the characteristics and relationships between his main figures. Such a change, while constituting a (moderate) betrayal of the film's narrative, allows the preservation of its emotional tone, its rhythm and critical edge. Skolimowski succeeds in creating what Nabokov termed his "bright brute": a movie that is ostensibly without artistic pretensions but succeeds on its own terms, being simultaneously funny and cruel, and commenting on the society and culture of its time. Of course, it is impossible to measure the film's fidelity to its original, but subjectively I find Skolimowski's film the most faithful of all the Nabokov adaptations and its "rough charm" sustains the passage of time.

However, this opinion is not widely shared by Nabokov specialists. Julian Connolly, who includes his assessment of the film in his essay on the book, writes:

> While the film has its amusing moments, Nabokov's dry wit and subtle irony often lie buried in scenes of slapstick action and forced hilarity. Although *King, Queen, Knave* is not one of Nabokov's major novels, the film version does not convey the scope or breath of Nabokov's distinctive vision. One cannot discern in the film the outlines of

those unique traits that become the hallmarks of Nabokov's mature fiction" [Connolly 1995: 214].

I will not dispute Connolly's claim that the hallmarks of Nabokov's mature fiction are absent from Skolimowski's version, but their lack does not undermine its value, not least because Skolimowski's *King, Queen, Knave* is an adaptation of this particular book, not of Nabokov's mature fiction. The elements of the film Connolly lists, such as the slapstick action, have a distinct narrative and ideological function, pointing to the absurdity of the lives of characters. Moreover, what was omitted from the book was compensated for by the changes the director introduced. These changes, especially Skolimowski's own unique handling of material objects, were appreciated by some reviewers (Milne 1973; Mosk 1972), while others, especially in his native Poland, accused him of making a trivial or unfunny film (Saniewski 1973; Radgowski 1973). Although I did not find even one review which was enthusiastic, the positive prevailed. Significantly, although some reviewers criticized the film for indulging in bad style, none accused Skolimowski of having no style, which characterized the critical reception of Richardson's *Laughter in the Dark*.

Skolimowski's own evaluation of *King, Queen, Knave*, however, is close to Connolly's assessment. In an interview given in 1990 he described it as the worst film of his career and an artistic disaster from which he could not recover for a long time (Uszyński 1990: 27–8). It appears that the reason for the director's contempt was his perception that it was an unfaithful adaptation, as well as short on substance, unserious and trite. As I have tried to demonstrate, however, the opposite is true — the film's substance is very rich, although it cannot be reduced merely to its plot. However, as with *Laughter in the Dark*, this film awaits its second coming — unavailable on DVD, ignored by television channels, it is practically inaccessible to the general public, and only the nerdiest of Nabokov or Skolimowski fans can find it on an old VHS.

# 4

# Escape into a Different Person, Escape into a Different Reality
## Despair *by Rainer Werner Fassbinder (1978)*

> *Literature and morality.* Imaginary evil is romantic and varied, real evil is miserable, monotonous, barren, boring. Imaginary goodness is boring; real goodness is always new, marvelous, intoxicating. Therefore "imaginative literature" is either boring or immoral (or a mixture of both). It only escapes from this alternative if in some way it passes over to the side of reality through the power of art — and only genius can do that. — Simone Weil, *Gravity and Grace*

*Despair*, set in Berlin of 1930–31, written by Nabokov in Russian in 1932 as *Otchayanie*, published serially in 1934 and as a book in 1936, is one of his earliest and most sophisticated novels in terms of constructing the narrative. However, because it was translated into English only in 1966, after the successes of such works as *Lolita* and *Pale Fire*, it is regarded as a shadow of Nabokov's masterpieces and rarely granted equal attention compared to them. When it is discussed at length, the focus is on its intertextual burden, especially its similarity to *Lolita*:

> For the reader of the 1966 English translation of *Despair* there is a certain intrusive echo from *Lolita*, though it is really a retrospective echo. It is present most of all, perhaps, in the rhetorical flourishes and sinister jollity of Hermann Karlovich which at times reproduces even the verbal meter of *Lolita*'s Humbert.... The reader who grasps the full, multi-faceted meaning of Hermann's carefully plotted assault on his double, Felix, in this simple Nabokov novel will most likely find himself thinking back to Humbert and Quilty and wondering if perchance he missed something in *Lolita* [Field 1967: 225].

Critics also note the connections with Dostoevski. Alexander Dolinin observes that when Nabokov wrote the original version of *Despair* he was able to see both strong points and shortcomings in Dostoevski's writing:

> Rereading *The Brothers Karamazov* through the prism of his own creative principles, Nabokov praises its cunning narrative techniques: intricate play with the reader (in the

tradition of *Eugene Onegin* and *Dead Souls*) whom the author "incessantly urges and teases, trying to arouse his curiosity in every possible way'; the crafty construction of the plot (*fabula*) based on deception, retardation and concealment of information; expressive and suggestive details. Dostoevski the artist, in Nabokov's view, fails only when he indulges in philosophizing through the mouthpiece of Alesha — "this mystical Ivan the Fool, the unhappy love of the author"— whose very presence "suddenly turns the other characters into talking mechanical dolls" [Dolinin 2008].

In the 1960s, when Nabokov prepared the English translation of *Despair*, this balanced view, which included qualified praise, gave way to an almost vitriolic attack on the author of *Crime and Punishment*. This attack, as Dolinin argues, had much to do with the standing of Dostoevski in the West, who was then an object of an "uncritical cult in America, which tended to reduce all Russian cultural heritage to the soul-searching of *Notes from the Underground, Crime and Punishment* and *The Brothers Karamazov*" (ibid.). For Nabokov in the 1960s, Dostoevsky was thus a clear peril, and he used the English translation of *Despair* as a weapon in his fight; with the book he meant to lampoon the darling of the existentialist crowd and thereby to overbear the artistic authority of his inflated compatriot (ibid.). The most visible sign of this parody are the titles which *Despair*'s protagonist, Hermann Karlovich, considers for his novel: "'The Double'? But Russian literature possessed one already. 'Crime and Pun'? Not bad — a little crude, though" (Des: 167).

Apart from lampooning Dostoevski, Nabokov attempted in *Despair* to develop certain motifs, that, although present in Dostoevski's *The Double* and *Crime and Punishment*, interested him as subjects in their own right. The most important is the motif of a man's attempt to escape from himself: from his social position, psychological limitations, his past — his whole identity. Apart from *Despair*, this motif is present, for example, in Nabokov's short stories, "Scenes from the Life of a Double Monster" and "An Affair of Honor." The first story retells the life of Siamese twins, whose freedom is drastically limited by their physical condition of being joined, and the attempts of their relatives to exploit it by displaying them as freaks to audiences willing to pay for the pitiful spectacle. In the later story, which I will discuss at length in Chapter 6, we find a man who, after lacking the courage to keep an appointment for a duel, imagines himself having a new life in which the signs of his cowardice are erased.

In all these stories, abandoning one's identity is presented as immensely tempting and extremely difficult. Tempting because such an escape equals total freedom or even, as Claire Rosenfeld argues in relation to *Despair*, promising immortality (Rosenfeld 1967). Difficult because external circumstances and internal factors conspire to keep a man in his place or reduce his room for maneuvering. The easiest way to escape from oneself appears to be through imagination and art, although this is always a short-lived and partial retreat.

## 4. Escape into a Different Person, Escape into a Different Reality

Reality, sooner rather than later, catches up with the refugee, making him even more miserable than before. Along with men who try to escape into a different identity, we find in Nabokov's prose those who resist the attempts of others to appropriate their personality or mold it to somebody else's image. For example, in *The Gift* the protagonist Fyodor resists the attempts of Mme Chernyshevski, the mother of Yasha, a boy his age who committed suicide, to make him a surrogate for her son. In his narrative Fyodor insists on having practically nothing in common with Yasha, and represents Yasha to the reader in a way that increases the distance between the two young men (Gift: 40–44). These stories, as well as many others, demonstrate that, ultimately, Nabokov does not believe in human doubles — either as entities in their own right or as an imaginary solution to the problem of being unhappy about oneself. This opinion is expressed most clearly by the writer himself, who in an interview with Alfred Appel, rejects any suggestions that there are doubles in his fiction, claiming that "Felix in *Despair* is really a *false* double" (SO: 83–4). Ellen Pifer elaborates on this statement but also softens it, claiming that in *Despair* the motif of a doppelgänger is a "deceptive shadow-theme, tracing delusions of Hermann's mad mind" (Pifer 1980: 97). Nabokov's take on the topic of doubles also shows that he has little in common with postmodernism, which perceives identity as flexible and fluent, an effect of various "identity games" in which people engage of their own free will, or even at their whim.

The protagonist of *Despair*, Hermann Karlovich Hermann, is a chocolate manufacturer and the son of a Russian-speaking German father and purely Russian mother, who has been living in Berlin since 1920. He attempts to escape from himself by killing another man, Felix Wohlfahrt, a tramp he meets during one of his journeys, and appropriating his identity. Hermann believes or pretends that Felix looks exactly like him — is his perfect double. However, from the way he describes the tramp, Felix's reaction to his announcement that they are alike, and other people's lack of recognition of their alleged similarity, we can deduce that they are, in fact, different. Subsequent events prove that they are not even similar, let alone identical. Felix is tall and of strong build, which conveys his working class background; Hermann is shorter and less muscular. Hermann is also considerably older than his "double." Some critics, however, who wrote about Fassbinder's film, claimed that the director markedly deflected from the literary original by immediately disclosing to viewers the lack of similarity between these two males (Elsaesser 1996: 76; Chamberlin 2008).

Nabokov does not explain why Hermann wants to part with his old self but merely offers the reader some clues. The most prosaic reason is an economic one. Hermann's business is on the verge of bankruptcy. By insuring his life for a large sum and then pretending to be dead, he can collect the insurance money through his wife and live comfortably in another country. Secondly, killing Felix will liberate Hermann sexually by allowing him to escape from his wife and her vulgar lover and live in a place where people do not know him. The third explanation can be described as artistic. By "killing" his old identity, Hermann hopes to commit the perfect murder, and in this way create a perfect object of art. It is possible to link the three reasons for Hermann's escape with three voices in the novel, which John Kimney identifies as "the voice of Hermann, the voice of a psychological novelist to whom Hermann plans to send the account of his murder of Felix, and the third as his 'rational memory,' who perceives 'flaws' in his resemblance to the double as well as his 'perfect crime'" (Kimney 1980: 101). Kimney argues that the three voices represent three different approaches to fiction — the social, the psychological and the artistic. Hermann associates murder with escaping from financial difficulties, with engaging in sexual abnormalities, and with creating a masterpiece (ibid.: 107). Although I agree with Kimney's explanation, for me the three reasons do not exhaust all motives for Hermann's actions. The last one is metaphysical: a desire to cross the boundaries of one's self. This desire, I believe, would exist in Hermann even if the other reasons for changing his identity had disappeared. It can be linked, as Claire Rosenfeld suggests, to the primitive human desire to create a body-soul, which a man can locate in his shadow, or in his reflection in the mirror as a means to save himself from death (Rosenfeld 1967: 68). Nabokov discusses such desire at length in his autobiography, saying that "nature expects a full-grown man to accept the two black voids, fore and aft, as stolidly as he accepts the extraordinary visions in between," but a man "rebels against this state of affairs" (SM: 17). The sign that in Hermann, as in Nabokov, such a desire is very strong is his addiction to telling new stories about himself, his continuous reinvention of the self, which surpasses his practical need to do so.

Hermann's discovery of Felix is not an impulse to make a plan to become somebody new, but a missing link in an already existing plan to find his "shadow" and give him his body, so to speak. However, because Felix is not really his double, and Hermann leaves a trace of his murder (the stick belonging to Felix), the police discover that it is, in fact, him who killed Felix and track him down in his retreat in the Swiss Alps. Or, perhaps, we should say that this is the most obvious interpretation of Nabokov's novel, because it is also possible that Hermann fabricated the story of Felix's murder in order to present it to us. Equally possible is that the story was written by the "émigré novelist" mentioned by Hermann, whom we identify as Nabokov. This writer invents Hermann simply as a character in his story, as a vehicle of his art

(Kimney 1980; Troubetzkoy 1995). I will return to these possibilities in due course, but first let me move to the novel's adaptation by Rainer Werner Fassbinder, based on a script by Tom Stoppard. Stoppard was hired because, as the director himself put it, *Despair* was "meant to be an English film" (Fassbinder, quoted in Thomsen 1980: 99). According to the director, Stoppard's main contribution was writing dialogue rather than providing the overall vision of the film (ibid.: 99; Robinson 1977: 216). When the actual shooting started, Fassbinder practically discarded the script, in which Hermann and his double were meant to be played by the same actor and "returned to the novel, which has that darkness and strangeness which wasn't in the script" (Fassbinder, quoted in Thomsen 1980: 99).

*Despair* follows in the footsteps of Skolimowski's *King, Queen, Knave*, being an international coproduction (West German and French), with the crew and cast coming from even more countries. It also closes a short cycle of films based on Nabokov's books and made in Germany in the 1970s. Its executive producer, Lutz Hengst, was also a producer of *King, Queen, Knave*. Before it, Hubert Vesely directed *Das Bastardzeichen* (*Bend Sinister*, 1970), and Horst Flick *Einladung zur Enthauptung* (*Invitation to a Beheading*, 1973). It is not difficult to see why these books by Nabokov, rather than others he wrote, made it to the screen in Germany in the 1970s: they lend themselves most to an interpretation in the context of totalitarian rule in Germany and Russia. The 1970s is also a period when Germany, after several decades of trying to forget about its past and move on, attempted to examine its Nazi history for the sake of learning about its past (examining its present day in order to avoid totalitarianism in future). The phenomenon of New German Cinema, which Fassbinder co-created and of which he was one of the pillars, is a fruit of this new approach. The directors belonging to this paradigm were less interested in the deeds of Hitler and other high ranking Nazis, and more (to use the phrase of one of the New German Cinema directors, Hans-Jürgen Syberberg) in the "Hitler in us." Nabokov's books, with their focus on "felt history,"—namely, on the direct physical impact of historical events on the body and senses of a single character (Foster 1995: 29) and their search for common characteristics of different political systems, personalities and cultures that might lead to totalitarianism and moral and physical destruction of individuals—were perfect vehicle's with which to talk about history and the present day in the way many German directors intended.

Taking this into account, it does not come as a surprise that Fassbinder, who, even against the backdrop of his fellow creators of New German Cinema, appeared to be particularly interested in the roots of Nazism and its influence on "ordinary citizens," had found *Despair*, which is set in 1930s Berlin, attractive.

**Dirk Bogarde as Hermann, Andréa Ferréol as Lydia, and Bernhard Wicki as Orlovius in *Despair* (1978), directed by Rainer Werner Fassbinder.**

He admitted that he was thinking about this novel for many years, and obtained the film rights early but struggled to find the right angle from which to tackle it (Rondi 1992: 124). His choice of *Despair* can also be explained by some other features of *Despair* pertaining to his interests and state of mind, such as self-alienation and doubling. We can derive this from the abundance of these phenomena in his films. Effi Briest in the film of the same title made in 1977, Ali in *Angst essen Seele auf* (*Fear Eats the Soul*, 1974) and many other characters in Fassbinder's films are unhappy in their bodies. They attempt to change their identity and typically fail, as Nabokov's Hermann fails. It was also suggested that doubling was Fassbinder's private obsession. Christian Braad Thomsen entitles the first chapter of his biography of Fassbinder, "The Double Man," arguing that the director in a sense multiplied himself by achieving more than could fill the lives of many less creative and driven individuals (Thomsen 1997). His output as a film director, which comprises over forty films and television productions, is astonishing, especially if we take into account that he died at the age of thirty-seven. Fassbinder also doubled himself by possessing contradictory features and revealing new facets of his personality. Even his bisexuality, claims Thomsen, was a form of doubling. Fassbinder's biographer quotes the director as saying shortly before his death, in relation to Genet's *Querelle*, that "the theme is the identity of an individual and how he acquires it. And that's connected to the fact, as Genet says, that in order to be complete, one needs to double himself" (Fassbinder, quoted in Thomsen 1997: 1).

Some authors also point to the personal crisis Fassbinder suffered prior to making *Despair* and during shooting, marked by suicidal thoughts. This crisis was rooted in factors such as the looming break-up with Fasbinder's long-term lover, Armin Meier, and the director's inability to control his drug use (Watson 1992: 28). The director himself revealed something of his state of mind at the time, saying:

> It's a point which comes in every life, when you realize that nothing more will happen — no new ideas or new sensations in your life. From this point you have to work really hard to like the things you like, to feel the things you feel.... Most people arrange themselves — compromise — when they realize they have reached this moment.... This man, Hermann, doesn't want to compromise; his solution is to enter a land of madness [Robinson 1977: 216].

The story of a man who goes insane could act both as a reflection of Fassbinder's state of mind and as a way of working through his problems. The various gaps in Nabokov's novel, including those referring to the central mystery of the film — namely, whether and why Hermann killed Felix (whose surname in the film is Weber, most likely because it is easier to pronounce by an English-speaking audience) — promised the director a chance to create his very own piece of work.

Like Nabokov, for Fassbinder the central issue is Hermann's identity: its alienation, dissipation and, finally, unsuccessful relocation through killing Felix. Fassbinder also avoids giving straightforward answers to why Hermann uses such an extreme measure to become somebody else, but provides clues which correspond to layers of Hermann's identity. These include Hermann's ethnicity and history, his professional and economic status, his artistic self, his sexual identity, his physical being and, finally, his "metaphysical core." Peter Ruppert and Thomas Elsaesser focus on some of these layers and reasons for escape (Elsaesser 1996; Ruppert 1984). Their analyses largely complement each other, as Ruppert foregrounds social factors in Hermann's decision to escape, while Elsaesser points mostly to his sexuality and family circumstances. In my discussion of the film I will draw on their arguments, as well as offering my own critique of them.

Fassbinder's Hermann is a Jewish-Russian emigrant in a Germany of escalating anti–Semitism, a fact practically absent from the novel. Such a background alienates him from and puts him in potential conflict with the mainstream of German society. There is little Hermann can do about his background to avoid the eruption of a conflict except hide his true self and escape from the increasingly oppressive surroundings into memories of better times. The film suggests that Hermann used or at least considered both strategies. During his life in Russia he was constantly using false documents. He says:

> When the war started I procured some papers which stated that I was a Blackshirt fighting the Reds in the White Army. But after the Revolution I got out as a Caucasian fighting the Brownshirts in the Red Army. All I really am is just a yellowbelly in a brown hat. But I'm holding on for myself.

These words testify to the life of deceit which Hermann was living, but also that, when he was pretending to be somebody else, he had a sense of his real self.

The possibility of a nostalgic return to Russia, as Ruppert maintains, is suggested in the early scene in which Hermann looks through the window at snow falling on the streets of Berlin and talks about winter in Russia. However, for me this scene does not reveal Hermann's nostalgia but rather his contempt for any nostalgic retreats. This ironic approach is suggested by the accumulation of clichés Hermann uses to describe life in Russia, the lack of any personal memories he shares with us, and the fact that his (pseudo)nostalgic outburst is not spontaneous but a reaction to his wife's longing look at the winter landscape from the window of their Berlin apartment. This scene does not have a direct equivalent in the novel, but early in the book Hermann mocks his wife's sentimental yearning for the old Russia. In this sense Hermann is similar to Nabokov, who also prided himself on not being nostalgic.

Hermann could try to counteract German anti-Semitism by political action, as did some people in Germany and elsewhere, but this possibility in the film remains theoretical due to his distaste for any human groupings, as well as any political position, and the simple fact that he does not know anybody whom he might join if he wanted to fight National Socialism. His initial alienation is the reason why Hermann wants to change his life, but it is also an obstacle to achieving this goal.

In common with his literary predecessor, Fassbinder's Hermann is also an unsuccessful businessman; his chocolate factory is on the verge of bankruptcy. Part of his failure appears to be his aristocratic disregard for business. Deep down he feels that he should not earn his living but live a life of leisure thanks to his inheritance. The story of his mother, who was meant to bring to her marriage to Hermann's father a dowry of gold coins as heavy as herself but in reality brought him only fake coins made of chocolate (and who subsequently died of diabetes), conveys Hermann's pretension to a life free of financial worries and explains his deep-seated contempt for chocolate. Even the way Hermann talks about chocolate, especially his conviction that it should be either bitter or very sweet, betrays the temperament of an aristocrat or an artist imprisoned in a capitalistic world of narrow-mindedness, moderation and mediocrity. There are also more prosaic and external causes for his lack of success in business: the economic crisis in the world and in Germany, which forces the bulk of the population to give up on luxuries, of which chocolate is an epitome. Of course, the natural reaction to such a decrease in demand would be production of a cheaper, less luxurious chocolate, but Hermann rejects such a possibility. He believes that if he is to be a businessman, he must occupy the "aristocratic" end of the capitalist spectrum. The symbol of Hermann's brand of chocolate is a woman in blue (in the book it is a lady in lilac), which alludes to the fact that the attachment to chocolate was passed to Hermann by his mother; and as a producer of this sweet he chiefly serves women. However, Hermann is not interested in women, and women are unfaithful to him. The symbol of Hermann's brand of chocolate thus acts as an omen of his failure as a businessman. This idea is explicitly presented in the novel when Hermann talks about the "lilac lady who had been untrue to me" (Des: 66).

Fassbinder represents Germany in the early 1930s as a country in decline. This is suggested by the recurrent images of cripples, beggars and street musicians lurking in the dingy streets against a background of dilapidated houses. He also shows that Nazism gradually permeates all spheres of German society and culture. The proliferation of men wearing Nazi uniforms, and the sight of stray dogs taken off in a truck to be exterminated, can be read as a precursor to the rounding up of "useless elements" in Nazi Germany, such as Jews, Gypsies, people with disabilities, the mentally ill and homosexuals, in order to send them to the gas chambers. Another sign that the people who do not fit the Nazi norm would be sent to the death camps is the huge pile of discarded chocolate figures that Hermann sees in the factory of his anti–Semitic potential business partner (Ruppert 1984: 57). Hermann is unhappy about this takeover of Germany by the Nazis, as conveyed by the expression of abhorrence he wears whenever he finds himself on the streets of Berlin. He finds the Nazis extremely vulgar; and the more homogenous they look and the more united they are in their actions, the more vulgar he finds them. He mocks the Nazi uniform of his manager, Miller, which he compares to a scout's attire, and looks in disgust as the Nazis destroy the shop windows of their political opponents and order beer in the cafés. The fact that the Brownshirts always act as a group and, in whatever they do, are very noisy, revealing a mob mentality, is especially disgusting for his individualistic taste. Hermann's contempt for Nazism can be regarded as a form of Russian contempt for Germans, to which Nabokov makes reference in his other works.[1] Nazism represents for Hermann the most debased form of German character and culture.

However, Hermann is put off by the aesthetic side of Nazi politics, not by its moral dimension, as some critics suggest (for example, Burdick 1982). In terms of morality, he shares the Nazi ideas, such as the right of the strong to achieve their objectives with any means, including taking the lives of other human beings. His betrayal and murder of Felix, despite befriending him, and his blaming the victim for the death, feels like the implementation of Nazi ideas and methods. Felix, like most victims of the Second World War and the Holocaust, especially Jews and Gypsies, dies not for what he does but because of who he is. Hermann is only put off by the industrial character and the haste of Nazi barbarities, which leave little scope for inventiveness. Accordingly, by killing Felix in an artistic way (in his opinion), Hermann wants to demonstrate to himself and to the world that he surpasses the totalitarian mob.

Aesthetic hell, in the book and in the film, is also encapsulated by Lydia and Ardalion, Hermann's wife's cousin. Hermann finds Ardalion's paintings sloppy, and unfinished, showing no desire to reach perfection and even no real interest in art. When Ardalion talks about art, the conversation immediately moves to money — he knows very well the financial value of each of his pictures and uses his position as an artist to sponge money from the Hermanns. Among Ardalion's pictures there is one with a swastika painted on the other side. This painting perplexes Hermann the most; on one occasion he visits Ardalion's studio uninvited to check if this picture is there. This double-sided picture symbolizes for Hermann the connection between art and politics in Nazi Germany. For him, they both are types of bad art, devoid of subtlety or charm. Ardalion's vulgar work is matched by his overdeveloped body and pseudo-bohemian attire, which includes long robes, colorful scarves and berets placed on one side of his head, all of them poignantly contrasting with the ascetic elegance of Hermann. Ardalion's style finds its equivalent in the pulp fiction devoured by Lydia, her inability to match the colors of her clothes, and her inability to make sense of politics or the economy, all of which Hermann continuously mocks. Ardalion and Lydia's all-encompassing kitsch finds its apogee in their sordid affair, which they are unable to conceal and which Hermann prefers to ignore.

Thomas Elsaesser, in his largely psychoanalytical analysis of *Despair*, suggests that the chief reason why Hermann wants to escape from himself is his unhappiness as husband and lover. He claims that his actions are motivated by his impotence — "his inability to satisfy his wife, or deal with the impudent flaunting of phallic potency on the part of his wife's cousin, which, by extension, signify his economic and political impotence" (Elsaesser 1996: 77). However, neither in the novel nor in the film do we find any suggestion that Hermann is sexually or sentimentally attached to Lydia. In the novel he openly states that he married her because she loved him, and the only type of love he is able to offer her is one resulting from his gratitude for her devotion. Lydia's role is thus to support and validate his narcissism. Nabokov's Hermann finds sex with Lydia uncomfortable, even repulsive. We learn that he never kisses her on the mouth and is unable to forget himself in the sexual act with her. Precisely during sexual intercourse with Lydia he begins to suffer dissociation from himself as described in this fragment:

> I would be in bed with Lydia, winding up the brief series of preparatory caresses she was supposed to be entitled to, when all at once I would become aware that imp Split had taken over. My face was buried in the folds of her neck, her legs had started to clamp me, the ashtray toppled off the bed table, the universe followed — but at the same time, incomprehensibly and delightfully, I was standing naked in the middle of the room, one hand resting on the back of the chair where she left her stockings and panties [Des: 32].

This passage points not only to the lack of passion on the part of Hermann, through the use of terms such "caresses she was supposed to be entitled to," but it alludes to the almost classical image of repressed homosexuality: a homosexual man looking at the heterosexual couple making love, secretly dreaming of being in the place of the woman. Hermann's reminiscences on his previous sexual encounters with women, the majority of them being prostitutes (not unlike the experiences of Humbert prior to meeting Lolita), also suggest that his sexual interest lies elsewhere. In the film, Hermann's lack of interest in Lydia is underscored by frequently showing her completely naked while Hermann behaves as if he has not noticed. The significance of such a scene is to point out that Lydia does not arouse her husband. Similarly, when Lydia and Hermann talk to each other, their conversations come across as artificial, as if they were only playing lovers rather than being in love. For example, Lydia announces with an exaggerated expression of outrage that she knows that Hermann and their maid are having an affair, to which Hermann replies that his wife is a complete idiot. It even appears that Lydia's infidelity is convenient for Hermann, as it allows him to indulge in his passion without arousing her suspicion or causing protest. Like Charlotte for Humbert, she acts as a smokescreen behind which he can play out his illicit erotic fantasies. Moreover, as Elsaesser himself admits, Lydia, played by Andréa Ferréol, an actress endowed with large breasts and wide hips, comes across more as a maternal figure than a lover.

Hermann even comments on his wife's similarity to his mother, perceiving both women as overweight and stupid (Elsaesser 1996: 77–8).

Hermann's description of his life with his fictitious brother, both in the novel and in the film, reads like a cliché of gay fantasy. He claims that his brother loved to put on his shirt when it was still warm, and the two shared a bed with a pillow at each end until it was discovered that the "brother" could not go to sleep without sucking Hermann's big toe. Hermann comes across as a wanderer, roaming through dark streets and cheap hotels in search of suitable men: handsome, virile and, if possible, of simple background, according to the rule that refined homosexual dandies find their perfect match in the opposite type. Felix, with his muscular physique and his strong language, in which he denounces women as useless whores (thus promising to Hermann a paradise free of women), perfectly fits this description. For this reason Hermann is immediately attracted to him and starts imagining that there is a "natural" bond between them. Take, for example this description:

> Grinning and grunting, perhaps a trifle shy of me, he stripped to the skin and proceeded to douche his armpits over the basin of the cupboardlike washstand. I shot glances at him, examining eagerly that stark-naked man, with a pinker coccyx and uglier buttocks. When he turned I could not help wincing at the sight of his big knobbed navel — but then mine is no beauty either.... I derived a keen pleasure from that survey; it set my mind at ease; no special marks stigmatized him [Des: 84].

We can also presume that after killing Felix and fleeing to Switzerland, Hermann would not live with his wife but rather stay away from her, allowing himself to solicit the sexual favors of men in anonymity. Casting Dirk Bogarde in the role of Hermann encourages a "homosexual" reading of Hermann. This actor, although he never "came out" as a homosexual, has become a gay icon and built his career on playing sexually repressed men in films such as *The Servant* (1963), directed by Joseph Losey, *Il Portiere di notte* (*The Night Porter*, 1974), directed by Liliana Cavani, and, most importantly, *Morte a Venezia* (*Death in Venice*, 1971), directed by Luchino Visconti and based on Thomas Mann's novella, which could have inspired Nabokov (Rosenfeld 1967: 67–8). Visconti's *Death in Venice* concerns the lack of sexual fulfilllment and yearning for lost youth of Gustav von Aschenbach. To such yearning, if we are to believe Susan Sontag, homosexuals are particularly prone (Sontag 1994a: 290–91). Equally, Bogarde's handsome but clearly wrinkled face and hands in *Despair*, which the camera investigates with poignant interest, excellently convey such yearning on the part of Hermann. Killing Felix, who is at the peak of his youthful and masculine power, might thus be regarded as Hermann's way to rejuvenate himself.[2]

I will also regard Hermann's killing of Felix as a means, paradoxically, to overcome his solitude resulting from possessing an individual identity, having only one history, knowing only one self, feeling only one's own pain. This metaphysical solitude pertains to every human being, but not everybody experiences it in the same measure. Hermann appears to suffer from it in the extreme; therefore his entire life is permeated by a desire to double himself. His conviction that killing Felix and stealing his identity will allow him to cross the boundaries of his individual selfhood is suggested by him equating "merger" with "murder" when talking about fusion with another chocolate factory as a way to avoid bankruptcy. The theme of the merging of two identities, or two metaphysical cores, is also introduced visually by the motif of preparing an eggnog, which opens the film and later recurs. To make this dish, two eggs are broken, beaten and mixed with other ingredients, such as milk and sugar, so that each egg loses its individual appearance as well as any chance to mature into a more distinctive entity. The experiment in merging eggs ultimately leads to the destruction of both eggs, which are consumed by Lydia and Ardalion. The fate of the eggs can be taken as a foretelling of Hermann's and Felix's "union," which does not prolong the existence of any of the participating elements but only serves Lydia and Ardalion, who, enriched by Hermann's insurance money, are able to continue their liaison.

Carl Proffer suggests that in the book Hermann's metaphysical loneliness is suggested by references to Shakespeare's Hamlet and King Lear, both characters experiencing loneliness in its utter horror: "There is the rub, there is the horror; the more so as the acting will go on and on, endlessly; never, never, never, never, never will your soul in that other world be quite sure ... and forever, and forever shall your soul remain in doubt" (Proffer 1968b: 265). Proffer also quotes Thomas Wolfe, who five years before Nabokov published *Despair* wrote in *Look Homeward Angel*:

> He understood that men were forever strangers to one another, that no one ever comes really to know any one, that imprisoned in the dark womb of our mother, we come to life without having seen her face, that we are given to her arms a stranger, and that, caught in that insoluble prison of being, we escape it never, no matter what arms may clasp us, what mouth may kiss us, what heart may warm us. Never, never, never, never, never [ibid. 265–6].

It is impossible to establish whether Nabokov knew these words, but even if he did not, it could be argued that they capture the atmosphere of *Despair*. Fassbinder discards references to Shakespeare and his followers but conveys their meaning by presenting Hermann's perceptions as entirely subjective: Hermann cannot share with anybody his dreams or even his simple sensations. The recurrent motif of walls and partitions which divide Hermann from fellow human beings and from himself underscores his metaphysical loneliness.

Hermann's escape from himself is unsuccessful because Felix does not look like him and the chocolatier leaves a trace of the murder. It is worth asking, however, what would happen to Hermann if things had gone according to his plan — if Felix looked exactly like him and there were no traces of his identity left. In this case, Hermann would have a chance to collect the insurance money (if it was not squandered earlier by Lydia and Ardalion), stop working and escape from the kitsch of Nazi Germany. However, it is doubtful that he would escape from his old self by merging with Felix in any way. The part of the film showing Hermann after the murder suggests rather that Hermann's method of escaping from himself leads not to a merger, to enriching his personality, but to losing any distinct identity, becoming nobody, a faceless and confused man.

The story of Hermann, both in Nabokov's and Fassbinder's version, can be conceptualized not only as a tale of escaping into a different identity but into a different universe. Glasses, mirrors and walls are recurrent in the novel and the film, and signify not only barriers between humans but also between different ontological orders. Yet, although Nabokov's and Fassbinder's Hermann want to escape into a different world, their itineraries are somewhat different. Hermann from the novel, as Wladimir Troubetzkoy observes, is a fictional character who strives to have a real life. He wants to write but is only written (by Nabokov) (Troubetzkoy 1995: 57). Troubetzkoy supports this opinion by drawing attention to the multitude of literary allusions that "force Hermann to keep his fictional status inside the narrative of which he thinks he is the author," making him a "shadow of many literary shadows" (ibid.: 58). In a similar vein, Kimney describes Hermann as a "monster in the service of art" (Kimney 1980: 106). Ultimately, the "play of shadows" employed by Nabokov makes the reader indifferent to the plight of any of the characters and skeptical about the reality of any event depicted in the book. As Troubetzkoy puts it, "We are unable to distinguish fiction from reality and what Hermann Karlovich says from the truth, we feel that we may be fooled by this strange narrator at any moment" (Troubetzkoy 1995: 55–6). The central occurrence, around which the narrative is built — the murder of Felix — is "so mysterious that in the end — April Fool's Day — the reader cannot be entirely certain that there was a murder" (Proffer 1968b: 266). Moreover, even if there was a murder, it pales into insignificance when compared to its rendition in art. A similar impression is yielded to many readers in *Lolita* because Humbert's description of his dealings with Lolita is so perfect that the reader tends to forget that behind Humbert's narrative is the "reality" of child abuse.

Contrary to the literary Hermann, who wants to escape from fiction to reality, Fassbinder's protagonist strives to escape from reality into fiction or a dream. This urge is conveyed by his pretending to be an actor — to Felix, to the police, and perhaps to himself. Unfortunately for Hermann, reality catches up with him again and again. People do not take him for an actor, even less a film director, but as a man who unsuccessfully plays an actor. Fassbinder also makes us believe that Hermann will end up in jail or be executed, as opposed to being transported to another film. The impossibility of Hermann's escape is signified by frequently shooting him from above, when he is enclosed by walls, as well as showing him watched by people whom he does not know, such as a street musician. By rendering Hermann as the object of a spy operation, Fassbinder also alludes to the Nazi period, when the authorities encouraged citizens to spy on each other. Together, the novel and the film demonstrate that movements between different ontological orders are impossible. Life remains life, art remains art, sealed off from each other.

The difference between the directions of escape of the characters in the book and the film has an implication for the emotional tone of the respective works and the type of pleasure they offer to their consumers. Nabokov's *Despair* comes across as a perfect, self-contained piece of art. In this sense it is probably the most postmodern of Nabokov's works — in my opinion, much more so than *King, Queen, Knave* or *Laughter in the Dark*. Fassbinder's film, on the other hand, invites a realistic interpretation: seeing the characters as real people, not characters in a film. This makes his film terrifying at times — for example, during the scene of Hermann killing Felix or waiting for the police at the end of the film. This realistic interpretation is strengthened by Fassbinder dedicating the film to the three artists Vincent van Gogh, Antonin Artaud and Unica Zürn who, in different ways, attempted to escape reality — through drugs, madness and suicide. Paradoxically, because of their dramatic attempts to flee from this world, they are remembered as much as people in "this world," with which they were in conflict, as for their successes in creating a parallel reality in art.

The difference between the literary and cinematic version of *Despair* might be attributed to the different attitude of Nabokov and Fassbinder toward realities presented in their work. The former regards it as his own creation, over which he has a total control. Therefore, although his books encourage sociological and historical readings, as many authors argued and I repeated elsewhere in this book, they equally lend themselves to metafictional interpretation too. Fassbinder, on the other hand, is a more "straightforward" and humble realist and moralist. To illuminate Fassbinder's moralistic approach, Peter Ruppert quotes Fassbinder as saying:

> When I show people on the screen the ways that things can go wrong, my aim is to warn them that that's the way things will go if they don't change their lives. Never

mind if a film ends pessimistically; if it exposes certain mechanisms clearly enough to show people how exactly they work, then the ultimate effect is not pessimistic [Ruppert 1984: 63].

Ruppert uses this quote to elucidate the subtitle of Fassbinder's film: "A Journey into Light," claiming, "There is no journey into the light here for the protagonist, but there is quite possibly such a journey for the viewer" (ibid.). However, the subtitle could be seen as augmenting the pessimistic component of the film's main title by referring to the journey taken by the film's protagonist — from his comfortable shadows, glass boxes, and mirrored chambers into the full light where he cannot hide himself. Such interpretation is also confirmed by the fact that the most ominous scenes in the film are set in full light. First, in his dream, Hermann, who looks like Felix, meets Lydia in a park saturated in light, looking as if taken from an impressionistic painting. This scene, however, instead of showing Hermann's liberation, confirms his entrapment by pointing to his dependence on the man whom he killed. It is also in full light when the police come to arrest Hermann, hiding in Switzerland. He attempts to avoid them by sitting in the shadow in his room, knowing that the shadow offers him some safety.

By and large, light in Fassbinder's films tends not to connote any blissful illumination but knowledge, which is painful because it shatters any pleasant illusions about the world and oneself, as well as finding oneself in a place from where there is no escape. The best example is *Veronica Voss* (1982), where, as Thomas Elsaesser observes, "the blacks, the greys promise just a little security and respite, but where the white is deadly" (Elsaesser 1996: 114). By employing the shadow-light dialectic, Fassbinder draws on the tradition of German Expressionism, the cinematic movement regarded by Siegfried Kracauer as anticipating Nazism (Kracauer 2004). It is worth adding that German Expressionism appears to have influenced Nabokov when writing *Despair*, although the writer himself denied any German influences on his work (Des: 10).

Experiencing Fassbinder's film as being in a more intimate relationship with reality than Nabokov's novel can also be attributed to the differences of media used by the respective artists. Cinema, even when presenting fantastical events and impossible characters, demands suspension of disbelief and identification with the represented world. Literature allows for a greater distance from the conjured reality.

While it is impossible to judge the overall fidelity of the film to the novel, there is no doubt that the director, assisted by the scriptwriter, preserved its linguistic complexity. As Dolores Burdick observes, "The film script is written by Czech-born Tom Stoppard, and the film stars British actor Dirk Bogarde, putting on a very slight German accent to match the good English uttered by an almost all-German-speaking cast. The movie features an American film-within-a-film, with English intertitles, subtitled in German" (Burdick 1982: 140). This multilingualism, as Burdick notes, universalizes the main themes present in the film, such as the motif of exile and alienation (ibid.).

Thomas Elsaesser situates Fassbinder's film against a background of movies about split identities, such as Alain Resnais' *L'Année dernière à Marienbad* (*Last Year in Marienbad*, 1961), Ingmar Bergman's *Persona* (1966), Federico Fellinini's *8½* (1963), Michelangelo Antonioni's *Il Deserto rosso* (*Red Desert*, 1964) and Visconti's *Death in Venice* (1971), the majority of them made in the 1960s (Elsaesser 1996: 75). While I see some connection between *Despair* and them, I will rather situate Fassbinder's film alongside some movies of the 1970s, such as *Performance* (1970) by Donald Cammell and Nicolas Roeg and *Mr. Klein* (1976) by Joseph Losey. In these films, dislocation of identity to another person is more discernible, inevitable and brutal, although, at the same time, somewhat more mysterious than in, let's say, *Death in Venice* or *8½*. One reason for this connection comes from *Despair* being a partly British film. Another might be a certain amorphism and withdrawal from public life characteristic of Europe of the 1970s. At the time, Europe, after the revolution of 1968, was searching for its new identity. This period thus can be compared to the end of the Weimar Republic, where the action of Nabokov's book and Fassbinder's film is set. Films such as *Performance*, *Mr. Klein* and *Despair* act as a warning against any attempts to dislocate or multiply oneself, by showing that, ultimately, such attempts lead to the destruction of identity. Identity, we realize when watching these films, is the greatest gift, one which should not be squandered.

*Despair* is an interesting example of a film adaptation where staying "faithful" to the letter of the original work results in making a film very different in its ontology. It is also an important film in Fassbinder's career due to its being a summary of his favorite themes. However, despite these qualities, it is one of his least viewed, discussed and appreciated works. The most important reason is that, despite the director's rooting it in a German context, for his admirers the film was not German enough. Such an opinion is expressed by Jean-Luc Godard, who regards Fassbinder as the last German director (or even the last director in Europe) whose films have such a strong national identity. Hence, for Godard, making *Despair*, which he describes as a "Hollywood film," is a sign of Fassbinder's betrayal of his own ethos (Godard, quoted in Witt 2000: 37). For me, it is rather a proof that film, in common with literature, can be both national and transnational, global and parochial.

# 5

# Remembrance of Things Unspoken
## Mademoiselle O
### *by Jérôme Foulon (1994)*

> Have I really salvaged her from fiction? — Vladimir Nabokov, "Mademoiselle O"

Readers of Nabokov are used to the multiple lives of his stories and characters, but *Mademoiselle O* and its heroine in this respect holds a record. J. E. Rivers counts as many as five versions of the story: one French, one Russian and three English ones, and several more incarnations of the character in Nabokov's novels and short stories, including "Easter Rain," (which is a Russian story by Nabokov from 1925, rediscovered in the 1990s, where the Swiss governess appeared for the first time), *The Defense*, *The Real Life of Sebastian Knight* and *Ada* (Rivers 2000: 95). Probably the best known version of "Mademoiselle O," and one which is of special importance for this study, constitutes Chapter V of Nabokov's autobiography, *Speak, Memory*. The multiple life of the story and, by extension, of its eponymous character, as well as other oddities pertaining to this text, was acknowledged first by John Burt Foster, who begins his essay by asking rhetorically:

> What kind of narrative is "Mademoiselle O," and can it be seen as a short story in any meaningful sense? Perhaps "memoir" is the better category, since in different variants the work appears as Chapter V in all three of Nabokov's autobiographies, first in *Conclusive Evidence* (1951), then in the Russian version known as *Drugie berega* (*Other Shores*, 1954), and finally in *Speak, Memory: An Autobiography Revisited* (1966). On the other hand, Nabokov had already published the 1951 version in *Nine Stories* (1947), his first short-story collection in English. And to this day the earlier version circulates as a story in *Nabokov's Dozen* (1958). Yet this book, in a final note, maintains that neither "Mademoiselle O" nor "First Love" (also part of the collection despite being Chapter VII of *Speak, Memory*) is fictitious: they "are (except for a change of names) true in every detail to the author's remembered life." Even this blanket statement, however,

has loopholes. Not only do name-changes preserve some fictionality but, more subtly, Nabokov's proclaimed fidelity to "remembered" life sidesteps the larger, more rigorous claim of being "true to life." No matter how much he wants meticulous veracity, he cannot rule out an element of story-telling in this memoir [Foster 1993a: 111].

J. E. Rivers observes that the "French Swiss" comes across as a more sympathetic and dignified person than her "English Swiss" followers. When attempting to account for the changes in the characterization of Mademoiselle, he suggests that she played an important role in the sexual development of the young Vladimir, and the subsequent versions testify to Nabokov's need to come to terms with this experience (Rivers 2000: 96–7). I find such an explanation plausible, but for me the most likely reason that the Mademoiselle in the French version is more sympathetic than her English counterparts is the fact that her portrayal was offered to the French audience. The fact that Nabokov was reading the story to French listeners in Paris must have made him especially cautious not to hurt the national pride of his listeners by debunking a person who introduced him to French language and culture. By contrast, when translating "Mademoiselle O" into English, he did not need to worry about offending patriotic feelings of his readers, as they were mostly British and American; he could even assume that some of them would enjoy his ridiculing of Mademoiselle.

The studies by Foster and Rivers suggest not only that there are many versions of "Mademoiselle O," but also that there is a certain ambiguity related to the ontological status of their protagonist. She can be regarded as a "real person," as a character in fiction or a liminal entity, suspended between reality, memory and imagination. Such ambiguous identity is acknowledged by Nabokov himself, who at the outset of his story presents it as his "desperate attempt to save what is left of poor Mademoiselle" (SM: 75) after using her in his fiction. His description on the one hand suggests a careful reconstruction of the true likeness of Mademoiselle, yet on the other hand warns the reader against putting too much trust in the truthfulness or honesty of the narrator. As we might know from other works by Nabokov, their narrators tend to be unreliable.

Mademoiselle's ontological status raises not only aesthetic but also ethical issues. If we regard Mademoiselle O as a true person, whose name was a thin disguise for his Swiss governess, Cécile Miauton (as Nabokov's biographer, Brian Boyd maintains (Boyd 1990: 60)), then the way Nabokov treats her shall be assessed against similar criteria to the way "real" people are presented in memoirs. If, by contrast, she is fictional, he had more right to construct her the way he wanted. Most likely, Nabokov wanted to have his cake and eat it: let us see Mademoiselle as "real," but at the same time use "fiction" as an excuse to treat her with harshness. Yet, the principal purpose of my examination is not establishing how close to reality was Nabokov's Mademoiselle O, but what values and ideas stand behind her construction, and whether the same values and ideas inform the screen adaptation of the story. In my comparison, I will privilege Mademoiselle O from *Speak, Memory*, partly because this is the governess with whom I am on most intimate terms, and partly because the narrative scope of Jérôme Foulon's film, by evoking other episodes from Nabokov's life, encourages us to choose Nabokov's biography as the main context of the study of this character.

Lets begin with her name, which is the clearest sign of Mademoiselle O's belonging to the world of fiction. Not only it is different from the real name and initial of Nabokov's governess, but it directs the reader to an earlier literary text: Heinrich von Kleist's short story "The Marquise of O" (Die Marquise von O), written and set at the beginning of the nineteenth century, during the period of the Napoleonic wars.[1] It concerns a recently widowed daughter of a citadel commander in northern Italy who was raped and impregnated while lying unconscious by an invading Russian officer of noble birth, Count F. He raped the marquise after saving her from the barbarous Russian troops who accompanied the Count in the storming of the citadel. It is worth mentioning in passing that "Mademoiselle O" begins with words that sound like an invitation to move the story to a different context: "Based on a true incident, the setting of which has been transposed from the north to the south" (von Kleist 2004: 68).

In the essay which compares the two works by von Kleist and Nabokov, Hal Rennert suggests that the representation of the Russians as barbarous was typical for the times the German writer composed his story (Rennert 1984: 332). I shall add that some of the connotations of Russia and Russians, as projected by von Kleist, existed earlier and survived until contemporary times. Iver Neumann claims that there was a long Western tradition, going back as far as the sixteenth century, of perceiving Russia as Europe's Orient, and attributing to its inhabitants such features as a predilection to totalitarian rule and, most relevant in this context, an immense appetite for sex, backwardness, bad manners and barbarity (Neumann 1999: 65–112). Yet, in line with the rule described by Edward Said in his famous book *Orientalism*, published for the first time in 1978, Orient is a Western creation; it is even a disguised self-reflection. Hence, those who created such a negative image of Russia projected onto this country those features which they rejected in themselves. Russia in such renditions was thus a spitting image of the West.

Von Kleist connects barbarity not only with Russia but also with the lower classes. In his description, Count F. comes across as more civilized than ordinary Russian soldiers. The latter "seize her [the marquise] with obscene gestures" and attempt to "assault her in the most shameful way" (von Kleist 2004: 69), and we are to believe that they have no sense of remorse. The rape committed by Count F. is, on the other hand, a result of his moment of madness, and he is later so ashamed of his act that he wants to die. Again, attributing barbarity to the lower classes is in line with the wider rule, identified by Said, that those who are in a position of power, (in this case the higher classes) tend to project their vices on those who are disempowered (in this case, the common folk) (Said 1985; 2003; Shohat 1997).

Rennert claims that Nabokov conceived his story as a way to symbolically revenge von Kleist's representation of Russia and the West, using Mademoiselle O as his vehicle (Rennert 1984). Rennert's main argument is that this revenge consists of conjuring up the woman as a beast and the Russian as a beauty (ibid.: 333). I agree with this view but want to develop it by arguing that simultaneously Nabokov represents Russia and the Russians as pure and civilized, and Mademoiselle O as Oriental. Such treatment of Mademoiselle is announced on the very first page of the story, where the author writes about "saving the poor Mademoiselle." The word "saving" evokes colonial discourse by suggesting that Mademoiselle needed rescuing, not unlike far-away lands which needed civilization, brought to them by Westerners (Shohat 1997: 39). Secondly, it implies that Mademoiselle could not represent herself: the writer has to do it for her by endowing her with a history. Again, this parallels the idea that the Orient is unable to represent itself, the West has to do the job (Said 2003: 21). In due course Nabokov also claims that his family had to help the governess in a more tangible way by providing her with income, a home and a whole *raison d'etre*, because on her arrival she was "a stranger, shipwrecked, penniless, ailing, in search of the blessed land where at last she would be understood" (SM: 77).

It is not surprising that Nabokov's Orient is female, as Orient tended to be feminized. As Said claims in one of his post–*Orientalism* essays:

> Orientalism is a praxis of the same sort, albeit in different territories, as male gender dominance, or patriarchy, in metropolitan societies: the Orient was routinely described as feminine, its riches as fertile, its main symbols the sensual woman, the harem and the despotic — but curiously attractive — ruler. Moreover, Orientals like Victorian housewives were confined to silence and to unlimited enriching production (Said 1985: 103).

The Orientalization of Mademoiselle, as undertaken by Nabokov, has several stages. Firstly, the writer orientalizes her physical appearance by mentioning her "abundant dark hair, three wrinkles on her austere forehead, beetling brows, the steely eyes, that blotchy complexion, which in moments of wrath develops an additional flush in the region of the third, and amplest, chin" (SM: 75). In another place he mentions her "Buddha-like bulk" and "impassive and simple symmetry of her face" (ibid.: 83). This description conveys darkness, severity towards others, stolidity and self-indulgence, leading to obesity and physical weakness — all features typical for Oriental people as construed by their Western colonizers. Furthermore, he evokes the governess' unpleasant hands due to the "froggy gloss on their tight skin besprinkled with brown ecchymotic spots" (ibid.: 82), which brings to mind the Western sense of disgust at touching Oriental people. As Rivers observes, some of the most off-putting details of the governess' appearance, including the "froggy gloss," Nabokov added during translation of the story from French to English (Rivers 2000: 96). Paradoxically, the evocation of a frog in this description, by its connotation of a "frog and a prince" fairytale, suggests also a possibility of a transformation of Mademoiselle into a beauty through the power of literature or art in general. Nabokov himself does not fulfill this possibility, but, as I will argue in due course, it was realized by the authors of the screen version of the story. The perception of Mademoiselle as Oriental is reinforced by Nabokov's depiction of Mademoiselle's manners as alien and repulsive to the young Vladimir. He mentions "her trick of peeling rather than sharpening a pencil, the point held toward her stupendous and sterile bosom swathed in green wool," "the way she had of inserting her little finger into her ear and vibrating it very rapidly" and "emitting in quick succession a series of asthmatic puffs" (SM: 82). Nabokov's reference to Mademoiselle's "open" ear might be regarded as a sign of his perceiving her body as grotesque: full of holes, potentially leaking and open to deformations, therefore contrasting with the Victorian concept of the female body as whole and perfect (on the grotesque body see Bakhtin 1984: 316–44).

After depicting Mademoiselle's body, Nabokov describes Mademoiselle's room, the most tangible product of her alien ways:

> Mademoiselle's room, both in the country and in town, was a weird place to me — a kind of hothouse sheltering a thick-leaved plant imbued with a heavy, enuretic odor. Although next to ours, when we were small, it did not seem to belong to our pleasant, well-aired home. In that sickening mist, reeking, among other woolier effluvia, of the brown smell of oxidized apple peel, the lamp burned low, and strange objects glimmered upon the writing desk: a lacquered box with licorice sticks, black segment of which she would hack off with her penknife and put to melt under her tongue [ibid.: 84–5].

This description conjures up Mademoiselle's room as an Oriental boudoir, associating its inhabitant with all typical features with which the Westerners furnished their representation of people from the East: predilection to sweets, heat and dirt. At the same time, it points to the division between Mademoiselle and the Nabokovs' space, almost belonging to different worlds.

Nabokov's emphasis on Mademoiselle's external appearance, bodily functions and her room at the expense of presenting her inner qualities, and representing them from the external perspective, is a further sign that he orientalizes her. As in the literature about the Orient, the function of this description is to allow the author to acquire a sense of superiority over the described person. At the same time, it shows that the author had only a superficial contact with the object of his study.

To avoid any doubts that Mademoiselle belongs more to the Orient than to the Western world, Nabokov concludes this portrayal by referring to her impression at night as "the ghastly Jézabel of Racine's absurd play stomped bare-footed into our bedroom" (ibid.: 85). Jezabel (or Jézabel) is a representative of paganism or of an alien religion who masquerades herself as a servant to god and attempts to corrupt the believers. Using this figure thus is meant to demonstrate that although the governess could mislead adults about her belonging to the Western world, perceptive Vladimir knew that her real allegiance was to an alien culture. Another connotation of Jezabel is that of a woman with uncontrollable sexuality. Hence, one can guess that in spite of pronouncing that Mademoiselle physically repulsed him, in reality Nabokov's attitude toward her was more complex: repulsion was mixed with physical attraction, which, again, is a common attitude of Westerners toward the Orient and, especially, toward Oriental women. A reading of Mademoiselle as sexually attractive is considered by Rivers, who, discussing her virtual passage from French to English, asks:

> Why this cooling toward the governess figure that ends at last in disgust? After reading an early draft of this essay, a friend suggested that perhaps Mademoiselle had sexually initiated the boy Nabokov, another friend, reacting to this suggestion, speculated that if so he could have repressed the memory only to have it surface partly or wholly in later life via "recovered memory syndrome." An interesting speculation, especially since sexual initiation by a governess is a hoary trope in both literature and life. By this logic Nabokov needed a language other than hers — English or Russian — to free himself from the lingering sexual tyranny and to express in coded words such as "unpleasant" (applied to her hands) his pent-up, still shaming, and perhaps not fully remembered experience of having been "abused" [Rivers 2000: 96–7].

It is also worth mentioning that Jezebel is a feminist icon, a symbol of a strong woman who does not allow men to dominate her and pays a high price for her independence. Reading Nabokov's story between the lines, we can also attribute this connotation to Mademoiselle. In such reading, the story is a way to come to terms with the fact that the young Nabokov found (sexually) attractive somebody whom he at the same time regarded as disgusting and whom he finds even more repulsive from a distance of sixty years. Being an object of such mixed feelings, Mademoiselle has something in common with Polenka, a peasant girl who was the first object of Vladimir's sexual attraction, and who equally repulsed him due to her alien (in this case) peasant ways. It is worth mentioning here that Russian class system is viewed by some authors as a colonial relationship. According to this perspective, Russian upper classes colonized the masses; they ruled over them but remained "foreign" to their peasant ways (Etkind 2003). This phenomenon, described as "internal colonization," to a certain extent is reflected in *Speak, Memory*, especially in the part devoted to Polenka. It concurs with, rather than being undermined by, the author's attempt to present his father as an excellent master revered by his peasants.

By evoking not just Jezabel but the reworking of this character by Racine, Nabokov tacitly admits that his perception of the governess was not direct but mediated by earlier colonial representations of the East, especially French ones. Equally, in this passage he makes reference to one of Mademoiselle's favorite writers, Racine, whom, as Jacqueline Hamrit observes, Nabokov loathed, "considering this type of writing both commonplace and poor" (Hamrit 2009). In the fragment comparing Mademoiselle to Jezabel we can also find a hint, confirmed in other parts of the story, that the governess perceived herself as a character from the literature, exemplified also by Corneille and marked by high drama and lofty style. The gap between Mademoiselle's self-perception as a tragic heroine of romance and her real life, marked by her unhealthy dietary habits and her unattractive appearance, provides Nabokov with abundant opportunities to mock the governess, of which he takes full advantage.

Nabokov further orientalizes, and thus undermines, Mademoiselle by comparing her with his mother, to whom he devotes Chapter II of his autobiography. There we learn how intelligent and sensitive, yet free of any traces of sentimentality or kitschy habits, his mother was. As Andrew Field observes, "Her habits and her moods and, most of all, her full parental involvement in the upbringing of her favored son are all vividly conveyed. His mother had taught him to be so passionate about remembering, and he shared with her the ability to experience various fragmentary moments of mental telepathy" (Field 1988: 255). In contrast to the perfect communication with his mother, the young Vladimir's life with Mademoiselle O is marked by mutual misunderstandings and mismatches, resulting from their differing tastes and behavioral traits. For example, the "oriental" openness of the governess contrasts with the distance of the young Nabokov.

As in an Oriental discourse, the positive qualities which Nabokov recognizes in Mademoiselle do not refer to her as an autonomous person, but to her usefulness to others or, to use the phrase of Pierre Bourdieu, to her "cultural capital" (1986), especially her ability to teach Nabokov her native language:

> What a number of volumes she read through to us on that veranda! Her slender voice sped on and on, never weakening, without the slightest hitch or hesitation, an admirable reading machine wholly independent of her sick bronchial tubes. We got it all: *Les Malheurs de Sophie, Le Tour du Monde en Quatre Vingt Jours, Le Petit Chose, Les Misérables, Le Comte de Monte Cristo,* many others. There she sat, distilling her reading voice from the still prison of her person [SM: 83].

The use of words such as "machine" and "prison" in this passage further undermine the value of Mademoiselle, almost stripping her of her basic humanity. Yet, at the same time, the word "prison," in common with the term "froggy gloss," suggests a potential of a more dignified and beautiful life for Mademoiselle, which was never realized, or even of her more attractive, hidden nature, which was never discovered by the boy Nabokov.

The next positive feature of the governess, fully acknowledged by the author, was the light she kept in her room which helped the young Nabokov cope with his sleeplessness and, as we might guess, helped develop his imagination, indispensable in his subsequent career as a writer. The connection between her light and his sleeplessness also suggests an unspoken fascination of the young Nabokov with the sexuality of a foreign woman. We can imagine, as Rivers suggests, that Nabokov could not sleep because at night he was thinking about Mademoiselle.

Lets return to "The Marquise of O," as von Kleist and Nabokov's stories are also linked, as Rennert observes, by the motif of a swan, which in both works symbolizes the eponymous female characters (although in each story it has different connotations). In "The Marquise of O," the swan stands for purity, which was violated by the Russian Count's despicable action. The Count, haunted by nightmares of remorse while recuperating from wounds suffered in a subsequent battle, compares the raped woman to a white swan at whom he had thrown dirt. In Nabokov's version, on the other hand, the swan is everything but an object of grace and beauty. It is an old bird, "a large, uncouth, dodo-like creature" making "ridiculous efforts to hoist himself into a moored boat" (SM: 92). These words confirm my view that in his story Nabokov tries to undermine Mademoiselle O by presenting her as strange and exotic.

The superiority of Vladimir over Mademoiselle is also based on their uneven access to the past. Mademoiselle's memories are presented as plainly inaccurate, typically due to her sentimentality and her tendency to exaggerate things. Nabokov's recollections, on the other hand, are true, if not to life then to some higher standard of truth. Hence, while on numerous occasions, as Forster observes, Nabokov draws attention to the blurring between memory and imagination, and fiction and reality (Forster 1993), he does not allow Mademoiselle to fictionalize or beautify her memories. Similarly, while he takes great liberties in transforming Mademoiselle into a grotesque character from an Orientalist text, he does not allow her to successfully orientalize her hosts or the country where she found herself. For example, he ridicules her naming the vicinity of the Nabokovs' Vyra estate "*le steppe*" (SM: 78), and when she recollects "the dead wax doll we once buried under the oak!," he corrects her with "No — a wool-stuffed Golliwogg" (ibid.:84), with Golliwogg having racist undertones.

The entire characterization of Mademoiselle is based on the contrast between the fit, healthy, emotionally balanced and "more Western than Westerners" Nabokovs, who constitute the norm, and the unhealthy, sentimental and Oriental Mademoiselle, who constitutes an aberration. At the same time, paradoxically, Nabokov demonstrates Russian cultural superiority over the West through developing motifs from French literature, such as the motif of the boy's sleeplessness, which can be found in Proust's *The Remembrance of Things Past*. This paradox can be explained by the idea of Russia as a "good learner," able to learn from the West, which was introduced during the reign of Peter the Great, the emperor responsible for modernizing Russia and moving its capital to Petersburg (Neumann 1999: 74–112), where Nabokov lived in his youth. The unsympathetic description of Mademoiselle O is accompanied by the writer's acknowledgment that he might be unfair towards her. This is conveyed in a passage following the claim that Mademoiselle's constant feeling of misery does not guarantee her a "permanent soul" and a place in eternity:

> Just before the rhythm I hear falters and fades, I catch myself wondering whether, during the years I knew her, I had not kept utterly missing something in her that was far more she than her chins or her ways or even her French — something perhaps akin to that last glimpse of her, to the radiant deceit she had used in order to have me depart pleased with my own kindness, or to the swan [SM: 92].

This sense of guilt resulting from missing something in a person, which deserved a better treatment both in real life and literature, perhaps more sympathy and attention, or even giving up one's deep-seated views and tastes, we also find in Nabokov's description of his homosexual brother Sergei: "It is one of those lives that hopelessly claim a belated something — compassion, understanding, no matter what — which the mere recognition of such a want can neither replace nor redeem" (SM: 199). In such recognition, however, Nabokov tacitly admits that he played no positive role in alleviating the misery of these people, and perhaps was even one of its sources.

In due course, however this "belated something" was offered to Sergei in an essay written by Lev Grossman (and quoted by me in the chapter devoted to *Despair*), which presents a more detailed and sympathetic portrayal of the "other Nabokov," largely at the expense of Vladimir, who comes across in this account as a cold and narcissistic genius. My main argument in the remaining part of this essay is that Foulon's film can also be seen as such a "belated something" offered to Mademoiselle and, to some extent, Sergei. It should be mentioned that Foulon is not the only reader of Nabokov's biography who closely links these two characters. Michael Wood, in his perceptive study of *Speak, Memory*, also places them in close proximity, connecting them by Nabokov's half-expressed, half-concealed guilt and regret (Wood 1994: 98).

However, before moving to the film's text, let's present its context. *Mademoiselle O* is a television film and, as with the bulk of television productions, almost at its birth was sentenced to a short and parochial existence. It is not commercially available in the Western world and does not have English subtitles; my own copy was presented to me by the film's producer. It was shot in 1993 and premiered in 1994, seven years after *Maschenka* (*Mary*, 1987) by John Goldschmidt, which was an international production (including French), and three years before the second American *Lolita* was made. It is unique in being the only film based on Nabokov's prose in which the French language prevails. However, it reveals significant thematic similarities to the two films between which it appeared, as well as to virtually all later adaptations of Nabokov's prose, resulting from the fact that it is set, so to speak, in the past tense. It concerns events and people who are remembered, not present here and now. This approach might be partly explained by the fashion for "retro," which started in cinema in the 1980s and never died out. Being written by a master of "time remembered," Nabokov's books perfectly lend themselves to such treatment, and *Mademoiselle O* is no exception.

*Mademoiselle O*'s production in 1993, coming almost immediately after the collapse of the Soviet Union and Russia's change of political regime, symbolizes Nabokov's return to free Russia (or at least free from the state communism). This return is rendered even more real by the fact that *Mademoiselle O* was shot on location in Russia, in places which look like the original locations of Nabokov's biography — outside the mansion of his uncle Ruka, the only one of the three houses depicted in *Speak, Memory* that has survived to the present day; in St. Petersburg; and in the misty Russian woods and parks. Moreover, although the film is described as French, and its budget of 7 million francs was provided by Telfrance and France 2, the majority of its cast and crew was Russian, including the actors playing the roles of Vladimir and Sergei and their parents. Moreover, it has an extended life in Russia, where it is available on DVD.

*Mademoiselle O* was only the second film in the career of Jérôme Foulon, who, in due course, became a successful television director. He co-wrote the script with Sandra Joxe, a scriptwriter with a special interest in women and children's stories. One can assume that the "feminization" of *Mademoiselle O* which took place on the road from book to film can be in part attributed to her feminine and feminist hand.

Foulon and Joxe's adaptation is an attempt to account for what Nabokov omits from his book and to present Mademoiselle from a different perspective, which I will described as multi-focal. This means that rather than privileging one point of view, be it of the young Vladimir or Mademoiselle herself, it juxtaposes different perspectives in order to afford a more accurate outlook on the story. Apart from the perspectives of Mademoiselle and Nabokov, we also receive the points of view of Nabokov's parents and other tutors of Vladimir and Sergei. Partly for this reason, and partly just to fill screen time, Foulon also includes episodes from the remaining chapters of *Speak, Memory* (for example, the imprisonment of Nabokov's father, the visits of uncle Ruka, and Vladimir's childhood infatuation with the peasant girl Polenka). One can also find some references to Nabokov's "fiction." Yet, these episodes are typically abbreviated and condensed to hardly more than an image. In this way Foulon not only recognizes that *Mademoiselle O* was the origin of the memoir, but also that it is crucial to his biography, or at least to the part documenting Nabokov's life in Russia. While doing that, the film also renders the relationship between the main characters differently, as we can expect from a film financed by a French company and made by a French director. Most likely, it will be difficult for him psychologically and politically to orientalize a French-speaking Swiss governess — namely, a person of a similar cultural heritage to him.[2] However, rather than reversing to the original scheme, as conveyed by von Kleist, in which the Russians are rendered barbarous and the Western person civilized, he complicates his portrayal by showing that neither of the characters fits the original stereotype well.

The film begins in December 1905 with the arrival of Mademoiselle at the Siverski station, from where she is taken to the Nabokovs' estate. We see first the enormous steaming wheels of the train, and then the governess alighting from the train. Such an image brings associations with *Anna Karenina*, especially since this image was reproduced in numerous film adaptations of this book. Consequently, when, in her first conversation with Elena Nabokov, Mademoiselle compares herself to the most famous heroine of Lev Tolstoy, saying, "There I was, abandoned by all, *comme la Comtesse Karenine*," her utterance, unlike in the literary version, does not invite ridicule. Upon her arrival, as in Nabokov's account, she also utters the dramatic cry, "Giddy-eh? Giddy-eh?" (Where? Where?). This cry features both in the book and in the film, where it expresses Mademoiselle's foreignness and helplessness; but in the original version it is also a sign of the governess' ignorance of Russia, which she did not overcome during her stay with the Nabokovs. This is conveyed by "giddy-eh" remaining the sole Russian word she took back to Switzerland. Foulon, on the other hand, does not repeat this remark or refer to it in any other way.

Mademoiselle brings with her an enormous trunk, upon which the camera lingers. The trunk, of course, contains the total material possessions of Mademoiselle, but also stands for her "cultural capital," to use again Bourdieu's phrase: something which makes her attractive in the job market in a foreign country. There she keeps many of the books and perhaps the spelling tests she did with Vladimir and Sergei. Mademoiselle's first contact with the Nabokovs' country house in Vyra begins with her encountering a stuffed bear, presumably from Siberia. Upon seeing it, she utters another cry, startled by the view of a "smiling" beast. This image gives the impression of a Westerner arriving in an Oriental land full of dangerous and exotic animals, which also reflects on its human inhabitants. The next episode, however, undermines and complicates this scheme. It shows separate encounters of Mademoiselle with two women who were looking after the Nabokovs' children: the outgoing English governess Miss Robinson, and Nabokov's mother Elena. The meetings are for Mademoiselle a source of discomfort and humiliation, which she, however, does not want to reveal. It is clear that the much slimmer and more elegant Miss Robinson feels superior to the overweight and plainer-looking outsider who is about to usurp her place. When introducing herself, she emphasizes that she is "from London," probably regarding it as the capital of the world, and fails to shake Mademoiselle O's hand. This rude behavior is understandable in the light of the fact that she was recently dismissed. Mademoiselle O, on the other hand, in this encounter introduces herself as coming from provincial Switzerland and attempts to sell one of her main assets — her sense of humor. She says, "I am Mademoiselle O. O tout court. O like O. O like sea-lion. O like platypus or orange, if you prefer" (*Moi, je suis Mademoiselle O. O tout court. O comme o. O comme otarie. O comme ornithorynque ou comme orange si vous préférez*).

What we see in the introduction of the two governesses is not an encounter between the Orient and the Occident, but a battle between two types of Occident — English and French — for the souls of the children, who both women probably regarded first as Oriental. Foulon presents it also as a competition between metropolitan and provincial styles. The women thus play the role of cultural colonizers attempting to mold the children to the image of the cultures which they represent, but their economic and social position renders them as inferior to the objects of their colonization. The early scene also introduces the Nabokov household as an arena in which different cultures, languages and people fight for the domination and sympathy of their masters. This makes it similar to a royal court, both Oriental and Occidental, or even a harem, with foreign women fighting for the attention and affection of their masters. In the light of this image, Mademoiselle's description of the Nabokovs' country home as a "*chateau*," which again Nabokov mocks in his biography, appears to be quite accurate.

Mademoiselle's manner of presenting herself on her arrival at Vyra, as well as her later comparison to Anna Karenina, also renders her as an instinctive cosmopolitan who attempts to feel at home everywhere she finds herself, adjusting her habits to those of her hosts. In a sense, it also renders her similar to Nabokov, who, through his story, suggests (albeit in a subtler way) that he is like Marcel from Proust's novel. Mademoiselle's openness to foreign influences is also conveyed in another early scene when she drinks some homemade wine she finds in the Nabokovs' house. First she approaches the glass with distrust, most likely expecting that it will be of low quality. However, after dipping her finger in and tasting it, she drinks the whole glass, and then we see a carafe full of the red liquid in her room. This early scene can also be regarded as a metaphor for Mademoiselle's whole attitude toward Russia. At first she is skeptical, then she tastes it a bit and likes it, and eventually she takes the whole "carafe," regarding the country as her own. Another scene demonstrating the transformation of her attitude toward Russia shows her playing with Sergei against the background of the same stuffed bear that startled her upon her arrival — as if the animal was their old friend. We also see Mademoiselle visiting a church, where she sees Elena praying. Although religion is typically represented as a crucial difference between Westerners and Easterners, and "us" and "them" in a wider sense, on this occasion the cultural connotations of the Russian Orthodox church are played down. It is presented simply as a place of privacy, which both women are seeking at times. The ability to accept her environment differentiates the cinematic Mademoiselle from her literary predecessor, who is represented as completely isolated from Russia and all things Russian until the very end of her stay.

Another difference concerns the physical appearance of the two Mademoiselles. Although the Mademoiselle played by Maïté Nahyr is overweight, she is not grotesquely obese, as Nabokov implies, and does not have a blotchy complexion, multiple chins, heavy breathing or a vestigial moustache. Similarly, her hands do not have the froggy or ecchymotic spots attributed to Mademoiselle by the writer. In spite of her excessive weight, she can be regarded as attractive, thanks to her abundant dark hair and lively eyes. Mademoiselle's physical allure is helped by her agility and dexterity, contrasting with the impression of sloth and physical slowness given by Nabokov. The sense that Mademoiselle is light despite her extra pounds is suggested by a caricature of her made by Vladimir, representing her as a butterfly. Although the governess takes great offence upon seeing it, it can be read as an appreciative rendition of her. The impression of Mademoiselle's overall attractiveness is also confirmed by Vladimir's attitude toward her. Although he usually talks about her in derogatory terms and makes caricatures of her, he also spies on her when she bathes and enjoys lying close to her (over)ripe body. His attraction to her body suggests that she plays in his life the role of a surrogate mother and the main source of his Oedipus complex, confirming the interpretation offered by Rivers.

The scene of spying, in which Sergei also participates, most likely on Vladimir's insistence, likewise shows that gaze is related to power and presents Mademoiselle in the way Oriental people, including Oriental women, were perceived by Westerners — as simultaneously appalling and appealing. Mademoiselle is herself aware of this ambiguity imbued in the boys' gaze and reciprocates their attention in an ambiguous way, showing both outrage and pleasure.

Furthermore, unlike her literary predecessor, the filmic Mademoiselle does not have affection for licorice sticks but for ordinary Swiss chocolate. This feature renders her more European and even more contemporary due to the widespread perception that for contemporary women chocolate is a surrogate for sex. Foulon also accentuates the compensatory character of chocolate. We see the governess eating the small dark squares every time she is humiliated or frustrated, and on most occasions it is men who cause her suffering. As such unpleasant occurrences are frequent, chocolate features extensively in the governess' life. Moreover, in one scene, when Vladimir is very sick, chocolate is depicted as a medicine or tonic because after receiving it from Mademoiselle the boy recovers. Thus, in contrast to the sweets described by Nabokov, which divided Mademoiselle from her Russian hosts, in Foulon's version they bring them together, symbolizing Vladimir's acceptance of Mademoiselle as a person and bearer of culture.

As previously mentioned, Elena Nabokov, along with Mademoiselle, is a character to whom Nabokov devoted the most attention in *Speak, Memory*, and whom he described with greatest talent, in contrast to Nabokov's father, who does not come across as equally vivid and distinctive. Yet, the two women are kept separate in the biography, perhaps reflecting the fact that they cared for the children at different times and places, and catered to their different needs. Foulon strengthens this impression, rendering Elena Nabokov as a perfect hostess and a "holiday mother" who, busy entertaining guests and with her own affairs, is absent from home most of the time; even when she is there, she typically observes others looking after her sons rather than engaging with them for a longer period of time. Yet, the fact that she is not with her children all the time makes her very attractive in her sons' eyes. We see that whenever the mother appears, the young Nabokovs abandon Mademoiselle to hug and kiss Elena. She comes across as naturally cheerful and warm, as well as elegant and beautiful. We can guess that it would be next to impossible for Mademoiselle to compete with her for their attention and affection. Moreover, during the first months of Mademoiselle's stay, Elena Nabokov is heavily pregnant. Her swollen belly invites comparison with the large figure of Mademoiselle, because in the case of Elena it signifies fertility and fulfilled femininity; in the case of Mademoiselle it points to her erotic disappointments and unsatisfied desires to have a family of her own, thus adding to the sense of her inferiority to Nabokov's mother.

And yet Foulon manages to convince the viewer, largely contrary to Nabokov's (conscious) intentions, that against the odds Mademoiselle succeeded in being somebody very important for the young Nabokovs. The features which shine best through the film are those which Nabokov does not recount (or does so only in a small way) in *Speak, Memory*: Mademoiselle's genuine love of children (which renders her own childlessness even more sad) and her warm personality. She is truly devoted to the young boys, getting up at night when her "Volodia," as she tenderly calls Vladimir, cannot sleep, and she is also, rather than their mother, at his side when he becomes seriously ill with pneumonia. Mademoiselle in the film is also an excellent governess, able to teach the children through showing things in a playful way. For example, she explains the meaning of words such as "dress" and "wash" by pretending that she washes and dresses herself, which immensely amuses Sergei and is even able to bring a smile to the otherwise sour lips of his brother. Moreover, although she often is offended, her offence does not last long. She tends to forgive people, especially "her" two boys, or is able to conceal her feelings.

Mademoiselle's warmth is most visible in her dealings with the younger of the two brothers, Sergei. Sergei is described by Nabokov as somebody who spent more time with the governors than he (SM: 198), and this assessment most likely refers to Sergei's time with Mademoiselle. His closeness to the French governess is confirmed by Brian Boyd, who writes that Sergei "adored Mademoiselle" (Boyd 1990: 70). In the film, the bond between them results from the fact that Sergei is the keener of the two to reciprocate Mademoiselle's affection, partly due to his younger age and partly due to his sweet nature, encapsulated by his fair hair and round face, contrasting with Vladimir's dark hair and long face that gives him the appearance of sulking.

## 5. Remembrance of Things Unspoken

It can be added here that in the film the difference in age between Sergei and Vladimir appears to be much greater than the ten-and-a-half months which in reality separated the two boys. Sergei comes across as a boy of five years, while Vladimir is ten or so years old. Moreover, as we can learn from Nabokov's biographies, the older of the boys was their parents,' and especially his mother's, favorite child, while Sergei was probably their least loved child. Although in the film the parents are treating both children with affection, it is clear that they regard their older son as a person of exceptional abilities, while at times they are exasperated by the lack of talents of their younger offspring. We see it most acutely in a scene of Sergei's playing the piano, where the mother and Volodia can hardly stand the sounds produced by Sergei, while Mademoiselle shows Sergei some appreciation. Sergei shows his attachment to the governess most clearly on the day of her departure, which is a heart-breaking experience for both the pupil and the governess. That day Sergei first chases the coach in which she is leaving Vyra for good, to give her the music box she forgot to take with her; then he hugs her, causing them both to cry. Vladimir, although he does not react in such an emotional way, is also strongly affected by her departure. The touching scene of Mademoiselle's leaving stands in contrast to the departure of the English governess, which left both boys unmoved.

Against the background of the simple and affectionate Sergei, in Foulon's film Vladimir comes across as a rather unappealing individual, short of being a monster. His difficult character is first revealed in an episode during Mademoiselle's arrival at the Nabokovs' country house. To introduce herself to the children, she strokes Sergei's face, to which he smiles. Vladimir, on the other hand, reacts to the same caress by brutally pushing away the woman's hand, adding to her pain of feeling unwelcome in the new place. The scene appears more drastic in the film than in the book for two reasons. Firstly, it is visualized rather than described. Secondly, in *Speak, Memory* Nabokov explains his reaction as the shock of being touched by a stranger, as it never happened to him before, and the unpleasant quality of Mademoiselle's hands. The whole film is punctuated by outbursts of Vladimir's hostility towards the governess, which, even when explained in the film, seems disproportionate to the acts committed by her. Moreover, in the film Mademoiselle's "sins" always ultimately turn out to be the fault of other people. For example, she sits on Vladimir's precious butterfly collection after being woken up by a white mouse put on her bed by the young Nabokovs. While Volodia is quick to punish Mademoiselle for her misdemeanors, he is much slower in showing her gratitude, while there are many things for which he should be grateful to her. One of them is the knowledge and appreciation he gains of French literature.

Unlike in the literary original, where Nabokov's taste for literature develops in opposition to that of Mademoiselle's allegedly kitschy inclinations, in the film she is represented as the sole gate to French and, indeed, any literature. As the director admits in an interview, he wanted to depict her as the one who helped Nabokov to become a writer (de Montvalon 1993) as, one might say, a midwife to his literary talent. This is conveyed in the passages where during her reading he starts to observe something intently, seeing things with utmost precision, a talent for which he later became renowned.

However, as I already indicated, even if Nabokov is initially prejudiced against Mademoiselle, in due course a bond of sorts is forged between them. It is revealed especially when Volodia falls ill. Not only he is then particularly close to Mademoiselle, who cares for him, but she also invades his dreams. She takes the shape of a swan, swimming on the same lake on which floats a boat in which Volodia is standing, moving away from the camera. The departure of a boat signifies (by its reference to Hades, to which Charon takes the deceased) his approaching death, while the swan might be seen as the guardian angel of the boy. Indeed, when Volodia wakes from his feverish dream, he finds Mademoiselle at his side, her presence being a sign that the illness is about to end.

The motif of a swan punctuates Foulon's film. In common with Nabokov, the director links the swan with Mademoiselle and makes it a symbol of "the second shore" one reaches at the hour of one's death. Yet, other connotations of the bird in the film are different than in *Speak, Memory* and closer to those evoked by von Kleist — namely, purity and Occident. The swan from a sketch hanging on the wall in Vladimir's room, and which appears in his dreams, is graceful rather than dodo-like, suggesting that behind the overripe body of Mademoiselle there is something pure and virginal. We also see a porcelain figure of a swan adorning a music box which Mademoiselle keeps in her study and which eventually is returned to her by Sergei. Although somewhat kitschy, this object, like the Swiss chocolates eaten by the governess, is viewed by the young Nabokovs as a precious, almost magical souvenir from the West. The swan also brings to mind numerous porcelain objects collected by Russian emperors and eventually put on display in the Hermitage to charm visitors.

Although Foulon shows that the Nabokovs were civil to the somewhat touchy Mademoiselle, he equally demonstrates that they rarely expressed gratitude to her and did not attempt to address the causes of her continuous sense of pain and humiliation. For example, following the performance of Sergei and Volodia, which Mademoiselle scripted and directed (and in which she also participated), the parents applaud the children but fail to acknowledge Mademoiselle's role. After the performance she remains on stage, alone, while

## 5. Remembrance of Things Unspoken 121

the children are hugged by the adults. Only later does Elena praise Mademoiselle's part in their children's theatrical success. Similarly, the few pleasures Mademoiselle can enjoy in Vyra are cut short. One of them is sleep. Mademoiselle appears to revel in her bed, unlike her talented pupil, Volodia, who suffers from insomnia. We can guess that her pleasure in sleep derives partly from her disappointment and the lack of excitement during the day. In her dreams she can make up for them. Mademoiselle's sleep is constantly interrupted — either by the boys (who put a white mouse in her bed) or other servants (who tickle her with a feather duster), or by the need to attend to children.

Although after the dismissal of Miss Robinson, Mademoiselle O occupies a privileged position among the servants, in due course she loses it to the succession of male Russian tutors and is relegated to caring for Volodia and Sergei's baby sister, Elena. The frustrated governess makes desperate attempts to regain her position by "assisting fate" to get rid of her competitors. She helps to expose the fact that one of them is infatuated with Elena Nabokov, and that another is too clumsy to ensure Vladimir and Sergei's safety in his care. Yet we, the audience, know that her efforts to keep her place in the Nabokovs' menage will ultimately be in vain because every failing Russian tutor (not unlike every failing English or French governess) can easily be replaced by a new one. This is because what matters to their employers are not their unique personalities but their cultural capital. As if to confirm this rule, after these two rather naïve and kind-hearted tutors, a third arrives — and embarks on a mission to eliminate Mademoiselle. He does so by using the caricature of Mademoiselle as a butterfly, which he finds by chance in Vladimir's drawer, in his cinematic projections, attended by the whole Nabokov household. Thanks to that, everybody can see Mademoiselle as an overweight butterfly. The fact that this humiliation is public, unlike the many earlier ones she suffered in private, makes it unbearable for the governess. She climbs the stage and denounces her tormentors. After this incident, she packs her belongings and leaves returning to her home country. Nabokov's parents, although embarrassed by the situation, don't try to stop her. We can even guess that deep down they are content that Mademoiselle decided to leave; otherwise they would have to dismiss her due to her dwindling usefulness, as they dismissed the other tutors. Similarly, we can assume that the victory of the Russian tutor, as Mademoiselle's previous victories over her competitors, will be short-lived; he will eventually give way to a more able teacher or be dismissed altogether if the children need a change. Or this would happen if not for the Bolshevik revolution, which drastically changed the definition of "cultural capital" in this country.

The portrayal of the Nabokov family, as offered by Foulon, is not exceptionally harsh. He simply presents how the system of servants was constructed and operated in an aristocratic house, in Russia and elsewhere. However, it does not concur with the image projected in *Speak, Memory*, where Nabokov attempted to project his family home as a harmonious, benevolent and "progressive" place in which no servant was ever harmed, many received more than they deserved and everybody loved their masters, who were too preoccupied with more interesting things to attend to the everyday business of housekeeping. The scarcity of such painful incidents in *Speak, Memory*, such as those showing the conflict between the tutors, can also be attributed to the fact that most likely children were spared from witnessing them. Foulon, by contrast, appears to be fascinated by the heated atmosphere in the employees' quarters and explores the role the adult Nabokovs played in creating the hierarchy of servants.

In contrast to Nabokov, who renders Mademoiselle as lacking insight — being unable to see or hear correctly and, consequently, interpret correctly, (which is a feature of many of Nabokov's characters who do not have the author's sympathy) — Foulon represents Mademoiselle as an excellent observer, often able to see what other characters fail to notice or attempt to conceal from her. The sharpness of her senses and her ability to read the situation correctly is the reason that she often feels offended and undermined, and eventually decides to leave the Nabokovs. Consequently, the gift of a hearing aid, offered to her in Montreux in Switzerland by Vladimir, who visits her there in 1930, when he is an émigré himself, feels like a superfluous present. Yet it is also symbolic of the fact that only then is he allowing Mademoiselle to hear well — previously he preferred to keep her in the dark.

During his visit to Mademoiselle, Nabokov, who at the time in reality led a rather modest life, comes across as a rich foreigner, even a playboy, enjoying the charms of the most beautiful parts of Europe. This is signaled by his coming to Mademoiselle in a luxurious car, in which he previously kissed a young woman. Mademoiselle, on the other hand, is an old woman visited by a dear acquaintance from her past, who might be her nephew or a grandson. In their encounter the colonial dimension of their relationship is finally overcome. Rather than one of them being a foreigner and the other at home, they both appear to be on neutral ground, neither particularly rooted nor painfully dislocated either. This is in contrast to Nabokov's rendition of this event, where both Vladimir and Mademoiselle are presented as strangers.

No doubt Foulon's portrayal of Mademoiselle is closer to the French version of the story than its English successors, although my argument is that the director goes further in "rehabilitating" Mademoiselle than simply following the French original. This opinion not only refers to the psychological characterization of the governess, but also to the visual aspect of the film. The director adds a French touch to the Russian locations by shooting them according to the conventions of Impressionist painting — it feels like there is always a layer of thick air between the camera and the object filmed, which softens the images. Furthermore, the style of clothes worn by the characters and the choice of certain images, such as picnics near the woods and lakes, evoke the favorite subjects of the Impressionist painters and their cinematic followers, for example, *Un Dimanche à la campagne* (*A Sunday in the Country*, 1984) by Bertrand Tavernier. Foulon's film could be named *A Sunday in the Russian Country*, as imagined by French people. Impressionism is also referenced by including an image of Nabokov's mother painting the nature outside her home, on incident that does not exist in *Speak, Memory*. Such pictorial convention de-orientalizes the story and suggests that Mademoiselle passed to Nabokov not only her knowledge of French language and passion for French literature, but also her way of looking at things. It should be added that the link between Nabokov's writing style and Impressionism, as suggested by Foulon, is well documented by critics (Ciancio 1999) and can be seen as an additional sign of his French heritage.

The Impressionist style in the film is combined with the conventions of television productions which can also be regarded as in some ways analogous to literary biography due to a preponderance of close-ups. Accordingly, Foulon often switches between extreme long shots and close-ups of the characters' faces to reveal the minute changes in their inner lives. The sense of the closeness between the film and the book also results from preserving the voice-over narration and the choice of child actor Anton Minachkine for the part of the young Vladimir. Not only is the boy physically similar to the young Nabokov, but he seems to accurately capture his character's aloofness and sense of superiority over others. Rarely does a child show so much empathy and so little sympathy to the character he is portraying in film as does the young Minachkine.

A previously mentioned, Foulon's film has an extended life thanks to its being shown on Russian television and being released on DVD in Russia. Browsing through the Internet in search of reviews, I discovered that its afterlife has been more extensive in Russia than in France, and in Russian than in French. Practically all opinions I found about it were very positive, and the film was praised especially for its infusion of warmth into the character of Mademoiselle and the authors' ability to evoke life in pre-revolutionary Russia. As I will argue in the following chapters, warmth is what characterizes practically all of the recent adaptations of Nabokov. From the perspective of some critics, this is unfortunate, because cruelty, or at least the lack of sentimentality, is at the core of Nabokov's prose. Others, however, might see the warmth enwrapping these films as coming from the very center of Nabokov's oeuvre. I am thinking especially about the chrysalis in the short story "Christmas," which was thought to be dead but transforms into a butterfly, acting as a symbol of human resurrection. Metaphorically speaking, Foulon found or inserted in *Mademoiselle O* the warmth or other ingredient which allowed Mademoiselle to become a butterfly, and one which, unlike the one used in the screening by the Russian tutor, would not upset her but make her smile.

# 6

# Duel in Contemporary Estonia
## An Affair of Honor
## *by Valentin Kuik (1999)*

> Put your trust in God and just press the trigger.—Vladimir Nabokov,
> "An Affair of Honor"

In the previous chapter I proposed to regard *Mademoiselle O* by Jérôme Foulon as the first attempt to "return" Nabokov to his native country. *An Affair of Honor* by Valentin Kuik can be seen as a second such attempt. This is also the only full-length film based on Nabokov's work that was made in the former Soviet Union, although meaningfully produced and shot not in Russia but in Estonia. It testifies both to the fact that Nabokov ceased to be a forbidden writer in the whole of the Soviet Union some time ago and at the same time, to the difficulty of Russian cinema embracing its regained literary genius.[1]

Before discussing the film, let's introduce its literary source. It was published in 1927 under the Russian title "Podlets" ("Cad" or "Scoundrel") and set in Berlin in 1926–27, among Russian emigrants. Following Priscilla Meyer's classification of Nabokov's short stories, I will regard it as a transitional piece. On the one hand, as in his early stories, which she describes as "variations on the theme of the loss of Russia" (Meyer 2005: 120), the motif of the lost country is still present in the narrative; but in line with a rule that "by 1926 Nabokov began to let go of the theme of the émigré's obsession with a lost Russia" (ibid.: 121), it is overshadowed by other issues, especially adultery, which would become one of the most persistent motifs in his prose. "An Affair of Honor" is a story of one Anton Petrovich, who, after finding that his wife is having an affair with a man named Berg, challenges him to a duel. However, being a coward, Anton Petrovich fails to attend the place of combat outside Berlin, seeking refuge in a hotel and imagining that his opponent flinched too, allowing him to save face and return home without feeling ashamed.

"An Affair of Honor" can be read as an insight into a mediocre character and the larger milieu of Russian emigrants in Berlin. Equally, it can be viewed as a variation on the subject of dueling, very popular in Russian literature and, one can say, in Russian life, with two of the country's greatest poets, Pushkin and Lermontov, being the victims of duels. Nabokov acknowledges his debt to Pushkin's *Eugene Onegin* and *The Shot*, and to Lermontov's *A Hero of Our Time*, by mentioning them in the text, and he cites in his editorial note "Chekhov's magnificent novella *Single Combat* (1891)" as a realization of a romantic theme on which his own story is a "belated variation" (AH: 83).

The dueling theme also links "An Affair of Honor" with other works by Nabokov. Among them is a semi-autobiographical short story "Orache," (in which a boy agonizes over his father's duel, only to learn in the end that his father emerged from it unharmed), and *Ada*. In the latter, as David Rampton observes, "Van fights a duel not because some plausible sequence of events makes it necessary, but because the duel is one of Russian literature's obligatory rites" (Rampton 1984: 134). As with many works by Nabokov, including those discussed in this book, the intertextual character of the story does not undermine its realism. This is largely because the characters look at each other and themselves through a prism of existing texts: books, films or myths. Texts are thus a link between their mental vision and the external world.

Anton Petrovich is aware that his attitudes and values belong to a different place and time. By choosing to resolve his problem through a duel, he demonstrates his harking back to nineteenth-century Russia. Understandably, he prefers this no-longer-existing country with its anachronistic codes of honor, to contemporary, Bolshevik-ruled Russia, from which he fled. Yet his lack of courage to stick to his original plan shows that he cannot measure up to the noble Russian traditions; he is an uprooted and thwarted Russian. His inferiority to the Russians of earlier epochs is signified also by his clumsiness and plumpness. Anton Petrovich is not the only debilitated Russian exile in Berlin. The vast majority of emigrants lead a miserable life, marked by alcohol abuse, near-poverty, a sense of temporariness and anomie, an index of which is extramarital sex. In comparison with fellow Russians, Anton Petrovich is somewhat fortunate, achieving the position of a bank clerk and wearing the same "fashionable" tie and handkerchief as fellow German clerks, who hurry in the morning to their offices. He is successful on his own terms, where success equals conventionality and mediocrity — features for which Nabokov has little sympathy.

The clerk does not stop being conventional even when he thinks about his death, as suggested by the following words: "When the duel starts, I shall turn up my jacket collar — that's the custom, I think.... That's how they did it in that film I saw" (AH: 100). As a weak and conventional man, who nevertheless at one point aspires to a more dignified life, he can be compared to Franz from *King, Queen, Knave*. Anton Petrovich's wife, Tanya, despite being hardly more than a vehicle to reveal her husband's mediocrity, bears some similarity to Martha Dreyer. Like Martha, she does not recognize individuals in people, only copies or types. In Berg she sees a similarity to an Englishman. In common with Martha, she also has an affinity for kitsch, for *poshlost*, as revealed in this fragment:

> She had a gypsy kind of voice, a bewitching voice ... happiness, a summer night, a guitar ... she sang that night seated on a cushion in the middle of the floor, and slitted her smiling eyes as she sang.... He had just proposed to her ... yes, happiness, a summer night, a moth bumping against the ceiling. "My soul I surrender to you, I love you with infinite passion..." [AH: 88].

Anton Petrovich's real position as a literally and metaphorically small man is revealed by his contrast with Berg, who is broad-shouldered rather than a fat, and a former White Army soldier who fought in the cavalry under General Denikin and killed more than five hundred Reds. Berg's strength, vitality, good humor and selfishness (when caught by Anton Petrovich he says "put yourself in my place") and his ability to get what he wants, likens him to Dreyer. Another connection between "An Affair of Honor" and *King, Queen, Knave* is the motif of water. In both works water is linked to illicit pleasures and bodily functions. In episodes when water appears the protagonists are ridiculed or undermined. One of the most memorable images in "An Affair of Honor" is a glove which flips against the wall and drops into a water pitcher. In *King, Queen, Knave* Franz moves out of the room he rents, leaving behind "a little dirty water at the bottom of the wash basin and a full chamber pot in the middle of the room" (KQK: 175).[2]

As Roy Johnson notes, Anton Petrovich compounds the farce of his duel by "choosing as seconds Mityushin and Gnushke, two drunken fools who come from the Rosencrantz and Guildenstern school of malevolent funsters — one of many such grotesque duos which crop up in Nabokov's work [two similar but more sinister thugs will appear shortly in "The Leonardo"]. He then goes back home, congratulates himself on his sangfroid — 'Extraordinary, how this man retains his composure — does not even forget to wind his watch,' then vomits all over the carpet with anxiety" (Johnson 2001). These farcical elements and grotesque elements do not allow the viewer to sympathize with Anton Petrovich. "The element of absurdity has too great a role in "Podlets" for Anton Petrovich to be seen as a tragic figure" (Turkevich Naumann 1978: 131).

The setting comes across as subjective; its function is to reflect the mood of Anton Petrovich. Turkevich Naumann observes, "The urban backdrop reflects his exhaustion and mental disorientation after he learns that Tanya has been unfaithful. The poplars are shadows. The bar from which he telephones Mityushin arises before him as in a dream and then recedes into the distance like the taillight of one of Nabokov's favorite trains" (ibid.: 133). Conversely, Berlin's historical, social and architectural specificity is of little importance for the story.[3] It would be possible to replace Berlin with, for example, Paris, and Russian emigrants with Polish emigrants, and change a couple of details, without violating Nabokov's portrait of a coward who would like to live a dignified life, and Nabokov's insight into a wider condition of cultural displacement. This sketchiness allows the potential adapter to fill the background with details of his/her choice, or even to transport Nabokov's stories to different places and times, without losing the plot. This quality was recognized by Valentin Kuik, the author of the screen version of "An Affair of Honor," who explains his choice of literary source by saying "Nabokov's stories are easy to adopt to Estonian circumstances; his stories, including "An Affair of Honor," could be set anywhere. "An Affair of Honor" was concise and dense, the conflict and moral stance were universal" (Kuik, quoted in Tuumalu 2005).

The background of Kuik's "affair" with Nabokov is his directing in the mid–1990s two plays for Estonian Television Theater — a department within the Estonian public television channel which was established in Soviet times and recorded theatrical productions for archival purposes, as well as producing performances on its own that were meant for broadcasting on TV. The latter, which were a kind of hybrid between film and play, were usually shot in a more elaborate manner than the regular theatrical productions and were taped on video. Kuik's plays were well received, and both of them won local awards for outstanding achievement in 1995 and 1996. After their success, the Television Theatre asked the director if he would be interested in adapting and directing something from Russian literature or drama for them. He decided that Nabokov's "An Affair of Honor" or "Lurjus," as it was known in Estonian after the original title "Podlets," would be a good candidate for a low-budget "chamber play." He wrote a script for an hour-long production; meanwhile, the Television Theatre had been reorganized and was no longer interested in his project. A year later he applied for funding from the Estonian Film Foundation (the main body financing film production in Estonia), using the script he had written earlier for the Television Theatre. The Foundation granted him support, and he could begin the actual production. Kuik, who owned a one-man studio called Onfilm, acted both as producer and director. He bought the film rights from Dmitri Nabokov via an agency, hired a crew and went into production. The total budget was about 147,000 Euros, making it most likely the cheapest full-length film based on Nabokov's prose. The tight budget of Kuik's *An Affair of Honor*, as I will argue in due course, is not betrayed by its "production values" or casting choices, but it affected its national and international distribution. The director/producer could afford only two exhibition copies of his film. In Estonia 4000 people went to see it in the cinema, and even fewer people watched it outside its borders. Yet, one of the copies circulated for some time on the B-festival circuit and won prizes at festivals in Riga and Minsk.[4] The film is also mentioned in the program of the Lübeck Film Festival in 1999, but was not shown there.

Valentin Kuik was well placed to undertake an adaptation of Nabokov to an Estonian setting. Although he is Estonian, he was born near Novgorod in Russia, (where his grandparents had relocated from Estonia in the late nineteenth century), only to return to Estonia in 1943 shortly after his birth. He graduated from the most famous film school in the Soviet Union, Moscow's VGIK (the All-Union State Institute of Cinematography). In his subsequent career as scriptwriter and director, Kuik imbued Estonian subjects and characters with universal meaning, examples being *Lurich* (1983), a film about Estonian wrestler Georg Lurich, and *Keskea rõõmud* (*Joys of the Middle Age*, 1986), directed by Lembit Ulfsak, about two married couples and a spinster who set off on a road trip from Tallinn to find a quack in southern Estonia. Largely due to this mixture of provincialism and universalism, which can be also observed in *An Affair of Honor*, his career was somehow protracted. Although he began working in the late 1970s, which saw the emergence of the "new new wave" of Estonian cinema (the first had occurred in the 1960s), and worked for Tallinnfilm, the main Estonian film studio, he was never recognized as a "true Estonian national filmmaker."

Kuik made *An Affair of Honor* in 1999, but his film is set in a slightly earlier period—namely, the middle 1990s. This was a period when Estonia, following the collapse of the Soviet Union and its regaining independence in 1991, was still in a state of confusion and transition to the new system (as it was all over the former Soviet Union). At this time the general social conditions were mostly determined by the early capitalist anarchy, with mafia-style business-making being the prevalent "mode" of economy. The already uncertain situation was exacerbated by the stock-market collapse in Russia in 1997, which had a serious effect on the Estonian economy, since Estonian businessmen had close ties with Russian markets. Estonia of this period, being a new and troubled democracy, thus bore a close link with the Weimar Republic, where Nabokov's story is set. For this reason, adapting it to this environment seemed natural. However, in other senses, moving "An Affair of Honor" to post–Soviet

Estonia was risky. This is because the occurrence of duels gets more and more unlikely the closer we are to the present. If duels were regarded as anachronistic in 1920s Berlin, then they must be seen as even more so in Estonia at the end of the twentieth century. We can thus deduce that choosing as the protagonist of a contemporary story a man who decides to resolve his heart problems in such a drastic way is a means to illuminate the discordance between him and his environment. This is indeed the case: dueling in Kuik's film testifies to the lack of harmony in the life of Henrik, the cinematic counterpart of Anton Petrovich. Equally, the troubled relationship between Henrik and his environment, rather than his psychological make-up per se, is the proper subject of Kuik's film. Kuik does not neglect Henrik's interior, but his insights and opinions are balanced with those of other characters, especially his wife Evelin. Unlike Anton Petrovich's wife, who does not have a voice of her own and is only spoken about in derogatory terms, Evelin is as important in Kuik's *An Affair of Honor* as her husband. Frequently we see her on her own, in episodes where the director adopts her perspective and reveal her thoughts. Metaphorically speaking, the original duel between Anton Petrovich and Berg in Kuik's film changes into a painful encounter between Henrik and Evelin, with the competition between Henrik and Berg only exposing and sharpening the conflict between the spouses.

By giving voice to the female character, Kuik also attests to the difference between Berlin of the 1920s and Tallinn of the 1990s; in the latter, women do not allow themselves to be silenced to the extent their grandmothers did. He also conveys his long-term interest in men-women dynamics and social constructions of gender, as conveyed in other films he directed or scripted, such as *Reigi õpetaja* (*Reigi's Teacher*, 1977), directed by Jüri Müür, a seventeenth century story about a vicar's wife sentenced to death for adultery. An Estonian critic, Andres Maimik, perfectly captured this interest and ideological position of Kuik's:

> Kuik has always dealt with the issue of manhood, with the socially constructed concept of masculinity, with the dramatic tensions between man's biological role and the society's expectations of him. [Yet] Kuik has never before preached "men's rights" in as self-ironical register as in *An Affair of Honor*, asking whether in the social interpretation of man, with the self-awareness constrained by the whipping of the gender roles, is there any room for soft values, a sense of security and warmth, helplessness, sincerity and emotional openness. Are we allowed to see a man wearing a dotted apron at a stove, pouring milk into a dotted mug? Or is "masculinity" only an armor, restricting the individual, in which every gap is carefully sealed with the cultivation of will? [Maimik 1999].

If we situate *An Affair of Honor* among other adaptations of Nabokov, then we can see that, by giving a voice to a silent heroine, Kuik follows in

## 6. Duel in Contemporary Estonia

Taavi Eelmaa as Henrik and Elina Reinold as Evelin in *An Affair of Honor* (1999), directed by Valentin Kuik.

the footsteps of Jérôme Foulon in *Mademoiselle O*. However, he goes further than Foulon because he grants his heroine full vision, so to speak, completely independent from Henrik. The importance of Evelin is announced in the first scene of the film, containing her dream, in which she goes to a cemetery, most likely to visit Henrik's grave. Her dream is juxtaposed with that of Henrik, who in it observes from a distance two men digging a grave for him. The meaning of this scene will be revealed later when we learn about Evelin's affair and Henrik's decision to challenge her lover to a duel. It turns out that he chose as his seconds the two men he saw in his dreams, one of them being his cousin. Rather than dissuading Henrik from fighting, they put pressure on him to take vengeance on the man who made him a cuckold and, metaphorically, prepare a grave for him. The initial sequence of dreams is significant not only because it acts as a premonition of things that will happen to the characters in their real life, but also because it conveys closeness between Henrik and Evelin; they not only share a bed but the whole unconscious (the language, the value system, the past). This motif brings to mind *King, Queen, Knave*, where Martha and Franz shared a dream about a motorcycle, but they squandered the gift of their closeness. The love of Evelin and Henrik will also be tested.

In the subsequent sequence we learn that Henrik, like his predecessor in Nabokov's story, is a clerk. He works in the newly established Estonian Pensions Department (shot on location in the real Estonian Pensions Department in Tallinn). In economical and social terms, he belongs to the middle class but is closer to its lower end. His job would be in the 1990s considered an appointment suitable for middle-aged women rather than young men with high aspirations, since the monthly salary was low. Henrik's lack of status is underscored by having a female boss who looks and behaves as a typical "auntie-like," low-ranking official. Henrik drives an old Soviet car, and the couple live in Lasnamäe, a Soviet residential district consisting of high-rising blocks of flats built during the 1980s (mainly for the workforce which the Soviet administration sent to Estonia to work in the heavy industry). Their estate has a low reputation, practically being regarded as a Russian ghetto. Moreover, Lasnamäe is seen as the epitome of everything that has lost touch with its past; its inhabitants, many of them Russians (although this is not the case with Henrik and Evelin, who are Estonians), are regarded as people without proper past and traditions (Näripea 2003). In this sense they provide an excellent contemporary parallel to the Russian emigrants of Nabokov's short story. Although Henrik's social and economic position is similar to that of Anton Petrovich (or even of a lower rung on a social ladder), this position is partly obscured by Kuik's casting choice — namely, the fact that the part is played by the best known and most charismatic Estonian actor, Taavi Eelmaa (b. 1971), who played major roles in such nationally and internationally renowned Estonian films as *Sügisball* (*Autumn Ball*, 2007) and *Püha Tõnu kiusamine* (*The Temptation of St. Tony*, 2009), both by Veiko Õunpuu. *An Affair of Honor* was Eelmaa's debut in a full-length film, and Kuik could not have known that his actor would become "the face of Estonian postcommunist cinema." Nevertheless, the fact that he cast him even at this early stage of his career is meaningful, as Eelmaa, being tall, well-built and having an aura of mystery about his appearance, is entirely different from Anton Petrovich.

Although Henrik's job connotes a lack of success, he wants to be a model employee and citizen. This is demonstrated by his attempt to memorize an oath on the Estonian constitution, which is a condition for his recognition as a fully-fledged civil servant, and his polite and patient treatment of his elderly customers, who often behave as if regarding him as personally responsible for their problems. Their behavior testifies to a certain backwardness in the citizens of Estonia, due to their attachment to the way things were done in the Soviet Union or even in nineteenth century Russia. For example, the inquiry of an older woman who wants to take care of her own death and take her name from the list of pensioners, brings to mind Gogol's *Dead Souls*. Equally, such amusing episodes can be viewed as subtle references to Nabokov, who published a study on Gogol in 1944 and in his own fiction drew on this writer (Fanger 1995).

While striving to become a model civil servant, Henrik betrays a lack of self-confidence and a sense of displacement, conveyed by the clumsiness with which he interacts with other people (on the one hand, with his customers and his female boss, and on the other, with Soviet-type "fixers" and brawlers, whom he chooses as his seconds). Neither at work nor outside work has he any real friends. Henrik's sense of displacement is also revealed by the state of his apartment, which looks as if it's undergoing renovation (with walls covered with newspapers), while, in fact, nobody is decorating it. The half-doneness of the apartment speaks of Henrik's inability to get rid of the past and keep up with the changes of time, to adapt to new social and economical conditions. It also reveals that Henrik and Evelin do not have enough money to finish the renovation, simply because they have such low-income jobs.

Moreover, although a "city man," Henrik reveals an attachment to the soil, to rural life. One sign of that is his sniffing and burying his face in the soil from the pot where he grows some flowers; another is his inquiring of one of his customers why he left his home village and moved to Tallinn. We can guess that, as with the vast majority of Estonians, he is only one or two generations away from the country. Henrik's attachment to the soil is also a sign of his desire to be a true Estonian, because countryside played a crucial role in preserving Estonian identity during the Soviet rule, and rural identity was an important factor in forging Estonian national identity post–1991 (Unwin 1999). Henrik also exhibits his transitory status from the country to the city, as well as from the backward, socialist Soviet Union to westernized Estonia, by showing that he is somewhat unfamiliar with the way the "big world" operates. For example, on the plane from Hamburg to Tallinn he asks the stewardess whether she sells flowers. His sense of being in-between contemporary and past Estonia is marked by his appearance: old-fashioned glasses, black hat, long coat and leather gloves. In such clothes he looks more like a character from some nineteenth-century Russian story than a citizen of a modern country at the end of the twentieth century. This look is not natural or accidental, but is cultivated by Henrik, as a means to acquire the distinct identity of a man with noble traditions. A similar function is played by his old-fashioned razor. When Evelin buys Henrik a packet of disposable razor blades before his trip to Germany, he takes offence, telling her that the razor is like an heirloom for him, and asks her angrily why she denies him this tradition. Although Henrik resembles Anton Petrovich in the special attention he pays to his appearance, he does not come across as kitschy, only eccentric.

The motif of a souvenir (or simply any material possession) which might or might not belong to the character's real past, functioning as a surrogate for the whole lost tradition, although not present in "An Affair of Honor," features in many other works by Nabokov set among Russian emigrants, such as *Mary*, *The Gift* or *The Luzhin Defense*. A desperate search for cultural roots and locating them in forgotten or even fake, pre-communist traditions is also a typical motif of the cinema of practically all old postcommunist countries. In this sense, *An Affair of Honor* belongs to a wider paradigm of the postcommunist cinema of nostalgia. However, rather than endorsing this yearning for idealized past, Kuik mocks it. In his critical attitude to the nostalgic pursuits of culturally displaced people, he is also close to Nabokov, who in his fiction and interviews denounced fellow Russian emigrants for locating in the past what was not really there or missing the loss of traditions which were not really worth missing.

Henrik's sense of displacement is also reflected in his wider environment. The white, almost monochromatic Pensions Department, devoid of any decorations or souvenirs, looks very official and sterile. The continuous presence and discreet surveillance of Henrik by his female boss adds to the sense that the workplace is not really his place. Kuik constructs Henrik's office as a crossing between a hospital and a milder, "feminized" version of panopticon; the latter being an institution very common in the U.S.S.R. When Henrik looks from his balcony at home, high in the apartment block, he sees only contours of the Old Town, looking as if immersed in fog. No part of the city or building attracts his attention; the whole town seen from his balcony appears equally blurred and distant. Similarly, when he walks through Tallinn, the city comes across as "neutered," without any landmarks or objects. Kuik foregrounds places signifying the transitory and mediated character of the lives of contemporary Estonians, such as a petrol station, a bus stop, a telephone box and wide, empty streets. The fact that most of the outdoor scenes are set at night adds to the indistinctiveness and neutrality of Tallinn. In the exterior scenes Kuik uses very little color and there is a prevalence of blue, which gives the impression of Tallinn as a cold city. As I argued elsewhere, representation of European cities as neutered, indistinct spaces is a typical feature of modern and postmodern cinema (Mazierska and Rascaroli 2003), but Kuik goes even further in the art of "neutering" the postmodern city than most directors.

Kuik's decision not to use his film as an opportunity to show more of Tallinn's stunning Old Town, instead leaving it either immersed in fog or in darkness, mirrors the way Nabokov represents Berlin in this story, as well as in his other works (for example, *King, Queen, Knave*). It can also be seen in the context of the previous Soviet cinematic tradition, when Tallinn's Old

Town was used as a (fake) historical decoration for innumerable Soviet productions and as a general historical referent of the West. At the time, every summer several film crews from all over the Soviet Union shot episodes for different movies there. The Old Town was used so many times as a film location that it became a cliché (Näripea 2004; 2009). In *An Affair of Honor*, during Henrik's walk through the city we also see the shooting of a film, which is an indication of this lineage. Kuik reveals his distance to or even contempt of this practice by suggesting that the movie is made by people who do not care what they are shooting, as its narrative does not have any connection with the Old Town. Most likely the film is made simply to make use of the location. Additionally, the Old Town was a money-making tourism device for the Soviet authorities, and it continued to be the main Estonian tourist attraction in the postcommunist years. Kuik thus sees the Old Town as something once noble, pointing to the pre–Soviet and pre-communist era and culture, which by now has been violated and corrupted by these Soviet and post–Soviet cultural and economic processes. The juxtaposition of the Old Town and the new residential district seems to connote a rupture — in tradition, culture, and environment — brought about by the Soviet occupation, which was not being undone in postcommunist times. Again, such representation echoes the theme of the rupture in culture and individual existence present in Nabokov's "German" short stories.

While the city comes across in the film as blurred, colorless and neutered, nature appears to be full of color and life, with water rushing in streams and birds singing. However, nature, to an even larger extent than the city, is represented by Kuik as subjective. We never get its unmediated image, but always see it through Henrik's eyes, and his perceptions are shaped by his naïve belief that life in the countryside is nobler and purer than in the city. Hence, the vision of nature in *An Affair of Honor*, being a simulacra of some mythical peasants' past, turns out to be more artificial than Tallinn observed from Henrik's balcony.

However, Henrik's story in Kuik's film is only half of the story. The second half belongs to Evelin. We learn that in common with Henrik, Evelin's economic status is low. From the brief scene at the beginning of the film we learn that she works for the National Library, which is not a job highly valued by the early post–Soviet standards. She works in the department of music, spending most of her time lending classical music on tapes and CDs. Classical music, also used extensively in the film's score, both diegetically and nondiegetically, indicates the characters' yearning for a better, more sublime sphere of life, which is difficult to reach in the new economic and social climate.

Kuik constructs Evelin as a loving wife who, nevertheless, becomes frustrated by her husband's behavior. Firstly, she is disappointed with his devotion to work. We see this in an episode when, after observing with pleasure a young couple listening to some music in the library where she works, she returns home and phones Henrik, expecting him to come home too, most likely to make love. When he refuses, she angrily removes the lipstick from her lips, as if she was punishing herself for beautifying her body for her husband and indicating a refusal of any future sexual services to him. Another scene which draws attention to Evelin's marital frustration takes place in a pub, where Henrik boasts to her about the approaching trip to Germany offered to him by his boss. She shares his joy but half-jokingly says that he should have agreed to go on the trip only on the condition of taking her with him. Henrik, however, ignores her words and carries on boasting about his success. Scenes such as these, which are missing from Nabokov's short story, shed light on the promiscuity of the female character, shifting blame for the crisis between the couple to the husband.

Henrik's failure to attend to his wife's erotic, psychological and material needs reaches a crisis point when the couple meet Berg, who in Kuik's film is Henrik's old school pal, in a pub. Unlike Henrik, Berg knows perfectly well how to impress women. He demands that a teenage boy remove the cap from his head out of respect for Evelin, teaches her how to play billiards, which is an excellent opportunity to touch each other's hands, and presents her with a lighter when she takes a cigarette from her bag. At the same time, Berg succeeds in humiliating Henrik, beating him at billiards and using this victory to reminisce on their school days past, when Berg was also the victor and Henrik the loser. Berg's success at billiards is a contemporary equivalent of Berg's victories in the war with the Bolsheviks in Nabokov's original. His old-fashioned gallantry, on the other hand, parallels the excellent sense of humor with which Nabokov's Berg impressed Anton Petrovich's wife. Not only in his relations with women but in any circumstances, Berg feels at home, despite him being, ultimately, only a small-time crook, a *cad* without any real achievements, professional or otherwise. Andrus Puustusmaa, who plays Berg, is shorter and less athletic than Taavi Eelmaa, thus underscoring his reality as somebody of fake, rather than real strength. In this context it should be mentioned that, although the original title of the film, *Lurjus*, which in Estonian means "cad" or "scoundrel," can be explained by it being the translation from the Russian version, it also better reflects the spirit of the film, which concerns a cad, who tricks a good couple, rather than a man who disgraces himself by deserting his place in a duel.

During her husband's trip to Germany, Evelin has an affair with Berg.

Elina Reinold as Evelin in *An Affair of Honor* (1999), directed by Valentin Kuik.

Henrik discovers it upon returning earlier than expected from the trip. He reacts by throwing his glove at Berg and demanding from Evelin that she moves out of their apartment, to which she complies, going to her sister's. Afterwards, Henrik prepares for the duel. He approaches his two mates, asking them to act as his seconds, visits the wood where he is supposed to shoot at Berg, attempts to buy a pistol, talks with Berg by phone, who humiliates him again, has his blood tested, writes a farewell letter to his office and attempts to take his own life by cutting his veins with his old-fashioned razor. It is difficult to say whether Henrik's suicide attempt is caused by his broken heart or his fear of facing a buoyant opponent. Lying in a bath with his wrists bleeding, Henrik cuts a pathetic figure, being a "cousin" of such characters as Miloš Hrma from *Ostře sledované vlaky* (*Closely Observed Trains*, 1966), directed by Jiři Menzel. Needless to say, his suicide attempt is unsuccessful. Thus, his razor betrays him twice—by failing to provide the link with the past and causing a rift with Evelin, and by failing to assure his dignified death.

In-between his preparations for the duel, Henrik imagines this event. On the first occasion, instead of shooting at Berg, he shoots himself in the head. Subsequently, Henrik imagines killing Evelin, who in her attempt to save Berg covers her lover with her own body, leaving Henrik devastated. The fact that, paradoxically, Berg is missing from these duels points to the importance of Evelin in Henrik's "affair of honor." His duel, unlike that depicted by Nabokov, is more about Evelin and him than the man with whom she had an affair. Such a representation also conforms to the way we think today about extra-marital affairs—namely, as problems between the married couples not between the lover and the cuckolded husband.

The style of these imaginary duels evokes descriptions of duels in the famous Russian works of the nineteenth century, especially *The Shot* by Alexander Pushkin. Evelin, in a long white dress and large hat, looks like a typical lady from the previous century. Berg, in his disrespect for his own life and complete lack of fear of his opponent, reminds us of the Count, who was eating cherries when Silvio was about to shoot at him for the first time. Evelin covering Berg with her own body so he cannot be killed can be seen as a variation of a scene in which the Countess begs Silvio to spare her husband (Pushkin 1994). As I mentioned, references to the classical Russian literary duels, including *The Shot*, were already present in Nabokov's story. Hence, in preserving and enhancing them we can see Kuik simply acting as an adapter trying to recreate the literary "original" onscreen. The fact that Henrik imagines his duel the way Pushkin and Lermontov described "affairs of honor" might also be regarded as a sign of the depth to which

Taavi Eelmaa in *An Affair of Honor.*

Russian culture permeates the minds of Estonians.[5] The link between dueling and Russian culture is also made visible by the character of one of the seconds, who puts the greatest pressure on Henrik to stick to his original plan of challenging Berg. He does it by making a connection between duels and good old times when "men were men," and to his own cultural heritage as the descendent of a Russian prince. Yet, this man, whose appearance and behavior is that of an ordinary brawler (immortalized in numerous Soviet films of the 1970s and 1980s, as well as epitomizing the mafia-style businessmen of the post–Soviet era), illuminates the absurdity of continuing this tradition.

Henrik, like his literary predecessor created by Nabokov, fails to take part in the "affair of honor," although it is not clear how he avoided his duel. Unlike Nabokov, who paid close attention to Anton Petrovich's desertion from the place of shooting (and in this way illuminating his character's weakness and lack of dignity), Kuik leaves the circumstances of Henrik's escape blurred, sparing us any details of his protagonist's cowardice. After his journey in a car driven by one of his seconds to the site of the duel and the series of imaginary duels, Henrik finds himself on the streets of Tallinn, drunken and confused. His walking through nocturnal Tallinn not only comes across as a more dignified reaction to his failing to defend his honor than Anton Petrovich's stuffing himself with food in a hotel, but suggests that life (understood as moral, as opposed to only biological activity) did not end for him with the aborted duel because it was only one of his many attempts to create himself. We expect that he will keep wandering and looking for new directions.

The fluidity of Henrik's identity, his potential to be a new person, is excellently suggested in the previous scene of a film crew shooting a movie. The film's director "fishes" Henrik out from a small group of onlookers and asks him to play an extra: a beggar with a hat. Henrik does not wait for the end of the shot, but leaves and goes home. This decision suggests that he is not so much a coward as a man of unfinished identity: a metaphorical tourist who enters various "scenes" to test himself, to check who he can play. For the English-speaking viewer the scene has added poignancy from using the same word — "shooting" — for both dueling and making a film. By making a connection between the two types of shooting, Kuik foregrounds the unreality of Henrik's duel.

The motif of shooting a film can also be viewed as a nod to Nabokov, who tends to furnish his novels and short stories with cinematic references. Yet we do not find them in "An Affair of Honor." Hence, paradoxically, while the majority of Nabokov's adapters purge their films of the cinematic elements present in their "originals," the one adapter who did not need to include them for the sake of fidelity to the literary original decided to use them. Kuik uses the cinematic reference in a similar way to the writer — as a symbol of a different, parallel reality that the characters risk to enter.

After his nocturnal peregrination, Henrik returns home and learns from his seconds that his honor was saved because Berg did not attend the duel either. However, unlike in the case of Anton Petrovich, who only imagines that his affair finished honorably for him, we get the impression that the humble Estonian clerk was truly lucky. In the last scene Henrik meets Evelin, who also returns to their apartment and puts her hand on his arm. It is impossible to say whether this tender gesture takes place in reality or is only imagined by Henrik, but a realistic reading is plausible. Kuik's film thus ends on a more optimistic note than Nabokov's short story, and its optimism results mostly from the couple beginning to overcome their marital problems.

*An Affair of Honor* can be interpreted not only as a story of a marital triangle and its resolution, but also as a metaphor for the conflict between different cultural strands and traditions for the privilege of creating the new face of Estonia. Seen from this perspective, Henrik comes across as the epitome of postcommunist Estonia searching for its new identity. He is uncertain whether it should stick to the old traditions or embrace the new ones; choose an urban or rural path; culture or nature; Russian ways or Western lifestyles. His uncertainty about the course of action, his opaqueness, finds its visual parallel in his apartment awaiting decoration and the blurred contours of Tallinn, which he sees from his balcony. Like the apartment, the city and Henrik himself, all need finishing. Henrik's problem, as Estonia's, appears to be that everything he touches turns out to be superficial or fake, like the film which is shot on the streets of Tallinn, whose director is not certain what he wants to shoot and tries to pack into his movie everything he encounters on the way, including beggars and prostitutes, and covers the set with smoke for better effect. The surrealistic style employed by the director throughout the film points to the sense of unreality of contemporary Estonia due to its troubled history. There is no obvious answer for Henrik's and Estonia's lack of identity, or perhaps the only answer is that they have to keep looking, trying various scenarios and putting on different masks.

However, the choice between the rural and the metropolitan, the old and the new, Western and Eastern, which perplexes Henrik, is experienced to a much lesser extent by female characters. Contrary to the tradition of equating the female element with nature and the country, and male with culture and the city, in *An Affair of Honor* men signify attachment to the country, while women, such as Evelin, Henrik's boss and Evelin's sister, as well as women only talked about in the film, belong firmly to the metropolitan world. Yet, paradoxically, in rejecting "nature," Kuik's women come across as more natural than men because they show that they do not need any extraneous elements to complete or enrich their identity: they accept themselves the way they are. By contrast, men's obsessive insisting on the need to obey traditions, blackmailing each other into sticking to the old rules and even faking one's own link with the noble past (like that of Henrik's second, who pretends that his ancestor was a Russian prince) suggests that they are uncomfortable and insecure in their own world.

In summary, Kuik's *An Affair of Honor*, more than any other film based on Nabokov's work, reveals, utilizes and updates the "Russian baggage" of his prose by preserving the links with classical Russian texts and focusing on characters who, even if they are not Russian, bring to mind characters depicted in the classical texts of Pushkin, Gogol, Lermontov and Chekhov, and appear to live in the shadow of Russian culture. Equally, *An Affair of Honor* demonstrates the transnational and transcultural potential of Nabokov's works due to dealing with uprooted characters and problems resulting from geographical and cultural dislocation. For readers familiar with Nabokov's anti-communism, it might seem paradoxical that his work is used to show Estonia's identity problems resulting from abandoning communism. However, in his writings

Nabokov never tackled communism as a located, historical phenomenon, but as a universal predicament. And more than regretting that the Bolsheviks seized power in Russia, which forced him and his family to leave his country and become displaced, he complained about the sudden, cataclysmic nature of this political and social change. Due to their suddenness, the transformations which swept ex-socialist Europe in the early 1990s are not that different to those which occurred in Russia in 1917. Both changes also caused similar reactions in people: on the one hand conformity and the need to be perceived as modern, resulting from the anxiety of being left behind, and on the other hand a search for traditions, modes of behavior, and symbols that could act as metaphorical "homes" for the newly displaced people. The overall conclusion of both Nabokov's and Kuik's work is that home and culture is never given; it has to be created from elements encountered by rambling through familiar and unfamiliar landscapes.

Unfortunately, however, as I indicated, Kuik's achievement in taking Nabokov's book on an interesting journey through space and time remained practically unknown beyond the borders of Estonia, and even in his native country did not receive the recognition it deserved. Perhaps Kuik's failure to enthuse Estonian audiences was its pointing to Estonia's cultural hybridity, which includes numerous Russian influences and was unwelcome at the time the young country was trying to unite around a nationalistic project.

# 7

# Nabokov as a Gentle Feminist

## The Luzhin Defence
## *by Marleen Gorris (2000)*

"The only way out," he said. "I have to drop out of the game."
— Vladimir Nabokov, *The Luzhin Defense*

The protagonist of *The Luzhin Defense*, the English version of *Zashchita Luzhina* (1930), Aleksandr Luzhin, is a chess master, in line with the principle that chess, chess problems, and chess players feature extensively in Nabokov's books.[1] Many authors also point to an analogy between Luzhin's life and chess (for example, Alexandrov 1995; de la Durantaye 2007: 166–67). Luzhin is known especially for inventing an excellent defense, which was named after him. In life, as in chess, he assumes a defensive position, reacting rather than acting. The persistence of chess motifs encouraged some critics to regard chess as Nabokov's favorite metaphor of art. This is because both playing chess and creating art demand economy and precision, which are qualities the writer valued highly. Nabokov also saw a conflict between life and chess, as between life and art (Gezari 1995; Alexandrov 1995). Yet, there is a limit to the chess-art analogy, and *The Luzhin Defense* illustrates this limit. The world of chess is self-contained and sterile, while art should be anchored in human reality. This idea is conveyed by Vladislav Khodasevich, who writes in the context of Nabokov's novel:

> The artist is doomed to sojourn in two worlds: in the real world and in the world of art he himself has created. The true master is always to be found at that line belonging to both worlds, where their planes intersect. Alienation from reality, absolute immersion in the world of art, where there is no flight, but only endless falling, is madness. It threatens the honest dilettante, but does not threaten the master, possessed of the gift of finding and never again losing the line of intersection. Genius is measure, harmony, perpetual balance [Khodasevich 1997].

In a similar vein, Leona Toker observes:

> Chess is a game that explores the infinitive potentialities of its own medium, whereas a truly great work of art explores its medium in order to reveal insufficiencies in the existing patterns of thought about the world. *The Defense* is an example of such a work of art. Its chess patterns stand for all the patterns and systems that prove tragically inadequate when preferred to or violently superimposed on the natural flow of life [Toker 1989: 67].

Toker warns against seeing too much similarity between chess and the life of Nabokov's protagonist, or chess and the structure of Nabokov's novel, claiming:

> The most salient of these analogies is the paradoxical symmetry (a chess phenomenon) of the plot and the structure of the novel: the protagonist's life only seems to submit to the rules of a chess game, and the novel itself only seems to be structured as a chess problem. Both the reality of Luzhin's predicament and the shape of the novel present too great a complexity to be described in terms of chess [ibid.: 68].

Thomas Karshan adopts a similar argument, drawing a parallel between *The Luzhin Defense* and Pushkin's *The Queen of Spades*, claiming that both works offer a similar lesson: "one cannot eliminate chance, or play, or spontaneous freedom, from the game of life, and the attempt to do so leads to madness and suicide" (Karshan 2009: 247). Accordingly, when studying Luzhin's life and persona, we should pay at least as much attention to their unique features as to the patterns they reveal. Moreover, these patterns might require a different explanation than the rules of chess.

Luzhin is treated with great sympathy by his creator, who in the Foreword to the novel admits, "He is uncouth, unwashed, uncomely — but as my gentle young lady (a dear girl in her own right) so quickly notices, there is something in him that transcends both the coarseness of his grey flesh and the sterility of his recondite genius" (Def: 10). We can sympathize with Luzhin either because of the hereditary or environmental factors of his life, or their combination. His nature is marked by an unwillingness to enter into relationships with the external world, and instead an urge to withdraw into his own world, epitomized by chess. Although such a detached and one-dimensional genius transcends time and cultures, and is almost a cliché, Toker observes that "his image is similar to that of the mad Jewish boy in Nabokov's "Signs and Symbols" (1948): even though the boy's family has escaped Germany to America, his acute paranoia, his sense of systematic hostility of the world, is a morbidly condensed literalization of the Jewish experience in Europe at the time of the Holocaust" (Toker 1989: 69).

As if confirming such a reading, Nabokov shows that Luzhin's environment reduced his chance of happiness, fulfilllment, even achieving maturity.

His parents did not understand him, he was bullied at school, and, eventually, he was exploited by Valentinov, his chess manager who did not see in him a human being, only a machine for winning chess tournaments. Luzhin's childhood and youth (not unlike a comparable period in Nabokov's life) was thus marked by loss. First Luzhin lost his "aunt," his father's lover, the only person who appeared to understand him and whom he loved more than his mother. It happened when Luzhin's mother forced her husband to finish his affair with her. In due course the chess master also lost his parents, and then his manager, who abandoned him when he seemed to lose his talent. Luzhin also lost his country as a consequence of the war and the Bolshevik revolution. Although, as Toker observes, Luzhin is "minimally affected by the irreversible changes in his fatherland" (ibid.: 69), it might be because he prepared himself for these losses by developing a defense mechanism: not seeing his surroundings and being addicted to chess. All the lost relationships with humans were never replaced by things of the same kind or value; the void each loss created was filled by chess. As a result of these multiple losses the sphere of the "real," in Luzhin's life diminished to the point where "real" for him became "unreal" and vice versa. As an adult person he takes the ghostly world of chess for the ultimate reality, while the (ordinary) reality becomes for him merely a distraction from chess or a reflection of the movements of chess figures, which take place in a parallel world.

Ontological confusion likens Luzhin to a madman, as well as to a child, as children tend to regard fairy tales and fantastical phenomena as reality. Not surprisingly, the adult Luzhin comes across as a child in a man's body. When Luzhin is thirty, his body, debilitated by excessive smoking and lack of physical exercise, appears to be much older, but his behavior comes across as childish. He pays no attention to manners and is ignorant about many adult pursuits, such as sex. The emptiness of Luzhin's existence is signified by the absence of his first name and patronymic in the novel. Michael Long notes:

> He is asked to become a man, assuming the dread patronymic, before he has ever filled out his personal name in childhood. The assumption of the patronymic is a symbolic closing of the door upon an Arcadia that he was promised. The personal name that never came to life in that vacant world is not revealed until the book's last sentences. But then the man is dead. "There was no Aleksandr Ivanovich" [Long 1984: 30].

However, although Luzhin belongs to the most distinctive characters in Nabokov's prose, there is no agreement among the critics whether the vivid characterization of the protagonist is accompanied by an equally careful development of the plot. John Updike finds the second part of the novel full of unnecessary detail (Updike 2000: 264) and Luzhin's death unconvincing: "I cannot see why, now that Luzhin is equipped with a willing if not enthusiastic female caretaker and furthermore a wealthy father-in-law, the grandmaster is hopelessly blocked from pursuing, this side of madness, his vocation" (Updike 1982: 158). Stuart Hampshire does not criticize the lack of consistency of the second part of the novel with its first part, but maintains that "the story is too monotonously black; taken as a whole, the novel may seem rather an exercise in proving a point" (Hampshire 1982: 160).

For Leona Toker, Luzhin's final total alienation and death is the logical conclusion of the shortcomings of both main characters — Luzhin and the nameless woman with whom he falls in love. In particular, her emotional development, as is his, "is incomplete:"

> The "mysterious ability of her soul to apprehend in life only that which had once attracted and tormented her in childhood, the time when the soul's instinct is infallible, tender pity for the creature whose life is helpless and unhappy" (Def: 105), is presented as both the most "captivating" thing about her and (as the word "only" suggests) a limitation. It is partly due to this limitation that the relationship which seems to possess the attributes of a protective castling turns out to be the second diversion of the double-rook sacrifice.... Mrs. Luzhin is guided by pity rather than by understanding; therefore, after her husband breaks down, she takes the advice of a psychiatrist to keep him away from chess.... Her defense against chess is as unnecessary and ineffectual as Luzhin's defense against life; instead of placing the game in proper perspective, she turns it into a lurking, destructive monster [ibid.: 75–6].

In Toker's interpretation, with which I agree, Luzhin's wife has good intentions but is somehow not up to the job of being the wife of a chess master. From this perspective, I regard *The Luzhin Defense* as similar to *King, Queen, Knave*, which preceded *The Luzhin Defence* by only two years. Both works, although different in emotional tone, concern absurdity — namely, discord resulting from a lack of understanding between people, despite living together and even, in this case, loving each other.

The role of Luzhin's wife, despite Nabokov describing her as a "dear girl in her own right," is a supporting one. She supports her husband and serves the writer to reveal the intricacies of Luzhin's character. At the same time, in her support of a man, she reveals a rejection of a social convention, a spirit of rebellion. Take this passage:

> She made his acquaintance on the third day after his arrival, made in the way they do in old movies or in motion pictures: she drops a handkerchief and he picks it up — with the sole difference that they interchanged roles. Luzhin was walking along a path in front of her and in succession shed: a large checked handkerchief that was unusually dirty and had all sorts of pocket debris sticking to it; then a broken and crushed cigarette minus half of its contents; a nut, and a French franc. She gathered up only the handkerchief and the coin and walked on, slowly catching up with him and curiously awaiting some new loss [Nabokov 2000: 86].

A scene like this brings joy to feminist readers who "glean" from classical literature moments when gender roles are challenged, either on social or individual level. A large proportion of film adaptations of classical literature of the last twenty years or so, including the widely discussed films based on the novels of Jane Austen, can be perceived as such attempts to find the moments of women's resistance to the roles prescribed to them by patriarchy (Vidal 2005). Marleen Gorris, the only female filmmaker who ever adapted Nabokov's work to the screen, belongs to this paradigm, and is even one of its main creators. Practically in all her films she focuses on the lives of strong women who oppose convention, be it a Dutch matron, a Russian Jewish woman who, during the Stalinist reign, was sent to a Siberian Gulag; or the first female doctor, who has to masquerade as a man in order to work in her chosen profession. It appears that her ultimate ambition is to create a history of female struggle against patriarchal oppression. In this stance we locate one reason why Gorris adapted *The Luzhin Defense*.

Another feature of Gorris" artistic biography that provides a clue to why she might have been attracted to Nabokov's novel is the fact that, in common with Jerzy Skolimowski and Tony Richardson, whose cases I discussed in earlier chapters, she is a model transnational director. Although she is Dutch, she made films in many different countries, including Germany, the U.S.A., the U.K., Poland and her native Holland. Perhaps the nomadic life is a consequence of her need to make films anywhere she finds funding; or, conversely, her desire to present people from different national and cultural backgrounds forces her to be a transnational director. Yet, as with many directors discussed in this book, she did not really choose Nabokov's novel. She was first offered the script by Peter Berry, a scriptwriter working mostly in television. She liked the screenplay more than the book, which she read only subsequently (Gorris, quoted in Blackwelder 2001).

Stylistically, Gorris' films, in common with the works of many women directors of her and younger generations, especially those who adapt literature (such as Jane Campion and Patricia Rozema), attempt to reconcile the demands of feminist and mainstream cinema. For this reason, unlike the works of her predecessors, such as Sue Clayton or early productions of Sally Potter (whose ambition was to produce feminist countercinema using Brechtian techniques of distancing the viewer), Gorris' films belong to women's cinema understood as minor cinema (on women's cinema as minor cinema see Butler 2002: 19–23). The sign of that is their use of the conventions of romance/adventure or heritage cinema. They lure the viewer with their picturesque setting and exquisite costumes, which both illustrate the period in which their films are set and play an important ideological function, typically epitomizing the "beautiful entrapment" of the female protagonists or their refuge from the oppressive male world. Significantly, Gorris' female protagonists demonstrate their independence not by breaking with the male world entirely, but by choosing a "different," unconventional man. Such construction of the narrative partly reflects the cultures in which the bulk of her films are set (where total independence is not a viable option for women) and partly a "new breed" of feminism to which she subscribes, which is sympathetic to close female-male relationships (even if in them women play supportive roles). Gorris' approach to feminine issues was first revealed in her Oscar-winning *Antonia* (*Antonia's Line*, 1995). In this film, Antonia is a matriarch, the epitome of nurturing and natural woman; but in the opinion of the majority of critics this does not make her subordinated or controlled by the forces of patriarchy (Bovkis 1997; Bainbridge 2008: 114–18). Caroline Bainbridge discusses Gorris' work in the context of the works of Luce Irigaray, who, inspired by Freud and Lacan, emphasizes the different roles played by women and men in society.

Another good illustration of Gorris' style and ideology is her widely praised adaptation of Virginia Woolf's *Mrs. Dalloway* (1997), which was her last film before embarking on Nabokov's novel. In this British-American production, an aging upper-class English woman, Clarissa Dalloway, during the day when she is about to give a lavish party, reminisces about her youth and reassesses her life. In reality, the only choice she had was a choice concerning her romantic life. She could either marry Peter Walsh, an adventurous, unconventional, but at the same time potentially less successful man who was madly in love with her, but with whom her future would be less certain, or tie the knot with Richard Dalloway, a stuffy, less dashing fellow, but one who promised her stability and prosperity. Clarissa opted for Dalloway, who subsequently became a Tory MP and a rich man. Although she is not free of a mild nostalgia or melancholy, and still has tender feelings towards Peter, she does not regret her choice because she loves her husband and her affluent and peaceful life. By contrast, Peter feels unfulfilled. His unhappiness, however, might be viewed as proof that Clarissa made the right choice, because with the man whom she truly loved she might have ended up as miserable as he. Along with Clarissa's narrative, Gorris presents the story of a man named Septimus Warren Smith, a veteran of the First World War who suffers a mental breakdown and commits suicide. This tragic event happens despite Septimus having by his side a loving wife who devotes her whole life to saving him from his inner demons.

*Mrs. Dalloway* is a seductive but somewhat unfaithful rendition of the eponymous character from the novel. Woolf's Clarissa chooses Mr. Dalloway over Peter not because she is, ultimately, more conventional and reconciled with patriarchy than she appears to be in her youth, but because she recognizes that if she gave in to the romantic passion offered to her by Peter, her ego would disappear, she would be swallowed up by the stronger character or even be destroyed by him (Waugh 1989: 116). Paradoxically, living with the more traditional Mr. Dalloway, merely as Mrs. Dalloway, she has more independence than if she married Peter, as expressed in this passage:

> For in marriage, a little license, a little independence there must be between people living together day in and day out in the same house, which Richard gave her, and she him. (Where was he this morning, for instance? Some committee, she never asked what.) But with Peter everything had to be shared; everything gone into ... she had to break with him or they would have been destroyed, both of them ruined, she was convinced (Woolf 1996: 5-6).

Paradoxically, from Woolf's book we can deduce that a certain type of patriarchal order is conducive to women's spiritual independence. Of course, such independence can only be achieved by upper class women.

The beautiful exteriors and interiors, full of flowers and tasteful ornaments, as well as a condemnation of the war which Britain did not start, makes Gorris' *Mrs. Dalloway* a paean to the gentle life of the English upper classes. This was, naturally, one reason why her film was favorably received in Britain and might even have been a condition of the director's obtaining British and American funding for this and her next project. *The Luzhin Defence*, like *Mrs. Dalloway*, is also a British-American production and is set at the end of the 1920s, a period of relative political calm and prosperity in Europe before the economic crisis and rise of fascism came to dominate its social and political life. It also intermingles the present with the past of the main character, on this occasion showing Luzhin as a boy in St. Petersburg. In common with *Mrs. Dalloway*, it deals with the issue of the woman's emancipation and asserting her identity through making a specific marital choice. This, of course, means that like in the literary original, where "Luzhin's girl" is a supporting character, Gorris grants her female protagonist autonomy and an equal role to that of her husband within the narrative. Taking this into account, it is not surprising that Gorris furnished her heroine with a name, Natalia Kharkov, as well as revealing at the beginning Luzhin's Christian name, Aleksandr. An additional, prosaic reason for doing so was to ensure that the dialogues sounded natural. However, having names also points to them having distinctive identities, which Nabokov questions in his book, rendering both somewhat unfinished.

Natalia's importance within the narrative is announced at the very beginning of the film, when we see her waiting for the train that will bring to Italy both her mother and her future husband. The camera juxtaposes the image of her careless wandering on the platform with Luzhin obsessively writing

**Emily Watson as Natalia in *The Luzhin Defence* (2000), directed by Marleen Gorris.**

down the chess moves in his notebook. In this scene Natalia comes across as both an active agent and an observer, unlike her future husband, who is represented as confined and "myopic." Moreover, she is represented as a full person, from head to toe, again unlike Luzhin, whose body is fragmented in the close-ups of his face and hands, suggesting that his entire life is concentrated in these two parts of his body. Luzhin, Natalia and her mother, without noticing each other's presence, proceed via a boat to a lavish hotel on an Italian lake (lake Como in reality). In this scene the presence of Natalia overshadows that of Luzhin, who sits in a corner of the boat curled, trembling and silent, like a lost child. Throughout the whole film Gorris sustains the difference between Natalia, who is always active and fully aware of her circumstances, and Luzhin, who is always lost when left to his own devices. Furnishing Luzhin with a cane, which Nabokov's Luzhin also carried, and a slight limp, which is the director's own addition, strengthens the sense of the chess master's struggle with physical space. Luzhin's limp likens him to other men in films with impaired legs — for example, James Stewart's character in Hitchcock's *Rear Window* (1954). On each occasion this physical defect requires a "phallic support" of a cane or crutch, and a metaphorical support of a strong and devoted woman, as in Luzhin's case. Luzhin comes across as active only in his memories, when he is rambling through St. Petersburg or running through his parents' large house, usually to avoid his mother and father, school and everything else that stands between him and chess.

From the questions the mother asks her daughter on her arrival we can deduce that Natalia's stay in Italy is meant to help her find a husband; this is at least what her mother hopes for. In due course, Natalia, in common with Clarissa from *Mrs. Dalloway*, is given two suitors — one more, other less conventional. The former is a handsome French aristocrat named Jean de Stassard, who immediately gains her mother's heart. The second is, of course, Luzhin. Natalia rejects Jean, partly because Luzhin proposes to her first (while the French aristocrat, if he would do it at all, will take more time, in line with convention as well as common sense). Natalia also rejects this man because she suspects that behind his polite veneer there is not enough substance, in contrast with the depth and mystery covered by the coarseness of Luzhin's manners. Another reason why she finds Luzhin attractive is that, as she herself puts it, he allows her to "breathe," be herself, as opposed to putting demands on her and molding her into a specific model. In her motivation she is thus similar to Clarissa, but such motivation leads her to make the opposite choice from her predecessor, who decided to give up on the adventurous Peter and marry the conventional Mr. Dalloway. However, it is not clear whether Natalia is right about Jean. This man, although obviously furnished with good manners and without any specific talents, as he himself admits, comes across as intelligent, sensitive and treats social conventions with some distance. Most likely he would allow Natalia to "breathe." For this very reason, however, de Stassard, paradoxically, accepts the fact that he is not her favorite choice, makes space for Luzhin and contents himself with the role of family friend and discreet observer of Natalia and Aleksandr's romance. The presence of de Stassard, even at a distance, increases Natalia's attractiveness and dignity.

Natalia and Aleksandr's romance blossoms against the backdrop of the chess tournament, held in the same lavish hotel on the Italian lake, where all the main characters stay. Its grounds include gardens and beautiful paths surrounded by weeping trees, where Natalia would play Alice to Luzhin's forgetful "Rabbit," as did her literary predecessor. Setting the film in such an exquisite environment is both in the tradition of "heritage cinema," to which Gorris' previous film belongs, and in the tradition of adapting Nabokov, where the physical environment in which his characters move gains in size and grandeur on the road from book to screen. To add splendor and drama, the tournament is upgraded from one of many chess events popular in Europe during the interwar years to the world chess championship. While the places in which the characters dwell gained in size, they themselves literally lost weight on the way from the novel to the film. Especially Luzhin, who in Nabokov's version is stout and gets fatter and fatter as the story develops; in the film is of slim build, which helps to awaken sympathy for him.

**John Turturro as Aleksandr Luzhin in *The Luzhin Defence* (2000).**

The events, included in the "Berlin" chapter of Luzhin's life, where he marries, has a mental breakdown and dies are either moved to the Italian setting or left out altogether. Such a change allows the director to take maximum advantage of the romantic surroundings and add (external) drama to the story by compressing the action. Gorris' version can thus be seen as an attempt to address the criticisms voiced by Updike and other authors, who found the book unnecessarily dragging and "monotonously black." An additional consequence of Gorris' decision to cut the Berlin chapter was a purging of the cinematic element present in Nabokov's novel, where Valentinov ends up working in the (metaphorically and literally shadowy) film business.

During the staging of the tournament, Luzhin and Natalia fall in love and prepare for their wedding. Also in the Italian hotel Luzhin meets Valentinov, who, during the championship, attempts to retake control of the life of his ex-pupil, discarded some years previously when Luzhin started to lose tournaments. To vindicate his own loss of faith in Luzhin and complete the destruction of this fragile man, Valentinov now wants to prevent his former pupil from winning the tournament. First he approaches Luzhin's main contestant, Turati, to give him advice on how, using psychological tricks, he can overpower his competitor. When it turns out that Turati is not willing to follow his helpful hints, Valentinov arranges Luzhin's abduction by car. Luzhin is left in a wood, completely disorientated, and, ironically, is rescued by a group of Italian fascists. Following this incident he suffers a mental breakdown and is asked by his fiancée to give up chess until his health improves. However, Valentinov abducts him again on the way to the church where he is to be married, to force him to finish the game. Unwilling to subordinate to Valentinov's force, and at the same time unable to resist his strong master (or simply tormented and disorientated), Luzhin commits suicide by jumping from the hotel window.

As this synopsis demonstrates, the role of Valentinov increased in comparison with his part in the novel. Thanks to this change, the director removed any suspicion that Luzhin's wife makes a mistake in dealing with her husband, resulting from a flaw in her character. Gorris' Natalia does all she could to rescue Luzhin, and if not for the circumstances — namely, Valentinov's relentless pursuit of his ex-pupil and his decision to destroy him — Luzhin most likely would have been saved and lived happily ever after, balancing chess with marital bliss, as Updike wished him to. In Gorris' version it is Natalia's well-meaning but misguided mother, rather than an objective narrator, who claims that her daughter fell for Luzhin because she pitied him (in the same way in her childhood she took pity on stray cats or lame ducks). Natalia, however, reacts to her mother's outburst with an ironic smile, showing her mother and the viewer that she knows this argument, does not agree with it and is exasperated by listening to it over and over again. By passing the opinion of the narrator of the novel to the character who is ridiculed during the course of the action, Gorris forces us to trust Natalia's judgment rather than Nabokov's.

By the same token, unlike Nabokov, who demonstrates that Luzhin and his wife cannot communicate on any deeper level, Gorris shows that the couple understand each other well. This is largely because Natalia in the film, in contrast to Nabokov's heroine, is not an enemy of chess. Shortly after their first meeting, she even boasts to Luzhin that she has learnt the basics of the game. Unlike her literary predecessor, who on the advice of the psychiatrists attempts to "liberate" Luzhin from chess for good, Natalia wants Luzhin to play in a tournament with Turati and win. She only objects to Valentinov's presence during her fiancé's play, knowing that he would try to mentally disturb and enslave him, perhaps even kill him. The ultimate testimony to Natalia's acceptance of the chess player in Luzhin is that, following his death, she finds his notes about the moves he planned to make in his game with Turati and finishes it in his place. Thus, she brings posthumous victory to Luzhin and affords herself a place as the curator of his memory. In her struggle to save Luzhin from Valentinov, she also reveals to Turati the whole scale of Valentinov's machinations and, by extension, helps the game preserve its honesty.

In the film, in Natalia's presence Luzhin does not grow passive and obese. On the contrary, Natalia succeeds in making him more mobile and active by identifying in him an interest that he can share better with her and which has the potential to balance his chess addiction: the love of dancing. Dancing, like playing chess, can be seen as a form of communication, where gestures replace words. Through teaching him to dance, Natalia thus expands his ability to share his thoughts and feelings, to "externalize himself," of which the Luzhin from the novel was incapable. During their dance Natalia asks him "to lead, to be in charge." In a different context such a request might suggest that deep down Natalia is a typical submissive girl, but in light of Luzhin's normal passivity and dependence, it should be viewed as her encouragement for him to gain identity and strength. Again, taking a clue from *Mrs. Dalloway*, we can deduce that only a strong and autonomous man is able to allow his wife to "breathe." By contrast, a weak or mentally disturbed husband, such as Septimus in *Mrs. Dalloway*, drastically reduces his wife's independence and makes her unhappy.

Ultimately, the love affair between Natalia and Luzhin is constructed by Gorris as a story of mutual emancipation. By falling in love with Natalia, Luzhin breaks with the one-sidedness of his existence; by choosing Luzhin as her husband, Natalia asserts her desire to live according to her values, not those of her mother. Their break with their previous existence is, in a sense, ultimate, because Natalia and Aleksandr have sex before their wedding. Natalia's mother is aware of that, telling her daughter with horror: "He defiled you. You are carrying his child." Natalia's possible pregnancy not only testifies to the passion of the couple, but also, like the notes which allow her to finish the match with Turati, prolongs the life of Luzhin, which in the book ends without a trace. Of course, the fact that Luzhin on the day of his death might already be a father makes using his name in the film more justifiable — by presenting him not only as a man with a distinct identity but an originator of someone else's life. Natalia and Luzhin's romance is also a story of growing mutual adjustment to each other. Contrary to many reviewers, I argue that they are compatible from the very beginning. For example, they both spurn social conventions, although Natalia is more self-conscious about her unconventionality than Luzhin. They both like games; Luzhin even proposes marriage to Natalia when she is playing tennis, and she asks him to wait until she finishes her game.

Gorris not only changed the character and narrative function of Luzhin's fiancée, but modified the roles of other female characters present in Nabokov's book, most importantly Luzhin's mother and his "aunt." The mother comes across as a more tragic figure than her literary predecessor because Gorris makes her a witness to her husband's affair with her real sister, and to his aunt stealing the heart of her only child. Hence, although Gorris shows the lack of affection and communication between the young Luzhin and his mother, she largely removes responsibility from the mother for this situation, relocating it to the boy's father. The mother is not overweight, but thin and pale, and dies by committing suicide rather than dying a natural death. The "aunt," from being a St. Petersburg's courtesan, changes into Aleksandr's real aunt, who visits the Luzhins at their home and, after the death of Luzhin's mother, marries his father. Gorris also increases the aunt's role in bringing up the boy. She takes him to funfairs, laughs with him and makes him happy. She also, like her literary predecessor, introduces Luzhin to chess. Her connection with the world of chess is even stronger than in the book because she gives the boy his first chess set, made of glass, and one of the figures, the king, he carries with him throughout his life. The figure in the film plays the role of a portal, a gate from one reality to another (on portals in *The Luzhin Defense* see Collins 2009: 195–98). In St. Petersburg it is a way to mentally escape life, in which the boy has to pay for his father's affair and mother's unhappiness, into a ghostly but more predictable and safer world. In Italy it brings to Luzhin's memory the icy winters in St. Petersburg and the crystal glass which fell from his mother's hand when he found her dead, thus being the metaphorical link with his childhood. The fact that the chess figure represents the king can be seen as a symbol of his waiting for somebody who would again love and nurture him: his queen.

While the women surrounding Luzhin, as represented by Gorris, play more positive roles in his life than the women in the book, the men on the way from book to film gained in viciousness. This applies primarily to Luzhin's "chess father," Valentinov. In the book his role is limited to exploiting his pupil, and his role in Luzhin's death, although crucial, is accidental. In the film, Valentinov embarks on a full-scale and premeditated destruction of Luzhin. This action, as already mentioned, results from his desire to prove that he was right in discarding Luzhin. Gorris also hints that Valentinov might be motivated by homosexual jealousy. His quasi-erotic interest in Luzhin is suggested by the way Valentinov looked at him from a distance, hidden, when the future master was a very pretty boy. Again he betrays it during the championship in Italy by putting himself firmly between Luzhin and Natalia, and attempting to convince Luzhin's fiancée that he was and still is the most important person in Luzhin's life: his mother, father and cook.

Another male character who gained negative qualities in comparison

**John Turturro, Stuart Wilson as Valentinov, and Emily Watson in *The Luzhin Defence*.**

with the novel is Luzhin's father. The father is made responsible for his wife's estrangement from her son and her untimely death. Throughout the whole film he also behaves as if he wants to be rid of his son in order to pursue an affair with his sister-in-law. Primarily for this reason he passes Aleksandr to Valentinov. Thus, each of Luzhin's fathers, his real father and his "chess father," come across as Laius in the Oedipus myth, who would sacrifice their son to realize their selfish goals. Accordingly, Luzhin in the film, to a larger extent than his literary predecessor, is given the position of an Oedipus who must free himself from his father to become a man.

By showing Luzhin as a boy aged ten or so, Gorris also demonstrates that his unhappy childhood — namely, his parents' unhappy marriage — as opposed to any peculiarities of his character to which Nabokov points, is responsible for his subsequent problems in adjusting to society. Even Luzhin's suicide is clearly preceded by the memory of his attempt to avoid his quarrelling parents by climbing out through a window onto a lawn. In the book there is also a link between Luzhin's deadly jumping from a window and his early "window experience," but it is more subdued, as it consists of climbing into a house through a window. Hence, the childhood in the film provides a matrix for Luzhin, explaining events which will happen to him in his adult life; it is also an important source of the structure of his identity. However, as Luzhin's meeting with Natalia shows, he has a chance to free himself from the clutches of his past. Natalia is thus given the role of a psychotherapist who helps the patient overcome family trauma. She identifies with this role practically from the beginning by asking Luzhin to tell her about his childhood.

One likely reason for Gorris cutting the Berlin chapter of Luzhin's life is to play down the fact that her characters are Russian emigrants trying, like the parents of Luzhin's fiancée, to recreate their lost country on foreign soil or, like Luzhin, re-live their Russian past in their head. The Russian nationality of Natalia and her parents is practically insignificant. They speak English, are played by British actors and never discuss anything Russian. Due to these changes they come across as English, or even English people evoking Gorris' *Mrs. Dalloway* and the British "heritage cinema" of Merchant Ivory (Macnab 2000: 50). Natalia might be compared to Lucy Honeychurch from James Ivory's *A Room with a View* (1985), for whom traveling to Italy also constituted a rite of passage — from innocent virgin to sexually awakened young woman, attracted to a man who does not fit into polite society. Equally, Natalia's restrained and well-mannered father perfectly fits the type of British gentleman rendered in this type of cinema. Unlike them, Luzhin does not come across as British; but if not for the Russian childhood and the name, his nationality would be difficult to pinpoint. Similarly, de Stassard, who is played by a British actor, in common with Luzhin, comes across as somewhat nationless. The only people with distinct national characteristics are the Italians, who are, again, represented according to the tradition of British "heritage cinema," as noisy, talkative and possessing mannerisms that provide an ample contrast to the more restrained behavior of British people.

Anglicization of Gorris' film can be explained by the fact that (as in the case of her previous film, as well as Ivory's movies), *The Luzhin Defence* is a British-American co-production geared toward British and American audiences who would not like to be drawn into the intricacies of many different national cultures. In an interview, Gorris herself admitted that initially she was planning to include flashbacks showing Natalia's past, but decided against it for the sake of a stronger dramatic effect (Gorris, quoted in Blackwelder 2001). The Anglicization of Gorris' film is signaled by giving the movie a title which is slightly different from the literary "original," with "c" replacing "s" in the eponymous "defense." Such a change, although fiercely objected to by some critics, is in accordance with the tradition of adapting Nabokov. In this respect, Gorris follows in the footsteps of Tony Richardson, who anglicized characters and the setting of *Laughter in the Dark*, and of Nabokov himself, who adapted his books for new types of readers.

Another change introduced in the film concerns representation of the chess tournament, and especially the game between Luzhin and Turati, which is rendered not so much as a chess game as a chess problem. As Janet Gezari observes, "In both chess problems and chess games, the sequence of events is controlled by predetermined principles, but in games, we play with chance and take advantage of our opponent's mistakes, while in problems, the element of uncertainty all but disappears along with the competition between players" (Gezari 1995: 48). For this reason there cannot be "Luzhin's defence," understood as a chess strategy which always works. Yet, Natalia finds among Luzhin's notes such a strategy, uses it in her encounter with Turati and wins. Her victory can be seen as a way of prolonging Luzhin's life and ensuring his lasting place in the history of chess. It can also be interpreted as replacing a masculine order with a feminine way of doing things: patriarchy by matriarchy. Such replacing takes place also in *Antonia's Line*, where Antonia is practically in charge of the whole village not because she defeated the men in combat, but simply because the weakened men are unable to stand to the challenge of everyday problems.

The representation of the chess game as a chess problem, and setting the story in a lavish hotel, brings additional context to the film, most likely one which neither the scriptwriter nor the director had foreseen: the reference to Nabokov's own life. This is because the hotel and its surroundings bear similarity to the Palace Hotel in Montreux, where the Nabokovs spent the last years of their lives. This impression is augmented by showing in the film the various pastimes with which Vladimir Nabokov is identified: chess, tennis, walking, traveling by train. The final gesture of Natalia, finishing her husband's job, can also be compared to the work of Véra Nabokov as the main custodian of her husband's memory following her husband's death, until this position was passed to the Nabokovs' son Dmitri following her own death.

For the main roles of Luzhin and Natalia, Gorris chose well-known actors John Turturro and Emily Watson. Such a casting choice, consisting of one American and one British actor, reflects the fact that *The Luzhin Defense* is a British-American coproduction. Inevitably, the actors brought to her film the baggage of their earlier roles. Turturro, who specializes in the roles of absent-minded, otherworldly and neurotic but decent men, furnishes his character with warmth, which the Luzhin from the last third of the novel lacks. Watson is renowned for playing strong and rebellious women, including in *Breaking the Waves* (1996) by Lars von Trier and *Hilary and Jackie* (1998) by Anand Tucker. Her heroines, like Natalia, are able to sacrifice everything for men, not because of patriarchal pressure but due to their own choice. Both actors are attractive, but not, especially Turturro, in a conventional Hollywood style.

**Emily Watson and John Turturro in *The Luzhin Defence*.**

The feminization of *The Luzhin Defence* invites comparison with *Mademoiselle O* and, especially, Vladimir Kuik's *An Affair of Honor*, which is almost contemporaneous with Gorris' film. In both movies we observe an attempt to present female characters as the male protagonists' true partners, as opposed to only pawns in male games. In both films the duels between men give way to a confrontation between a man and a woman in which each side must realize and reveal to their partner his or her expectations and needs. This feminization points to the new ways of reading classical literature, and Nabokov's books especially, by finding in them and reconstructing the unheard voices of women. The work of Kuik and Gorris can thus be compared to feminist criticism of *Lolita*, as well as the artistic reworkings of this novel (for example, *Poems for Men who Dream of Lolita* by Kim Morrissey).

As with almost all films in this book, *The Luzhin Defence* met with mixed reviews. There was a remarkable consistency in what the reviewers praised and what they criticized. The positive opinions concerned the visual side of the film: the beauty of the settings and their lighting, the exquisite costumes, the fluency of the camera, the careful framing, rendering almost every image a piece of art. There appeared to be a consensus that in terms of visual qualities, *The Luzhin Defence* surpassed Gorris' *Mrs. Dalloway*, creating one of the most successful "heritage" or costume films of the decade. There was also much praise directed towards the actors, especially Watson and Turturro, for their ability to convey convincingly the love affair between the central couple. For example, the distinguished British critic Philip French labeled in *The Guardian* Gorris' film "a work of considerable intellectual and physical elegance," and praised Turturro for being "utterly convincing as the 30-ish Aleksandr Luzhin" (French 2000). A. O. Scott of *The New York Times* wrote about Watson and Turturro that "Their odd, attractive faces and slightly nervous performing styles seem perfectly complementary, and their romance is a welcome respite from the usual mechanistic movie star courtship" (Scott 2001).

The praise for the "heritage" element was especially strong in American reviews, confirming the view that an American audience is more easily lured by the beauty of exquisite mansions, gardens and costumes, most likely on account of having little comparable treasures in their own country. We find typical praise in *The New York Times*:

> *The Luzhin Defence* takes place in what looks, at first glance, like familiar movie territory. The chugging locomotive, the cloche hats and elegant summer suits, the picturesque limestone villa all denote Europe between the world wars. But the literary source of Marleen Gorris' elegant, tenderhearted film is not Waugh or Maugham but Nabokov; the lush scenery and period costumes are not vehicles of historical reckoning or social observation but rather the scaffolding for a delicate fable about memory, devotion and the vulnerability of genius in a cruelly ordinary world [Scott 2001].

The Russian reviewer Valeri Kitchin also praised the film in similar terms, underscoring the superb roles of Turturro and Watson, and the exquisite setting, which he compared to *Morte a Venezia* (*Death in Venice*, 1971) by Luchino Visconti. Not surprisingly, he also addressed the issue of Luzhin's Russian identity. Although he commented with some irony that, according to the long Western tradition of representing Russians, Luzhin is more otherworldly and alien to Westerners than Black people, he did not criticize this attitude, regarding it as a "fact of nature" and pointing out with some pride that Luzhin's genius belongs to the same mysterious category as Russian ballet (Kitchin 2000).

On the other hand, the reviewers were almost unanimous in chastising Gorris for rendering chess games unrealistically and making her film more romantic than the book. Symptomatic in this respect is a review written by a chess specialist, Tim Krabbé, who illuminates the link between the two perceived weaknesses of the film:

The infantile plot makes you wonder whether the disrespect is greater towards the book or towards chess. It takes a sad sort of guts to turn a novel about the tragic enchantment of chess into a feminist pamphlet; man is too weak, woman must finish his work for him. There was a *chess consultant*, Jon (John in the credits) Speelman, but he has not been able to prevent this movie–Luzhin from out-caricaturing all the weirdos the chess world has ever known.... Or the players from battering away at the clocks like furious postal workers who have decided that today, finally, they will gorgeously stamp *all* fragile items to smithereens.... It is strange that after the adjournment, Turati and Valentinov insist on finishing the game — apparently, in all the days that must have passed between Luzhin's breakdown and his marriage, they haven't seen that move Rh3. It *is* a brilliant move, but it would be found by any reasonable chess player who looked at the position for longer than a quarter of an hour. Beside that, we may assume that an adjourned position deciding a world championship would have been in the papers all over the world — thousands of chess players would have looked at it for hours, for days. And nobody, nobody has seen Rh3, or has cared to send a telegram. And even when Natalia plays Rh3, Turati still doesn't see it coming [Krabbé 2001].

Of course, Krabbé's review demonstrates that he expects a film about chess to be faithful to the mechanics of the game rather than its psychology. In a somewhat similar vein, Alan Stone, who was also very critical of Adrian Lyne's *Lolita* (see Chapter 1), wrote in the *Boston Review*:

The most stunning transformation made in bringing the novel to the screen is what made *The Luzhin Defence* a film to be shown at the International Women's Film Festival. Gorris's Luzhin kills himself in the middle of the world championship match. The pieces remained in place in a game that no one thought Luzhin could win. In the film, Luzhin has in fact solved the impossible puzzle, noting the winning solution on a piece of paper that Natalia finds in the dead man's pocket. Luzhin's opponent Turati graciously agrees to finish the game. He and Natalia sit in the great hall at the chessboard and, following her husband's notations, she wins the game and proves that Luzhin was in fact a world champion. So she redeems the genius of her dead husband, her decision to marry him, and her own integrity — all of which Nabokov left in doubt at the instant when Luzhin unclenched his hand, at the instant when icy air gushed into his mouth.

Over the past decade ambitious directors have brought a whole spate of twentieth-century novels to the screen. I can think of none that is more disrespectful to the spirit of its author than *The Luzhin Defence*. Gorris, who started her career as a fiercely independent feminist, has made a cinematographically beautiful film empty of Nabokov's ecstatic genius, his prescient psychology, and her own original talent [Stone 2001].

The extent to which Gorris "lightened" the story of Luzhin also caused uneasiness among ordinary viewers, as reflected in an opinion published on the IMBD website:

There is only one problem: the film has nothing to do with the novel. Indeed, how would they make a commercially successful movie about a fat unattractive man who marries a dull woman who doesn't understand him? Yeah, let's turn the loser into a winner, even after death, substitute the dull wife for an understanding fiancée, throw in an antagonist, add costumes, remove thoughts and we have an "amazing, definitely worth seeing" movie. Who cares about being faithful to Nabokov — he's dead.

In all three reviews the authors position themselves as custodians of the literary works, which they perceive as true originals rather than anterior texts on which the filmmaker draws according to his or her needs. Such an attitude, as I argued in the previous chapters, is a typical position taken by the reviewers, although the closer we come to the present day the more examples we find of journalism that acknowledges the gap between the texts but assesses the film as a work in its own right. This approach is taken by Philip French, among those I quoted. In the opinion of Belén Vidal, who also in her discussion of *The Luzhin Defence* refers to Krabbé's condemnation of Gorris' film, the resistance towards granting a film based on a literary work the status of an autonomous work is especially great when the film's director is female (Vidal 2005).[2] I believe it is directed both towards the female director usurping the position of an author and towards offering a feminist reading of a novel written by a highly respected male author of conservative views.

However, I will not dismiss the negative opinions of the film simply as anti-female rants or an old-fashioned defense of fidelity to the literary text. Behind them there is an advocacy of certain values in art which are not media specific and which one can find in Nabokov's novel. I will discuss them in greater detail in the chapter comparing Nabokov and Godard, but now I will mention just one — artistic economy or "saturation," as Leona Toker puts it (Toker 2005: 233–34): using the minimum of artistic means for the maximum effect. Watching *The Luzhin Defence*, one often feels that too much is said and shown to achieve the expected outcome; less could be more. For this reason I regard *An Affair of Honor* by Valentin Kuik as a superior film to *The Luzhin Defence* because it accomplishes a greater artistic effect with modest means. At the same time, I am saying that with an awareness that my judgment is also a product of cultural forces, including an easy grasp of the codes used by Gorris, knowing many other films belonging to "heritage cinema" and her own works, and knowing much less about Estonian cinema and about the films Kuik directed and scripted.

Returning to the issue of "feminist" bias in the adaptations of Nabokov, judging by the films made in the last twenty years, this is what became the rule. Hence, one can hypothesize that if his prose will be screened again, the resulting film will be closer to the reading offered by Kuik and Gorris than by Kubrick.

# 8

# From B-Movie Script to Greek Tragedy

*"The Assistant Producer" by Vladimir Nabokov, and* Triple Agent *by Eric Rohmer (2004)*

*Triple agent* (*Triple Agent*) by Eric Rohmer, unlike the other films discussed so far, is not an adaptation of any book by Nabokov. Nevertheless, similarities between this film and "The Assistant Producer," a short story Nabokov published in 1943, invite discussion. By including these two works in one chapter I am not implying that Rohmer borrowed anything from Nabokov's story. The probability of such an occurrence is small because "The Assistant Producer" belongs to Nabokov's less known stories and was published for the first time in French only in 1982. The links between these two works can be sufficiently explained by the fact that the book and the film are themselves "adaptations": artistic retellings of the Skoblin-Miller affair—a real event which took place in Paris in 1937. Rohmer himself claimed that the scenario for *Triple Agent* was inspired by a story he found in a historical journal (Rohmer, quoted in Jeffries 2004). However, being born in 1920, he was old enough in 1937 to be able to take note of this event.

Although not an adaptation of Nabokov's prose, *Triple Agent* looks no less an adaptation than, for example, *An Affair of Honor* by Valentin Kuik. Moreover, it gives an insight into how Rohmer would have approached Nabokov had he decided to adapt any of his books. I shall add that even if Rohmer had never made a film which lends itself to comparison with a particular Nabokov novel or short story, I would still like to evoke Rohmer's name in this book because these two authors have much in common. First, both are preoccupied with the precise description of the places and spaces where the action of their works is set. Nabokov claims that his students "had to know the map of Dublin for *Ulysses*" (LL: 55). As Maxim Shrayer observes, the experience of reading many of Nabokov's short stories "can be compared to that of finding one's way around a given space (a city, a region, a country) via a travel guide" (Shrayer 1997: 625).[1] The same can be said about watching Rohmer's films, which prompted one critic to say that the director "might have ended up a travel agent" (Wrathal 1996: 53).

Second, both authors prove difficult to place on the realism/anti-realism scale, which is of crucial importance for modernists and postmodernists. Nabokov's vivid descriptions of characters and settings, and his famous attention to detail, link him with the great realistic fiction. At the same time, his works tend to be played on different ontological planes, which is a feature of anti-realism. He himself eschewed the problems of realism altogether by insisting on reality's subjectivity (SO: 10). Rohmer openly advocated realism in his critical writings and insisted that a film's categorization as "modern" or "high art" should not depend on its self-reflexivity or, in a wider sense, the rejection of realism (Rohmer 1986). At the same time, despite his professed attachment to realism, many viewers regard Rohmer as one of the most unrealistic directors among the creators of *Nouvelle Vague* due to the literary character of his films, which is marked by the prevalence of words over (physical) action (Crisp 1988).

Third, both authors have created their own languages. The one by Nabokov tends to be described as "Nabokese." As for Rohmer, Derek Schilling, the author of the most recent monograph on the director, maintains that Rohmer's characters speak "French as heard by Rohmer":

> It is fitting that perhaps the greatest legacy of this former professor of letters should be the creation of a language unto itself: *le rohmérien*, that unfailingly clear, but not always concise tongue that in its immoderate respect for grammar and its melodic intonations seems to chastise and seduce at one and the same time [Schilling 2007: 193].

Fourth, both authors were unwilling to make sweeping aesthetic judgments and were prejudiced against those who did so. Nabokov refused to talk about literary schools, especially modernism, instead preferring to talk about individual authors or works, saying that what interests him in art is "not general ideas, but the individual contribution" (LL: 33). Rohmer in his critical writing showed reluctance towards discussing the cinema of whole nations and aesthetic formations (Rohmer 1986; Crisp 1988: 1–13). This reluctance towards generalizations, seen in both artists, can be traced to their respect for detail and precision, revealed in their own works.

Finally, and most importantly from my perspective, there is a similarity between Rohmer's and Nabokov's political views. Both can be described as having conservative or right-wing views (SO; Rohmer 1986: 92). Both were also against art which serves specific political groupings or purposes, arguing at the same time that it can be a useful weapon against certain types of politics insofar as it develops critical judgment in individual readers or viewers. Nabokov said:

> I believe that one day a reappraiser will come and declare that, far from having been a frivolous firebird, I was a rigid moralist kicking sin, cuffing stupidity, ridiculing the vulgar and cruel — and assigning sovereign power to tenderness, talent, and pride [SO: 193].

Rohmer's views on the relationship between art and politics are best conveyed in his answer to the question posed in an interview: "Do you think that a filmmaker should be indifferent to his times?":

> No, not at all. Quite the reverse. I'd even say that he can and must be committed, but not politically in the narrow, traditional sense of the term. What does art give people? Pleasure. The artist should be committed to the organization of that pleasure, and since we're told we are entering an age of leisure, perhaps he will be able to discover for himself an important, exciting role that is completely worthy of him [Rohmer 1986: 92].

As a consequence of these factors, both authors place themselves somewhat outside artistic schools, paradigms and fashions. Many of these features shine through in "The Assistant Producer" and *Triple Agent*, which retell the story of the 1937 Paris disappearance of an ex–White Army general and activist of the Russian émigré organization ROVS (Russian Armed Services' Union), Evgenii Miller, kidnapped by another ex–White Army general, Nikolai Skoblin, aided by his wife, the singer Nadezhda Plevitskaya.

According to the prevailing version of history, Skoblin and Plevitskaya were both secret agents working for the Soviet and possibly German authorities. It was Plevitskaya who was first approached by the Soviet secret services (NKVD) through one of her admirers, a Russian millionaire. She persuaded her husband to work for the Soviet Union, regarding it as a way to boost their income and allow her to indulge her taste for luxuries. As Alexander Orlov writes, "While most of the White officers had a hard time struggling for a living, the Skoblins lived well due to her singing engagements in various capitals of Europe and the 6,000 French francs which he earned monthly as an NKVD informer" (Orlov 2004: 194). It is accepted that Skoblin organized the kidnapping of Miller with Plevitskaya's knowledge and under her advice, although it is not clear whether the action went according to his plans or whether he was outsmarted by those for whom he worked, namely the Soviets.

In common with her husband, who was not an average soldier but a general, Plevitskaya was not an average singer. Hubertus Jahn describes her as the superstar among the singers of popular songs during World War I. Among her admirers were Nikolai I and a host of theater and opera personalities, such as the bass Fëdor Shaliapin and the editor of *Teatr i iskusstvo*, Aleksandr Kugel. As one of the first gramophone stars, she had the largest audience of any *estrada* artist of the time, triggering "Plevitskomania" all over the country and in all social strata (Jahn 1995: 100). Plevitskaya modeled herself on a Gypsy singer, performing traditional or pseudo-traditional songs with gypsy bands, although she was born to a peasant family in a village near Kursk, and her first husband, the dancer Edmond Plevitsky, was Polish. After the October Revolution, Plevitskaya switched sides and sang for the troops of the Red Army. In 1919 she was captured by a unit of the White Army under the command of Skoblin, who married her while in exile in Turkey after the defeat of the White military forces. She then became the most popular female Russian singer of the White émigré era. In the 1920s, Plevitskya made concert tours throughout Europe and in 1926 to the United States, where she was accompanied by Sergei Rachmaninoff. Her fame and celebrity ambitions, as Orlov suggests, partly explain Plevitskaya's willingness to work as a spy. On the other hand, it beggars belief that somebody so successful in her profession would risk her fame and good name by engaging in such disreputable activities as betraying fellow citizens and friends.

According to Nabokov's biographers, Nabokov knew Plevitskaya personally. He visited her when she was living in Berlin in the 1920s, and met her and her husband at parties in Paris. Moreover, Nabokov was friendly with Ivan Lukash, an aspiring writer (including scriptwriter) who, in due course, left Berlin and went to Paris to ghost write Plevitskaya's autobiography (Field 1987: 123–5; Boyd 1990: 261). Andrew Field maintains that "it was then assumed among Berlin émigrés that the guileless and talkative Lukash must have told Plevitskaya at least as much as he heard from her, for Lukash knew every Russian in literary Berlin, and the Soviets were interested not only in wooing émigré writers, but also in keeping track of their activities" (Field 1987: 125). Nabokov also knew other prominent émigrés who turned out to be Soviet spies. The literary journal *The Rudder*, where Nabokov published some of his short stories, and "which was virtually a large family unit of Russian liberals most of whom had known and worked with each other for more than a decade, was nearly penetrated by the NKVD" (ibid.: 126). The shock of discovering her secret activities could be an important reason why Nabokov did not write about Plevitskaya's affair during his émigré years. Instead, in 1943, he devoted to it his first short story written in English, which suggests that geographic and cultural distance allowed him to approach the subject with a cool head. As I will argue in due course, for some readers, including this one, the head proved somewhat too cool; the treatment of the characters is too cruel.

The fact that Nabokov knew about the affair is sufficient explanation why he wrote about it. An additional factor, however, was the fact that the marriage of Plevitskaya and Skoblin, who in "The Assistant Producer" are turned into La Slavska and General Golubkov, was a union of art and politics, which interested Nabokov throughout his working life, as demonstrated by, for example, *Invitation to a Beheading* and *Pale Fire*. Plevitskaya's art both facilitated and camouflaged Skoblin's secret political activities, for it allowed him to travel and gather intelligence during her concerts in private homes. Skoblin's work as a secret agent, on the other hand, allowed his wife to indulge in a style fit for a star.

In his story, Nabokov, who remained consistent in his anti-communist views throughout his life and regarded violence as one of the greatest evils, scorns Golubkov's political actions as governed by opportunism, not convictions, and causing the suffering of innocent people, most importantly the hapless General Fedchenko (who stands in the story for General Miller), whose counterpoint in real life was handed over to the Bolsheviks, tortured and executed (Bailey 1961: 227–67).[2] By spying for different political parties, Golubkov also disgraces the White Warriors Union (the literary equivalent of ROVS) in the eyes of both Russian émigrés and "native" Russians who remained anti-communist and held this organization in high esteem, as suggested by the following passage:

> The dreams of simple Russian folk, hardworking families in remote parts of the Russian diaspora, plying their humble but honest trades, as they would in Saratov or Tver, bearing fragile children, and naively believing that the W.W. was a kind of King Arthur's Round Table that stood for all that had been, and would be, sweet and decent and strong in fairy-tale Russia — these dreams may well strike the film pruners as an excrescence upon the main theme [AP: 550].

Although this idea is not fully spelled out in the story, we can also guess that the activities of people such as Skoblin/Golubkov made Nabokov distrustful of or even frankly hostile towards any institutional or political life.

However, the main object of the author's derision is not Golubkov, who is only gently mocked, but Slavska. She appears to be the repository of all the features Nabokov detested in life and art. He describes her practically exclusively in derogatory terms, beginning with the fake Slavic name "La Slavska," which connotes unfounded pretence to talent, style and importance:

> Not opera, not even *Cavalleria Rusticana*, not anything like that. "La Slavska"— that is what the French called her. Style: one-tenth *tzigane*, one-seventh Russian peasant girl (she had been that herself originally) and five-ninths popular — and by popular I mean a hodgepodge of artificial folklore, military melodrama, and official patriotism. The fraction left unfilled seems sufficient to represent the physical splendor of her prodigious voice.... Her artistic taste was nowhere, her technique haphazard, her general style atrocious [ibid.: 546 and 552].

The vulgarity of Slavska's performance is accompanied by the vulgarity of her demeanor and entire character. In common with other female characters conjured up by Nabokov to arouse negative emotions in the reader, like the Swiss governess Mademoiselle O or Lolita's mother, Slavska is overweight, has a flair for flashy clothes and indulges in sentimental gestures. As with Mademoiselle O and Martha in *King, Queen, Knave*, Nabokov compares her to Anna Karenina — not to edify her but to underscore her distance from Tolstoy's famous heroine. On this occasion we learn that Slavska is slightly nearsighted, like Karenina.

For Slavska, art is not the autonomous area, as it is for her creator, but a vehicle to earn a good living and the admiration of her audience. Moreover, the singer, like her husband, is shown to be a political opportunist who would sing for any political grouping if it brought her advantages. In addition, Slavska is for Nabokov a prism through which he views and criticizes the Russian émigré milieu, as conveyed in the second part of this sentence: "But the kind of people for whom music and sentiment are one, or who like songs to be mediums for the spirits of circumstances under which they had been first apprehended in an individual past, gratefully found in the tremendous sonorities of her voice both a nostalgic solace and a patriotic kick" (ibid.: 552). Slavska not only responds to the audiences' needs but perpetuates them.

All in all, Slavska perfectly illustrates ideas developed both in Nabokov's fiction, such as *Invitation to a Beheading* and *Lolita*, and non-fiction works, like in his essay "Philistines and Philistinism." In this essay Nabokov focuses on the smug philistinism known as *poshlism*:

> *Poshlism* is not only the obviously trashy but mainly the falsely beautiful, the falsely clever, the falsely attractive. To apply the deadly label of *poshlism* to something is not only an aesthetic judgment but also a moral indictment. The genuine, the guileless, the good is never *poshlust*. It is possible to maintain that a simple, uncivilized man is seldom if ever a *poshlust* since *poshlism* presupposes the veneer of civilisation. A painted necktie has to hide the honest Adam's apple in order to produce *poshlism* [LRL: 313].

Nabokov adds that *poshlism* was a rare phenomenon in his native country because of the "cult of simplicity and good taste in old Russia" (ibid.: 313). This state of affairs changed with the victory of Bolshevism. For Nabokov, Bolshevism involved a reduction of the wealth of moral and aesthetic values to a handful of utilitarian concerns, which blinded people to any true values and killed their spirituality.

Slavska embodies the double corruption of moral and aesthetic values that is brought about by Bolshevism. Although she lives in Paris and performs for the supporters of the Whites, in her heart she is what Nabokov regards as a typical Bolshevik: vulgar, sentimental, dishonest, perhaps even with herself.

In a wider sense, she illustrates the idea that politics which does not recognize the uniqueness of every human being becomes vulgar, and that art which accepts or serves such politics is condemned to immorality. In line with his hostile attitude towards her, Nabokov does not grant his heroine a dignified ending. Preceded by a long imprisonment, Slavska's death, like her life, comes across as no less kitschy and meaningless than her life:

> We get a few glimpses of the Slavska in prison. Meekly knitting in a corner. Writing to Mrs. Fedchenko tear-stained letters in which she said that they were sisters now, because both their husbands had been captured by the Bolsheviks. Begging to be allowed the use of a lipstick.... Some time after the outbreak of World War II, she developed an obscure internal trouble and when, one summer morning, three German officers arrived at the prison hospital and desired to see her, at once they were told she was dead — which possibly was the truth [AP: 558–59].

The unabashed cruelty with which Nabokov treats his heroine can be viewed not so much as a consequence of his desire to render truthfully the episode from the lives of White émigrés, but rather a result of his anti–Bolshevism and misogyny. Firstly, Nabokov's biased attitude towards Slavska can be detected in a number of aspects of the short story. His portrayal of Slavska is notably more critical than her description by other authors, such as the previously quoted Bailey, Orlov and Jahn, and is even harsher than his assessment of Plevitskaya offered to his biographer, Andrew Field: "Plevitskaya had a fine voice. I think she had some talent, but she was rather trite. She was a corny singer" (Nabokov, quoted in Field 1987: 125). A sign of Nabokov's appreciation of Plevitskaya's talent is also his composing a poem in her honor when he was living in Berlin (Boyd 1990: 494).

Secondly, in "The Assistant Producer," Slavska does not have a voice of her own, which is somewhat ironic given that she makes her living by using her voice. She is being narrated rather than narrating her own story. Moreover, unlike some other female characters in Nabokov's fiction, especially Lolita, whose "true stories" shine through the unreliable descriptions of male narrators, Slavska's version of events is completely thwarted in the narrative. Perhaps for this reason, no commentators seem to take pity on the character, but accept the writer's rendition (Appel 1974: 288–96, Nicol 1993).

Nabokov gives the lives of Slavska and Golubkov the form of a kitschy, sensationalist B-movie script. This quasi-cinematic form, conveyed by the very title of the story, has attracted the greatest attention among critics, including Alfred Appel and Charles Nicol. Nicol observes that the narrator, a "Russian émigré living in America and familiar with geographical features of California, is very much like Nabokov himself, not only in these features of his life story but also in his [ironic] tone and his political attitudes" (Nicol 1993: 157).

Appel quotes Nabokov replying to the question "'Who exactly is this narrator?' with, 'It's me, of course, disguised as a priest.'" ... "Why a priest?" asks Appel. "He tells the truth," answers Nabokov (Appel 1974: 291).

At the same time as identifying the narrator of the story as Nabokov in disguise, Nicol detects in the titular character Golubkov himself, who survives the events of the 1930s and relocates to California where he becomes an assistant producer in a movie about his own life. Nicol and Appel argue that such a fate was not uncommon among Russian emigrants, and Nabokov was not the only author to write about it. Appel writes:

> The theme [of playing oneself in a movie] is memorably orchestrated in Josef von Sternberg's *The Last Command* (1928), in which Emil Jannings plays an ex-tsarist general who, now a poor old man in Hollywood, applies for work as an extra and is cast to replay his glorious former self in the film-within-the-film. The cruel, dizzying commission and that film's Communist director (William Powell) combine to drive Jannings insane. (Sternberg's scenario was inspired by a "true story" rather than, say, Pirandello's play *Henry IV*, 1922).... "I had fortified my image of the Russian Revolution by including in my cast of extra players an assortment of Russian ex-admirals and generals, a dozen Cossacks, and two former members of the Duma, all victims of the Bolsheviks, and, in particular, an expert on borscht by the name of Koblianski. These men, especially one Cossack general who insisted on keeping my car spotless, viewed Jannings' effort to be Russian with such disdain that I had to order them to conceal it," writes Field Marshal von Sternberg in his autobiography, *Fun in Chinese Laundry* (1965) [Appel 1974: 275–76].

Nicol also mentions F. Scott Fitzgerald's *The Last Tycoon*, which he considers a major inspiration for "The Assistant Producer," quoting the following fragment:

> "But the man's good. Can't we use him as the old Russian Prince in *Steppes*?"
> "He is an old Russian prince," said the casting director, "but he's ashamed of it. He's a Red. And that's one part he says he wouldn't play."
> "It's the only part he could play," said Stahr" [Fitzgerald, quoted in Nicol 1993: 161].

It is also a well-known fact, commented upon by Appel, Field, Boyd and Nicol, that Nabokov himself, when living in Berlin, boosted his meager income by working as an extra in the movies. Not surprisingly, the idea that life imitates film which imitates life is a frequent motif in his works, used previously in *Despair* and *Laughter in the Dark*, as discussed in previous chapters. The effect in all these works is of a house of mirrors, in which the characters are forever entrapped. The "house of mirrors" motif lends Nabokov's "The Assistant Producer" a dreamlike, surrealistic atmosphere. Other aspects of the story, however, bring "The Assistant Producer" closer to journalism than to fiction (Johnson 2001). These include references to newspapers which reported the episode of Fedchenko's disappearance in such terms:

> The French police displayed a queer listlessness in dealing with possible

clues as if it assumed that the disappearance of Russian generals was a kind of curious local custom, an Oriental phenomenon, a dissolving process which perhaps ought not to occur but which could not be prevented [AP: 557].

Moreover, as an experienced political commentator rather than a writer of fiction, Nabokov makes comparisons between Bolshevism and Hitlerism, regarding both as cruel and kitschy. I will suggest that an important reason for Nabokov's interest in the Skoblin-Plevitskaya-Miller affair was the opportunity it offered to compare and denounce these two systems, of which he was a victim. Following Hannah Arendt's book *The Origins of Totalitarianism*, published for the first time in 1951, we tend to take the similarity between these two systems for granted; but when Nabokov wrote his story it was far from obvious.

Nabokov's description of the events surrounding the disappearance of Miller was so persuasive that it is likely that it affected Geoffrey Bailey, the author of the previously mentioned book *The Conspirators*, which is devoted to a number of mysterious events from the period between the two world wars, involving Soviet spies. Although Bailey does not cite Nabokov, he dedicates his book "to V., who knows," which tempts the reader to regard it as based, at least in part, on Nabokov's investigation. Moreover, as Charles Nicol observes, "While that story is never directly mentioned in his text, Bailey seems to take pains to elaborate on a number of its details, establishing a closer parallel between its reality and actual events than any other source either inside or outside of Nabokov scholarship" (Nicol 1993: 156).

The credits of *Triple Agent* cite Rohmer as the sole author of its script, and, as I mentioned, the possibility that Rohmer was familiar with Nabokov's short story about Pleavitskaya and Skoblin is small. However, what interests me in this book is not so much an adaptation in its rigid form, but intertextuality.[3] For this reason it is also worth mentioning that Rohmer and Nabokov are linked by Alfred Hitchcock. Not only are there many textual similarities between Hitchcock and Nabokov, but these two authors discussed a possible collaboration on a film (Boyd 1991: 401–2). Hitchcock was also a great influence on Rohmer. Hence, *Triple Agent* can be regarded as a kind of substitution for the film that Hitchcock and Nabokov never made together. Yet, as with all substitutions it is rather different from what it was meant to replace.

The most likely reason why the director chose to film this story is that it serves as a perfect vehicle with which to condemn in one blow two systems — Russian communism and Nazism — towards which Rohmer held an attitude similar to Nabokov. Moreover, *Triple Agent* fits well the pattern of Rohmer's later works, which also include *L'Anglaise et le duc* (*The Lady and the Duke*, 2001) and *Les Amours d'Astrée et de Céladon* (*Romance of Astrea and*

*Celadon*, 2007). All these films are set in the past (in the case of *Romance of Astrea and Celadon*, even a mythical past) and concern fidelity in love or politics. Needless to say, they reflect the director's desire to escape from the present day, which one can also identify in the late works by Nabokov. At the same time, Rohmer's strong position as an auteur allowed him to make these films with a considerable degree of freedom, disregarding cinematic fashion of the day. Hence, there is a timeless feel to *Triple Agent*, which, paradoxically, makes it a closer relative to Nabokov's prose than practically any other film discussed in this book, which are to a much larger degree the children of their times.

In common with Nabokov, and in accordance with his longstanding interests, Rohmer uses the story of Skoblin and Plevitskaya as a means to focus on women, art and politics. However, he constructs his heroine, her art and her position within the narrative differently than Nabokov. The difference between Arsinoé and Slavska is the more striking because Rohmer's Voronin fits perfectly Nabokov's description of Golubkov, being somewhat dry and boring. These similarities and differences between the characters of the respective works suggest that while in his views on men Rohmer does not differ from Nabokov, in their attitudes toward women they are worlds apart. In *Triple Agent* the Russian Plevitskaya changed into Arsinoé, a Greek and the second wife of Voronin, Rohmer's Skoblin. As a number of authors observed, the change of nationality allowed Rohmer to make his characters converse in French without undermining the realism of the film (Vincendeau 2004: 38; Schilling 2007: 183). It is a convincing explanation, but in my opinion the change also helps to convey Arsinoé's detachment not only from French society, but from Russian as well, including from her own husband. Her Greekness makes her a double outsider — in France and in her own home.

In stark contrast to Nabokov's Slavska, Rohmer's Arsinoé is not overweight and does not strive for material goods and fame, but instead is slim and modest in her needs. Yet, despite having few dresses, all rather old, she looks attractive thanks to her good taste and grace. Furthermore, she is introverted. She admits that she has no courage to paint outdoors, and while in public places with her husband she is never first to strike up a conversation, but limits herself to listening to others and answering their questions. As one might expect, the couple did not meet in such unusual and adventurous circumstances as Golubkov and Slavska, but in a sanatorium where Golubkov was convalescing from his war injuries and Arsinoé was curing her generally fragile health.

Unlike Slavska and Plevitskaya, Arsinoé does not encourage Voronin to spy, and almost until the end of the film (and certainly it is too late) she does not know about his activities as a secret agent, much less a triple one, because

Cyrielle Clair as Maguy, and Katerina Didaskalou as Arsinoé in *Triple Agent* (2004), directed by Eric Rohmer.

Voronin lies to her or withholds important information from her. She learns about his secret life from third parties and from Voronin's conversations with his friends, in which he comes across as more open than when talking to Arsinoé. As a wife kept in the dark, she is similar to a number of women, presented or alluded to by Rohmer in his earlier films, such as Françoise, whom Jean-Louis is to marry in *Ma Nuit chez Maud* (*My Night with Maud*, 1969); the wife in *L'Amour l'après-midi* (*Love in the Afternoon*, 1972), whom the protagonist, Fréderic, is about to betray with a flamboyant Chloe; and the eponymous aviator's wife from *La Femme de l'aviateur* (*The Aviator's Wife*, 1981), who is only talked about by the aviator's ex-girlfriend, Anne. In all these films the greatest guilt of the men, as with Voronin, is their sinful thoughts and lies; these thoughts and lies, rather than physical acts, make them unfaithful.

Arsinoé plays a similar role in her husband's life to that of the loving and steadfast wife of Fréderic, but she occupies a different position within the narrative. In *Love in the Afternoon* (and other Rohmer works) the director does not focus on faithful women who are cheated on by unfaithful men, but on the men or on those women who attempt to seduce men away from their previous partners. Consequently, the betrayed women appear unimportant and unremarkable; they are often kept off-screen, thus preventing the viewer from identifying with their plight. Their narrative and ideological function is thus limited to arousing moral scruples in their men. By contrast, Arsinoé is the main character in the film, and we see almost all represented events through her eyes, with the exception of newsreels that are woven into the main narrative. I suggest that in *Triple Agent* Rohmer metaphorically repays the silent and duped wives by bringing one of them out of the shadows, giving her a voice and allowing her to present her version of the story. The fact that Arsinoé pays such a heavy price for her husband's crimes and misdemeanors casts a new light on the situation of the characters from Rohmer's earlier films, rendering the crimes of the unfaithful men greater than they originally appeared. Arsinoé also harks back to women from Rohmer's earlier films because she attempts to preserve her dignity and grace in adverse circumstances, caused primarily by the compromising behavior of a man she loves, trusts and on whom she depends. In this respect she is most similar to the eponymous Marquise of O from Rohmer's adaptation of Heinrich von Kleist's novel *La Marquise d'O ...* (*The Marquise of O...*, 1976), who is rescued by a Russian officer from the danger of being raped by his countrymen only to be raped and impregnated by him while she lies unconscious.

As Arsinoé's story, *Triple Agent* is different from "The Assistant Producer," which is told by an external and omniscient narrator whose voice we can identify as Nabokov's. Arsinoé's point of view is already privileged in the first scene of the film, in which Fiodor listens to the radio news, observed by his wife. Soon somebody phones him and he leaves, but the camera stays with Arsinoé, who does not know where her husband went and on what errand. We appear to look at Voronin through her eyes and gradually, in common with her, realize the extent to which Voronin is involved in spying for what turns out to be totalitarian regimes. Thanks to always being with Arsinoé, we are assured that, unlike Slavska, she did not encourage her husband to behave immorally; on the contrary, she urged him to behave honorably in whatever circumstances.

This does not mean that Arsinoé's position is morally straightforward, far from it. The more she understands her husband's activities, the more worried she becomes — not only about the couple's wellbeing and safety, but also her involvement in Fiodor's dubious affairs. Although, as Arsinoé puts it, she is wrapped up in her work, she is honest enough to realize that ignorance or partial knowledge is not an excuse. She suffers a dilemma: either to remain a loyal wife and accept everything her husband tells her, or to follow her principles, especially her distaste for totalitarian regimes and keep her distance from Voronin, even abandon him. However, Arsinoé is denied the chance to make an informed choice in these matters because life goes faster than she can think. Even before she is able to find out what role Fiodor played in General Dobrinsky's abduction (Rohmer's Miller), her husband disappears and the police come to arrest her. As we learn, her sentence is very harsh and she dies in prison. However, unlike her predecessors, Plevitskaya and Slavska, who are punished for their own sins, Arsinoé suffers because of her loyalty and naiveté rather than perversion. Hence, if there is any moral lesson for women in *Triple Agent*, it is not to trust a man, and especially not to allow oneself to be blinded by love. This is also the lesson which "the aviators' wives" and other women of their kind could derive from Rohmer's earlier moral tales.

*Triple Agent* includes not only a moral lesson for straightforward, faithful, good women who fall prey to their cheating husbands, be it in love or in other matters, but also for those spouses and people in general who, thanks to their cunning skills, regard themselves as superior to others. This is certainly true of Voronin, who arrogantly announces to Arsinoé (in a way which links him to Humbert from *Lolita* and Hermann from *Despair*): "I pull strings behind the scenes." No doubt he believes that he is able to control others, but does not realize that other people do not adjust to his plans but follow their own agenda; he is not only a triple agent, but an agent in triple or more numerous affairs. As a result of the entanglement of these various "strings," most likely he falls into a trap he himself created. In this respect he is similar to characters such as Adrien in *La Collectionneuse* (*The Collector*, 1966) or Marion in *Pauline à la plage* (*Pauline at the Beach*, 1983) who also feel superior to others but become defeated in the end. However, Voronin's situation is different in the sense that his downfall has a catastrophic consequence for another person. His defeat testifies to the broader idea that intelligence without morality is stupid, similarly as morality without intelligence leads to destructive acts.

The last and most important difference between Nabokov's Slavska and Rohmer's Arsinoé lies in their occupations: Arsinoé is not a singer but a painter. Giving Arsinoé such a profession helps to render her story as that of a woman locked in her house and kept in the dark about her husband's affairs. No less significantly, it also allows Rohmer to transmit his views on art. In contrast to Slavska, who represents a discipline of art and a style most alien to Nabokov's interests and tastes — and therefore easy to condemn — Arsinoé stands for art very close to Rohmer's own.

Unlike Nabokov, for Rohmer the crucial division within artistic production is not between popular (therefore vulgar) art on the one hand and elitist (and original) art on the other, but between art which gives access to reality and that which emphasizes its artifice. Practically throughout his entire career, both as a critic and filmmaker, Rohmer defended the former — for example, in this polemic against Pasolini's claim that the specificity of modern cinema is self-reflexivity:

> I don't believe at all that modern cinema is necessarily a cinema in which you have to be aware of the camera's presence. It so happens that at the moment there are plenty of films where you are aware of the camera, and so there were in earlier days. But I don't believe that the distinction between modern and classical cinema can lie in that statement. I don't think that modern cinema is a "cinema" of poetry and that the old cinema was no more than a prose or narrative cinema. For me there is a modern form of the prose and "romance" cinema in which poetry is present although it was not directly intended. It comes as an extra without being expressly solicited.... It seems to me that that *Cahiers* on the one hand and the critics on the other tend to be too much concerned with cinema which makes one aware of the camera and the *auteur*— which doesn't make it the *only* kind of *auteur* cinema there is — at the expense of another kind of cinema, the narrative cinema, which is immediately regarded as classical [Rohmer 1986: 85].

Rohmer's words refer specifically to film, but they reflect a wider position confirmed in *Triple Agent*. In this film, in an analogous way to his polemic against Pasolini, Rohmer compares "poetic" with "narrative" painting, arguing that there should be a place for both in the history of art and people's homes. Poetic painting in this film is represented predominantly by Picasso, although the names of other modernist artists, such as Juan Gris, are also mentioned by the characters. Picasso's paintings make the viewer aware that s/he is viewing a picture (and this impression was even stronger in the 1930s, when Rohmer's film is set) due to their distortions of the represented objects or the difference between the prevailing representations of such objects. As a consequence, a viewer of Picasso's work is conscious of the painter and the tools he uses, just as the viewer of a self-reflexive film is aware of the director and the camera. Moreover, in Picasso's pictures the literal background of the painted object is rendered unimportant; the artist attempts to capture the "essence" of represented reality in a small number of strokes or lines at the expense of showing details. Part of Picasso's art is also political in an obvious way, conveyed most famously in *Guernica*, produced during the period when *Triple Agent* is set. Not surprisingly, Arsinoé's neighbors, who are communists and supporters of the National Front, love Picasso and even have one of his (unsigned) graphics in their apartment. They believe that there is a natural link between "progressive" art and "progressive" politics, both of which they advocate. Arsinoé, by contrast, feels somewhat taken aback by Picasso's abstractions and is embarrassed by the idea of the artist being so closely involved in politics. However, she does not deny Picasso's works have artistic value, only admits that she does not understand them. Voronin, on the other hand, calls Picasso and his ilk "awful" and makes no attempt to understand them. His philistinism brings to memory Stalin, who rejected high modernism and any type of art which he was unable to understand, showing his preference for traditional, "prosaic" art, but at the same time contrasts with the avant-garde art that flourished immediately after the victory of the Bolshevik Revolution and that was associated most strongly with the films of Dziga Vertov and Sergei Einsenstein.

Unlike in Picasso's art, in Arsinoé's paintings the author is effaced and the represented reality takes central stage. As all her viewers note, there is a striking similarity between her paintings and reality. She captures the faces of people, such as Dani, the daughter of their neighbors, and places she observes during her walks in Paris and in the countryside. Arsinoé's pictures, as she herself puts it, present "people in their natural settings," which is also, as Ginette Vincendeau observes, a perfect description of Rohmer's own films (Vincendeau 2004: 39). Although Arsinoé is a realist for whom faithfulness to observed reality is of paramount concern, she does not simply copy what she sees, but "thickens" her canvasses by capturing in one scene people she encountered in different locations and adding a story to them. For example, after painting Dani's portrait, she includes the child in a number of paintings she describes as "genre painting," (for example, one presenting people visiting a Paris market). Arsinoé attempts to preserve their ordinariness but at the same time tries to make them look interesting. When we look at her paintings for the first time, they appear old-fashioned. However, the longer we look, the more charming and extraordinary they become. It is certainly true of portraits of Dani; thanks to looking at them we realize how serious, pensive and beautiful she is. If it were not for the portrait, most likely we would overlook the girl. Another function of Arsinoé's art is to immortalize the physical and social environment of people: buildings, ways of going shopping, bathing costumes. Rohmer suggests that without the work of people like Arsinoé we would not be able to reconstruct the past. Again, the reconstruction of the past, as well as capturing the present, can be seen as Rohmer's specific concern. The director chooses to film Arsinoé's paintings as if he was offering them to a leisurely admirer rather than a rushing tourist. Again, such an approach can be seen as paralleling the way he wants us to see his own works: with attention and patience. Importantly for my study, this is also an attitude Nabokov expects from his readers, as conveyed most famously in his "Good Readers and Good Writers" (LL: 1–6).

In my opinion, Rohmer includes characters of such varied attitudes to art to reiterate his point that producing art of high quality does not depend on appropriating a specific political position or a specific attitude to represented reality. Realism for him can be both classical and modern, and realize the synthesis between the good, the beautiful and the true.

The form of *Triple Agent* in a sense parallels that of "The Assistant Producer." In common with Nabokov's work, it is divided into two intertwined strands: "artistic" and "journalistic." The first strand consists of the action proper — namely, representation of the domestic life of Fiodor and Arsinoé, and their relationship with their neighbors and friends. The second strand is made up of fragments of old newsreels from the times concurrent with the Miller-Skoblin affair. They include information about, for example, the victory of the National Front and the World's Fair in Paris. Like Nabokov's musings about the fate of various White Army generals who disappeared in Paris, their function is to provide a wider political and cultural context to the story of Arsinoé and her husband. In particular, they demonstrate the existence of a close link between "grand politics" and the lives of ordinary people, at least at the momentous period preceding the Second World War. The fact that in Rohmer's work we find this type of "extraneous" material, (which fragments the main narrative and draws attention to the fact that it is not a "slice of life" but its representation) might suggest that he is less of a realist than he likes to present himself. However, as Derek Schilling observes, the anti-realistic device was a consequence of Rohmer's failure to integrate archival and fictional materials in the way he did in his earlier *The Lady and the Duke*:

> The actors, he surmised, could be filmed on a sound stage and then be digitally embedded in decors selected from stock film footage of the 1930s and 40s. The *Zelig*-like idea was jettisoned for want of shots of sufficient length and proper composition. As it stands, *Triple Agent* pushes the viewer imaginatively to breach the gap between the two filmic registers and to recognize the newsreel images as belonging simultaneously to a collective historical past and to the fictional present in which the characters dwell [Schilling 2007: 183–84].

Another similarity between the form of *Triple Agent* and "The Assistant Producer" is containing a coda. In Rohmer's film two White Russians discuss the ultimate fate of the characters. We learn from their talk that the wife of the triple agent died in prison during the Second World War and that *his* fate remains unknown. Metaphorically speaking, in both works the spy lurks in the shadow. Such codas are not uncommon features in Nabokov's prose, and they point to the fact that the writer wants to have the "last word" in his books. In Rohmer's works such a device is unusual, and in my opinion, in *Triple Agent* it plays a different function than in "The Assistant Producer." It reveals the author's helplessness in relation to history; he can recreate it, and express his solidarity with its victims, but he cannot change the past or even learn more than the basic facts (in this case, that Arsinoé died). Tamara Tracz compares the men talking about the war's events to the choruses of Greek Tragedies, who describe and lament the deaths of heroes. In light of that, it is fitting that Arsinoé is Greek (Tracz 2005). It is not only the ending but the whole film which bears resemblance to that type of play, due to its serious, somber tone and the sense that the historical "actors" are powerless in relation to historical forces.

Simultaneously, Rohmer's film evokes Hitchcock's cinema. The situation in which Arsinoé finds herself, as Derek Schilling observes,

> recalls Hitchcock's *Suspicion* (1941), in which the timid Lina (Jean Fontaine) elopes with playboy Johnny Aysgarth (Cary Grant) without doing the requisite background check. Upon returning from their honeymoon, Lina discovers that her husband has never held down a job and is a gambler and thief to boot. Put on her guard by third parties, she begins to suspect her husband, who is an avid reader of detective stories, of plotting to murder his friend and business partner Beaky, and to do her as well. By adopting Lina's perspective throughout, Hitchcock leaves Johnny's presumptive guilt open to question [Schilling 2007: 185].

However, in comparison with this or other films by Hitchcock, and even with Rohmer's earlier films, *Triple Agent* feels static and devoid of action. It is a spy film without car chases or even spying, and the entire "action" transpires off-screen. Consequently, as many reviewers noted, it is the antithesis of the spy genre (for example, Elley 2004; Jeffries 2004; Tracz 2005). However, by not showing how the spy operates, Rohmer also makes a perfect film about spies. If they are to be effective, they must keep their double or triple lives separate from each other. Moreover, Rohmer staunchly adopts the perspective of a wife who is kept in the dark about her husband's affairs. This mode of narrating allows Rohmer to present the story of Arsinoé and Voronin as a moral tale, bearing particular resemblance to *My Night with Maud*. Moral dilemmas and choices do not reveal themselves in situations of frantic action. In action films moral problems are bracketed off, so to speak, and regarded as irrelevant. Only when characters discuss their moral positions and we have a chance to compare them with their actions are we able to see the moral dimensions of their deeds. In "The Assistant Producer" the moral aspect of the characters' acts is presented as largely unimportant because Nabokov holds them in too much contempt to give them the privilege of suffering moral dilemmas.

As previously mentioned, *Triple Agent* is not an adaptation of "The Assistant Producer," and I would prefer that Rohmer did not know Nabokov's story. Comparing them as independent re-workings of the same event is an excellent tool for revealing specificities of the two artists' attitude toward life and art. Such comparison points to Nabokov's misogyny, prejudice against popular art, willingness to engage in self-reflexive games and a preoccupation with situations in real life when life is thwarted by its representation — simulacra triumphs over original. Rohmer's *Triple Agent*, by comparison, is a testimony to the director's deep sympathy for and identification with women, his conviction that realistic art is not inferior to any form of anti-realism, and his unwillingness to see the world as a "hall of mirrors" in which reflections appear more real or beautiful than the original. The fact that both artists embarked on screening the story of Plevitskaya and Skoblin demonstrates a common negative attitude toward fascism and communism and the conviction that essentially these two systems were similar because they ultimately produced the same results: widespread misery and moral corruption. Although this conviction is nowadays widely held, it would be difficult to find another story which illustrates it so perfectly.

# 9

# Vladimir Nabokov and Jean-Luc Godard

> We shall do our best to avoid the fatal error of looking for so-called "real life" in novels. Let us not try and reconcile the fiction of facts with the facts of fiction. *Don Quixote* is a fairy tale, so is *Bleak House*, so is *Dead Souls*. *Madame Bovary* and *Anna Karenin* are supreme fairy tales. But without these fairy tales the world would not be real.—Vladimir Nabokov, *Lectures on Don Quixote*

> I like to see things for the first time. Just as ordinary people like to see a world record broken because it's for the first time; the second time they're less interested. Pictures are made to make seen the unseen.—Jean-Luc Godard in a conversation with Jonathan Cott

So far I have compared Nabokov's individual books with individual films by various directors. In the last chapter of my book I will present the results of my hunt for a film director whose life and works resemble Nabokov's. I am not the first person who searched for a cinematic double of Nabokov. A number of authors did it before me, reaching a conclusion that the closest to Nabokov's double is Alfred Hitchcock (Stringer-Hye 2002; Davidson 2007; Straumann 2008). I have no intention to undermine this claim. Indeed, there are many connections between these two authors, such as similar dates of birth and death (1899–1977 in the case of Nabokov, 1899–1980 in the case of Hitchcock), shared interest in a figure of exile, or a penchant for doubles and cameo appearances. If we take into account Nabokov in the last decade or so of his life, when he put on weight and his face gained an expression of arrogance or mischief, then we can also see some physical resemblance between these two men, excellently captured in a collage of their photographs accompanying James Davidson's essay (Davidson 2007). Nabokov himself acknowledges his resemblance to Hitchcock, writing that at the gala premiere of Kubrick's *Lolita*, he was "as eager and innocent as the fans who peered into my car hoping to glimpse James Mason but finding only the placid profile of a stand-in for Hitchcock" (LoS: xii).

However, rather than repeating the well-worn arguments, I wish to draw here a less explored and obvious parallel — that between Nabokov and Jean-Luc Godard.[1] My comparison will cut across many aspects of these artists' lives and work: from their biographies and the contents and forms of their works, to their *Weltanschauung*, as conveyed in their fiction work and discursive prose, such as interviews, answers to questions from the public, reviews and lectures. I am comparing Nabokov to Godard with full awareness that the former might find it demeaning to be linked to somebody of strongly left-wing persuasion and a penchant for unpolished, sketchy work. Also Nabokov might reject my comparison on account on his dislike of literary studies or, indeed, any type of studies based on comparisons. It is worth quoting in this context his words: "Lenin's life differs from, say, James Joyce's as much as a handful of gravel does from a blue diamond, although both men were exiles in Switzerland and both wrote a vast number of words" (SO: 118–19). For me, however, brought up on the Foucaldian concept of "discourse," there is nothing outrageous in comparing Joyce's life with that of Lenin. On the contrary, I believe that such comparisons allow us to make precious discoveries. As I will argue in due course, the idea of bringing together and opening to comparison distant objects was, in fact, not at all alien to Nabokov.

## *Biographies*

Nabokov and Godard are one generation apart. The former was born in 1899, the latter in 1930. This difference affected the relationship between these two artists. From his youth Godard knew about Nabokov and referred to his works; Nabokov most likely never watched any of Godard's films. However, thanks to being born thirty years after Nabokov (and Hitchcock), Godard's experience of cinema was analogous to Nabokov's relationship to literature. In his youth Nabokov had an opportunity to learn about different types of literary modernisms (Foster 2005). As a young critic, and then filmmaker, Godard experienced cinema's maturity; he was situated, as Serge Daney puts it, "in midcinema — neither too early nor too late" (Daney 1992: 159), which allowed him to develop a sense of cinema's history. This is something which Hitchcock, who was born at the same time as Nabokov and almost at the same time as the cinematograph, had no chance to achieve in his youth.

Nabokov and Godard came from affluent families with a distinctive ethos — Nabokov from the Russian liberal and well-educated aristocracy,

Godard from Swiss and French Protestant bourgeoisie. Both families had literary connections. Nabokov's great grandmother was a friend of Heinrich von Kleist (SM: 44); Godard's ancestors from his mother's side were friends of Paul Valéry and André Gide (MacCabe 2003: 7–8). Both artists were especially close to their mothers, who had artistic interests, and remember their grandparents as awesome, almost mythical figures (SO: 28–41; MacCabe 2003: 24). Nabokov was one of five children, Godard one of four. Their large families spent their summer holidays on country estates belonging to their relatives, in Vyra near Petersburg and in Anthy on Lake Geneva in Switzerland, respectively. They also prided themselves on being good at sports, having special interests in tennis and soccer, where both played as goalkeepers (SO: 198; MacCabe 2003: 23). Both remember their childhood as a place of utter happiness, which they had to leave promptly. Nabokov was brutally expelled by the Bolsheviks; Godard blames his departure on the blemishes in his own character, which led to his drifting and petty crime, and drove a wedge between him and his family. Another factor in Godard losing his childhood paradise was the divorce of his parents and his mother's sudden death (MacCabe 2003: 41).

Nabokov confesses that "nothing short of a replica of my childhood surroundings would have satisfied me" (SO: 27). Godard talks about his childhood in similar terms:

> Now I can look on it as paradise. I was very healthy and even if my own family was not that rich, we had access to all the resources or the wealth of my mother's family, as did all the grandchildren. It was one of those huge Protestant families that behave like a tribe with their own ritual, their own ceremonies.... You were protected. It was like a Greek legend, my grandfather and grandmother were gods, my parents were demi-gods and we children were humans [Godard, quoted in MacCabe 2003: 18].

Nabokov sets many of his stories in places he knew in his past and furnishes his characters with his own childhood experiences. The connection between Godard's childhood and his films is less obvious. However, from the late 1970s, when Godard relocated to Switzerland, the landscapes of his childhood feature extensively in his films. Deserving special attention in this context is *Nouvelle Vague* (1990), set on a country estate of the kind his grandparents owned. *For Ever Mozart* (1996) was, in fact, shot on this estate, now completely deserted and desolated. Taken together, these films simultaneously testify to the presence and absence of childhood in Godard's adult life.

Childhood experiences provided these authors with a metaphorical capital which they were able to use throughout their entire careers. One aspect of this is a sense of individualism: following one's own interests and values rather than being a member of a horde. The affluence experienced early in life also led Nabokov and Godard to neglect the material side of their existence, not even caring about having their own home. Nabokov, when asked why he did not own a house in America, despite spending twenty years there, responded, "I don't much care for furniture, for tables and chairs and lamps and rugs and things — perhaps because in my opulent childhood I was taught to regard with amused contempt any too-earnest attachment to material wealth, which is why I felt no regret and no bitterness when the Revolution abolished the wealth" (SO: 27–8). Godard confessed, "When I was young I was part of a huge, rich family, with a lot of cousins and uncles. I had so much in my youth that today I think it's justice that I have less" (Smith 1998: 183). On another occasion, when comparing himself to the fellow creator of the French New Wave, François Truffaut, Godard said, "I came from a very rich family; he came from a very poor family. To have a success was very important for him and I didn't need that.... For me, the way to succeed was to be unsuccessful, but to make a living on that" (Rosenbaum 1998: 55). Both artists also needed the capital of their happy past to sustain them through many difficult years marked by instability and a lack of success. These years they survived in " good style," never coming across as victims, never asking for sympathy or pity. Michael Wood gives as an example of this by describing Nabokov's reaction to his father's death:

> The night his father was assassinated in Berlin in 1922 Nabokov remembers as "something *outside life*, monstrously slow, like those mathematical puzzles that torment us in feverish half-sleep." This is an entry in a diary, not meant for publication. The torment must have been terrible, must have remained terrible, but this private language already holds it at bay, subordinates it to an imagery of distance and unreality. Nabokov's "coldness" in novels and interviews is among other things a continuing act of courage, a refusal to be bullied by the rages and accidents of history, or by the possible pity of others [Wood 1994: 17].

Equally, one gets a sense that in Godard there is also no gap between the private and public persona. No external calamity appears to impact on the director's frequency or quality of work. Moreover, the reader of his biographies and public prose learns that one cannot be really close to Godard, not because he likes to keep his distance from intruders, but because the "real Godard" is in his works, not outside them.

Another connection between the biographies of Nabokov and Godard concerns their final destination, so to speak. Since the mid–1970s, Godard has lived in Rolle, Switzerland, on the northwestern shore of Lake Geneva, which is not far from Montreux on its northeast shore, where Nabokov and his wife spent their final years. For a short time the writer and the director were thus almost neighbors. The relocation to this part of Europe, from the United States in the case of Nabokov and Paris in the case of Godard (via Grenoble, where the director lived for some time in the 1970s), had a similar effect on their work and outlook on the world. During this period Nabokov lived on the top floor of the Montreux Palace Hotel and enjoyed the exclusive company of guests carefully monitored for their political views. The books he wrote during this period, especially *Ada*, convey his desire to detach himself from the world outside his direct proximity and create his own chronotope (Norman 2009).[2] His relocation to Switzerland can be viewed as almost reaching, figuratively and truly, his ideal of living "in the much abused ivory tower" (LL: 370).

The "Swiss Godard" also lives the detached life of "a wise old man" (Smith 2007) and although he still travels with a frequency unusual for men of his age, his social life is more stable and limited than in the past. Unlike Nabokov, Godard never projected himself as a man from an ivory tower. On the contrary, his ideal was working in a cooperative, and, as much as possible, engage with political and social issues. During his Rolle period, however, the reality and ideal started to diverge. The beginning of his life in Switzerland coincides with the so called "cosmic period" of his career (Cerisuelo 1989: 207–31). Indeed, although in films such as *Passion* (1981) and *Prénom Carmen* (1983) the director still reveals interest in the nature of capitalism and the struggles of the working classes, which preoccupied him previously, he puts less emphasis on their contemporary context and intertwines them with a meditation on metaphysical questions.

To conclude this part, Nabokov's and Godard's lives and careers reveal a large degree of semblance, with a paradise buzzing with life at the beginning, frequent changing of locations in the middle part, and a kind of quiet paradise regained in the final chapter.

## *Structures, Characters, Stories*

As I argued in the previous chapters, Nabokov is an excellent storyteller. Brian Boyd observes, "For all his compulsive originality, he relies on the salient events of story that arise out of the biological necessities of reproduction and survival: love or death, or both: intense, consuming, sometimes perverse passion; and murder, suicide, execution, assassination, violent death by fire, water, or air (Boyd 2005: 33). Godard attracted similar opinions. Despite his ostentatious disrespect for tradition and penchant for formal experiments, the director also relies on plots, and in constructing his narratives he uses the same ingredients as Nabokov. The narratives of these two authors also reveal structural similarities, being full of significant details and clues which become visible only on repeated readings and viewings. Often within one story we find another one, concealed behind the first. The characters who appear marginal at first contact turn out to be very important, as argued, for example, by Richard Rorty in his essay on the barber of Kasbeam in *Lolita* (Rorty 1989). By the same token, in Godard's *Scénario de Sauve qui peut (la vie)* a character openly claims that secondary characters are more important than those at the first plane of action. Even the simplest of Nabokov's stories turn out to be puzzles (at least in the eyes of some of his critics), and the same has been argued in relation to Godard's films. For example, Kristin Thompson maintains that even a movie such as *Sauve qui peut (la vie)* (1980), marking Godard's return to traditional filmmaking after a period of experimentation with video, is, in fact, a "parametric film": a work of a highly complex structure whose patterns are as important as its syuzhet (Thompson 1988: 247).

What is the purpose of using such complicated structures? One can identify two complementary answers to this question: "aesthetic" and "epistemological." The first explains them via the artists' pleasure in creating problems for the readers/viewers to solve (Gezari 1995; Blackwell 2009); the second by the way these authors see the world. According to this reading, Nabokov's and Godard's arts are fundamentally mimetic, but not in a sense of following a crude realism or naturalism, but thanks to capturing what is hidden from the "naked eye" (Thompson 1988; Blackwell 2009; Boyd 2009; de la Durantaye 2009). I shall return to these issues when discussing Nabokov's and Godard's aesthetic and epistemological views.

Let's now look at the characters and stories of these two authors in detail. While Nabokov, not knowing Godard's work, could not borrow from it, Godard's characters are frequently based on Nabokov's creations. We can observe it in Godard's full-length feature debut film, *À bout de souffle* (*Breathless*, 1960). The French director Jean-Pierre Melville, who plays in the film a writer named Parvulesco who is interviewed by Patricia, modeled himself on Nabokov. Melville reminisced on this role by saying, "I had seen Nabokov in a televised interview, and being, like him, subtle, pretentious, pedantic, a bit cynical, naive, etc., I based the character on him" (Melville, quoted in Nogueira 1971: 76). Two features of Melville's character link him most to the writer. One is an affinity to pun, revealed by short and clever responses, as exemplified by the answer to the question "What is your greatest ambition?": "To become immortal, and then die," (which, as Glenn Kenny observes, is worthy of Nabokov himself (Kenny 2007)). The second is Parvulesco's awareness, also revealed by writers and philosophers in many of Godard's subsequent films, that creators of high culture cannot afford to ignore popular culture, even if they treat it with contempt. A sign of this attitude is Parvulesco's very presence at a press conference attended by journalists from the popular press. His behavior suggests that he has no desire to discuss his books but, as Nabokov put it, "to construct in the presence of my audience the semblance of what I hope is a plausible and not altogether displeasing personality" (SO: 158). Godard also helps the viewers see Nabokov in Parvulesco by having the journalists ask the writers questions about a book which appears to be *Lolita*, being popular, scandalous, and yet high art.

While Parvulesco is similar to Nabokov, Patricia in *Breathless* resembles Nabokov's America seen through European eyes. She is superficial and pragmatic, yet fashionable and beautiful and very attractive to Europeans — in this case a small crook, Michel Poiccard, who wants to escape with her to Italy and start there a new life.

The motif of a couple's escape from a suffocating existence, present in a number of Nabokov's works but most strongly associated with *Lolita*, became a staple feature of Godard's early films. After *Breathless*, we encounter it in *Le*

Jean Seberg as Patricia, and Jean-Paul Belmondo as Michel in ***Breathless*** (1960), directed by Jean-Luc Godard.

*Mépris* (*Contempt*, 1963), *Bande à part* (1964) and *Pierrot le fou* (1965). The last of these three movies is also the first Godard film where the connections with *Lolita* were acknowledged by the director and the critics. Asked what was the source of this film, Godard answered:

> A *Lolita*-style novel whose rights I had bought two years earlier. The film was to have been made with Sylvie Vartan. She refused. Instead I made *Bande à part*. Then I tried to set the film up again with Anna Karina and Richard Burton. Burton, alas, had become too Hollywood. In the end the whole thing was changed by the casting of Anna and Belmondo. I thought about *You Only Live Once*; and instead of the *Lolita* or *La Chienne* kind of couple, I wanted to tell a story of the last romantic couple, the last descendants of *La Nouvelle Héloïse*, *Werther* and *Herrmann and Dorothea* [Godard, quoted in Milne and Narboni 1972: 25–16].

Although this comment testifies to the difference between the characters of Godard's film and the original *Lolita*, the narrative of *Pierrot le fou* contains many elements which are closer to Nabokov's book than Kubrick's adaptation was. Examples are the shabby hotels the couple visits, the hallucinatory character of some of the episodes, and the sense of the finality of their journey. Moreover, the male protagonist of the film, Pierrot-Ferdinand, not unlike Humbert, constantly reads books and quotes from them, exasperating Marianne, his companion and lover. He also initially compares Marianne to the women from Pierre-Auguste Renoir's paintings (although there is no physical similarity between them), and to the Marianne from the past (like Humbert compares Lolita to Annabel Lee, the heroine of Edgar Allan Poe, and to his own childhood love). The women whom Humbert and Pierrot-Ferdinand love are thus not really the ones who travel with them, but some kind of mental image they project on real women.

*Contempt* concerns an attempt to adapt Homer's *Odyssey*, which in part is a story of a man chasing nymphs, not unlike *Lolita*. The film production is depicted as a power game for the body and soul of a beautiful woman named Camille, a contemporary nymph (not least because she is played by Brigitte Bardot, a "supe-nymph" of Western cinema in the 1960)s. Equally, it is a power game between Europe and America, epitomized by Camille's French screenwriter husband, Paul, and the film's American producer, Prokosch, (Godard's Humbert and Quilty, respectively). Camille leaves Paul for the more self-confident and richer Prokosch, and eventually the couple die on the road. These duels between two men and two cultures are observed by the director named Lang (played by Fritz Lang), who, like Nabokov, is personally not interested in the "nymphs" and is detached from the earthly conflicts he directs. In addition, in common with Nabokov, he is an emigrant who fled to America from Nazi Germany and speaks several languages.

*Vivre sa vie* (1962) does not utilize the trope of the road, but, in common

## 9. Vladimir Nabokov and Jean-Luc Godard

**Brigitte Bardot as Camille, Jack Palance as Prokosch and Giorgia Moll as Francesca in *Contempt* (1963), directed by Jean-Luc Godard.**

with *Pierrot le fou* and *Contempt*, it shares a number of thematic similarities with *Lolita*. The name of the main character, Nana, can be compared to Lolita, as it also sounds somewhat childish (with the two repeated syllables). Godard's Nana is a young woman who, like Lolita, would like to be an actress but ends up as a captive woman — a prostitute and a slave to a succession of unscrupulous pimps. She is also a victim of a society that is indifferent to her plight, although this motif, as in *Lolita*, is subdued. Moreover, like Lolita, Nana attempts to resist her circumstances. Her watching of Dreyer's *La Passion de Jeanne d'Arc* (*The Passion of Joan of Arc*, 1928), which presents the suffering and resistance of a young woman to male oppression; the stories which she tells in the film and the conversation she strikes up with the philosopher Brice Parain testify to her desire to preserve her autonomy. Yet, other texts Godard quotes in his film, such as a fragment of "The Oval Portrait" (by Humbert's idol, Edgar Allan Poe), point to the idea that a woman has no chance to survive physically or morally when she is used by an artist. The film finishes when Nana's pimp sells her on to another pimp. This exchange parallels Lolita's passing between Humbert and Quilty, although its outcome is more tragic because Nana is killed during the exchange between her masters, while Lolita dies as a "semi-free" person — in childbirth.³ Through the use of self-referential techniques, such as beginning the film with an almost still portrait of Nana, Godard suggests that although his heroine physically dies, her portrait survives, as does the portrait of Lolita.

However, there is a crucial difference between the women from Godard's early films and Lolita: all of Godard's females are adult. In three later Godard films, *Sauve qui peut (la vie)*, *Détective* (*Detective*, 1984) and *Prénom Carmen*, the director refers to the relationship between an older man and a child. In *Sauve qui peut (la vie)*, where this motif is most developed, a film director named Paul Godard lusts after his own daughter, Cecile. In a widely quoted scene, Paul even asks another man if he, like Paul, ever wanted to "fuck his daughter up the ass." Yet, despite this shocking confession, Paul does not come across as a repulsive figure — as, in the eyes of contemporary readers, Humbert does — because, unlike Nabokov's character, Paul does not act on his desire. He avoids sex with his daughter, despite the fact that he is sometimes alone with her, including in a car, which serves Humbert as an important "vehicle" for fulfilling his unhealthy passion. Another reason why the viewer is more willing to forgive Paul is, as Peter Harcourt suggests, the painful sense of fragmentation of his life (Harcourt 1981/2). He lives in a hotel rather than in a proper house, is no longer with his long-term girlfriend, and has sex with prostitutes. Moreover, he has only intermittent contact with his ex-wife and his daughter; therefore, he has little chance to sustain a deeper, more spiritual bond with the girl and to see her as a full person rather than a collection of body parts. Paul yearns to have such a holistic relationship, as revealed by his pleading with his ex-wife and daughter to let him see them more often. Yet, only a short while after saying that, Paul dies, knocked down by a car. Such an ending brings to mind the death of the pedophile in Nabokov's *The Enchanter*, but is rendered more poignant by the fact that his wife and daughter witness the accident and ignore it. Paul's ex-wife even says to Cecile, "This does not concern us." Yet, the accompaniment of mournful music, and the camera showing Cecile in long shot while she walks away from the scene of her father's death, suggests otherwise: the father's death concerns the girl deeply.

According to Harcourt, the ultimate reason why Paul has incestuous inclinations towards Cecile is the nature of capitalism itself, which fractures communities, making wholesome and "organic" social relations, even with one's family, difficult (ibid.). A sign of this is the father and daughter's communication through material objects rather than through words or intimate gestures. During their meetings, Cecile asks her father whether he brought her a present, and he throws a tee-shirt at her, commenting how she would look in it. Needless to say, Harcourt's explanation why men become pedophiles, somewhat in the style of John Ray, Jr., would be mercilessly mocked by Nabokov; but some scholars, contrary to Nabokov's own reading of his book, bring into relief the relationship between Humbert and Lolita's behavior, and the social and economic environment in which they live (Brand 1987; Collins 2009).

Paul Godard is a film director and has the same surname as the director of *Sauve qui peut (la vie) otion*, with the first name borrowed from Jean-Luc's father. The implied similarity between the director and his protagonist might suggest that Godard himself reveals an unhealthy appetite for adolescent girls. Equally, it might be seen as a way of teasing the viewers who are all too willing to indulge in biographical interpretations of films, seeing reality in fiction. Without dismissing these interpretations, I propose to see such biographical hints as an indication of Godard's awareness that by including in his works images and stories of exploited girls and young women, he is complicit in their exploitation and providing immoral pleasure to the consumers of art. In this respect he differs from the author of *Lolita*, who refused to acknowledge, much less take responsibility for, any comfort he yielded through his book to child molesters or fans of pornography. He did so despite admitting that, after his book was published, he used to meet men who introduced themselves as Humbert's brotherly souls and assumed that he also belonged to their secret "club of nympholepts" (SO: 24). Of course, any possible guilt of a filmmaker in this respect is greater than that of a writer, because in order to construct fictitious characters the filmmaker must use bodies and the minds of real people; the writer, as Nabokov emphasized, might rely solely on his imagination. The difference, as I attempted to show in the first chapter of this book, is of crucial importance for making a film based on a work such as *Lolita*, perhaps making its faithful adaptation impossible.

The next Godard film with the motif of Lolita is *Detective*, where we see an elderly man who walks into a hotel with a girl no older than nine years, with long, blond hair and a long dress. This is the youngest "Lolita" we find in Godard's films, with the oldest "Humbert" accompanying her, and it takes the viewer some time to realize that there is an erotic relationship between them. Although the girl is only beginning to become a nymphet, her guardian, a mafia boss nicknamed Prince with intellectual pretensions and a disdain for contemporary French culture (paralleling Humbert's contempt for trashy American culture), is already worried that she will soon grow up and become a vicious and demanding woman. Touching her silky hair, he says, "This is the hair of a future witch." The setting in a large and anonymous hotel brings to mind the key episode in *Lolita*, set in the Enchanted Hunters.

The physical appearance of the girl in *Detective* likens her to a girl from Diego Velázquez's opus magnum *Las Meninas* (1656). Although in Nabokov's masterpiece we do not find reference to Velázquez, Godard's idea of styling his nymphet on its earlier artistic image constitutes an analogy to *Lolita* because Humbert also sees in Lolita the incarnation of an eternal nymphet, as captured by artists and poets of the earlier generations, especially Edgar Allan Poe. Moreover, Velázquez bears resemblance to Nabokov and Poe because of his preoccupation with light and shadow, especially the change in objects when they are moved from light to shadow. The issue of light and shadow, as I will argue in due course, also constitutes an important motif in Godard's own work. By evoking Velázquez, Godard also refers to his earlier film *Pierrot le fou*, in which the double-named protagonist, Pierrot-Ferdinand, lying in a bath, reads to his young daughter fragments of *Histoire de l'art*, devoted to the use of light and shadow in Velázquez's paintings. Those who remember this film might see in a girl accompanying the aged mafioso in *Detective* Ferdinand's small daughter, captured by the gangsters as punishment for her father's numerous transgressions.

Finally, in *Prénom Carmen* Godard includes two characters who we can regard as the analogues of Humbert and Lolita, or even Quilty and Lolita, but ten or so years later: Carmen and her film director uncle, named Jean-Luc and played by Godard himself. It should be mentioned that *Carmen* is evoked in Nabokov's novel too: Humbert frequently calls Lolita "Carmen" or "Carmencita" (for example, Lo: 273). Carmen in *Prénom Carmen* claims that she was Jean-Luc's favorite niece and they used to have sex when she was a child or a teenage girl. However, she does not appear traumatized by this occurrence nor bear any grudge against her uncle. She only wants him to allow her to use his apartment (where subsequently she has sex with another man) and help her in a bank robbery, all for old times sake. Her uncle agrees to her request, not out of guilt or because of his continuing infatuation with Carmen, but most likely to get rid of her and be left in peace. In terms of the narrative, *Prénom Carmen* can thus be regarded as an updated version of the last part of Nabokov's *Lolita*. It pertains to the times when the victims of child abuse demand financial compensation from their perpetrators, rather than contenting themselves merely with escaping the clutches of their predatory lovers.[4] Visually, however, *Prénom Carmen* testifies to uncle Jean-Luc's (and the director's) continuing fascination with the young woman. As one reviewer observed, "One is on occasion made disturbingly aware of the director's almost lascivious thralldom to his actress' naked body and its most basic functions. Has Godard, one even finds oneself wondering, turned into a dirty old man?" (Adair 1984: 31). This hypothesis cannot be excluded, but what is more interesting from my perspective is, again, Godard's provocative claim that in cinema one cannot discuss "dirty sex" without becoming dirty oneself.

In this part I also want to mention Godard's *Passion* because this film can be seen as an adaptation of an early part of Nabokov's *Laughter in the Dark*, concerning Albinus' desire to animate some paintings by old masters, as conveyed in this passage:

> How fascinating it would be, he thought, if one could use this method for having some well-known picture, preferably of the Dutch School, perfectly reproduced on the screen in vivid colors and brought to life — movement and gesture graphically developed in complete harmony with their static state in the picture, say, a pot-house with little people drinking lustily at wooden tables and a sunny glimpse of a courtyard with saddled horses — all suddenly coming to life.... And the designer would not only have to possess a thorough knowledge of the given painter and his period, but be blessed with talent enough to avoid any clash between the movements produced and those fixed by the Old Master [Laugh: 5–6].

To realize this dream Albinus invites to Berlin Axel Rex, a professional cartoonist living abroad, but in due course he gives up on this plan, becoming more interested in Margot, who introduces more motion into his life than any living pictures might do and better encapsulates for him the idea of eternal beauty. In *Passion*, a foreign artist, a director from Poland named Jerzy, arrives in Switzerland to make a film consisting of *tableaux vivants* based on the masterpieces of European art. Like Axel Rex, Jerzy is a callous man who will sacrifice everything and everybody to realize his artistic experiments. We see him having affairs with a succession of women (while having a wife in Poland) and making actors and extras wait for long hours until he makes up his mind how to use them. In common with the film planned by Albinus, Jerzy's *Passion* also remains uncompleted, most likely because its producer ultimately chooses a film with a story and drama over one which is merely a succession of *tableaux vivants*. Both works thus point to the victory of art with stories and popular appeal over those which are purely aesthetic and elitist.

## *Approaches to Language*

Nabokov and Godard can also be linked because of their interest in and attitude toward language. Elizabeth Klosty Beaujour describes the former as "one of the most distinctive twentieth-century examples of a category once widespread and now almost extinct: the bilingual, or in Nabokov's case, the trilingual, writer" (Beaujour 1995: 37). She further observes:

> Bilingual or polyglot writers have more in common with each other, whatever their national origins, than they do with monolinguals who write in any one of their

languages.... Bilingualism confers advantages for cognitive tasks involving metalinguistic awareness, separating word sound and meaning, and generating synonyms and original uses. Sensitivity to the pleasures of redundancy and play is fostered by bilinguals" awareness of the inherent separability of sign and referent, an awareness which Nabokov developed into a mastery of the potential for defamiliarization provided by even slight variations in vocabulary and levels of language.... Bilinguals are less inclined to rely on rigid and unvarying processing strategies and are particularly good at seeking out patterns. They also demonstrate a hightened sense of the "relativity of things" and greater than usual tolerance for certain kinds of ambiguity [ibid.: 37].

Nabokov's talent to express himself perfectly in three languages he learnt in his childhood, and at the same time to mould the existing languages into his own, idiosyncratic language, is a subject of many studies, and I do not wish to repeat the arguments presented in them (for example Grayson 1977; Wood 1994; Beaujour 1995). What is more interesting for me here is that Godard shares with him this characteristic. In common with the author of *Lolita*, Godard can be described as a polyglot. He made films in a number of different languages, including French and English, which was often spoken at home by his parents. Moreover, as with Nabokov, he is "at home" in any language he uses – his *British Sounds* (1969) and *King Lear* (1987), shot in English, appear no more foreign than *Pierrot le fou* or *Sauve qui peut (la vie)*. Irrespective of who produces his films, typically we hear more than one language. French and English prevail, but there are also traces of Russian, Italian, Czech, Polish and German. Godard, like Nabokov, is also interested in different styles of talking and modes of address. Alan Williams identifies reading aloud, composing aloud for transcription, interviewing, giving a prepared speech or lecture, free association and translation (Williams 1982: 193). One reason to include these different forms of verbal communication is to show that there are different languages even within one ethnic language, of which polyglots are more aware than those who do not know any foreign language.

Godard's films are also full of reproduced or simulated texts: citations of literary and historical works, paintings, and words and fragments of words taken out of context and furnished with a new meaning. An early example is the singling out of the letters "SS" from the sign "Esso" in *Pierrot le fou*. Such action might suggest that the oil companies (or all capitalist companies) are the new fascists trying to subjugate ordinary people to their political program and, as did the original fascists, conceal their real intentions. The play with words offered in *Pierrot le fou* has been compared to the Situationists' *détournement*, which consisted of using a fragment of a dominant culture in a way opposing the assumptions and purposes of this culture (Williams 2000: 54–6). In his subsequent films, however, Godard went further that the Situationists, who, while criticizing the dominant culture, nevertheless acknowledged its hegemonic status. He, on the other hand, due to the extremity of his linguistic games — his willingness and preparedness to sever virtually every word from its natural context, cutting it into pieces and leaving the fragments for the viewer to deal with — confuses the viewer/reader about what is the linguistic norm and what is an aberration. Godard's ideal seems not to be a new and better language, but a never ending destruction/construction of language: language in a state of flux.

Although Nabokov and Godard do similar things with words, cutting and reassembling them, and seeking unexpected connections, their linguistic games are informed by different ideologies. When discussing Nabokov's attitude toward English, Klosty Beaujour uses the contrasting terms "verbal adventure" and "linguistic violence." She argues that in his first American novel, *Bend Sinister*, "mixing of languages, code-switching, and hybridization of tongues are negatively marked, and paronomasia, cross-linguistic puns, neologisms, and spoonerisms are linguistic practices associated with a vile totalitarian country whose language Nabokov describes as a 'mongrel blend of Slavic and Germanic with a strong strain of ancient Kuranian running through it'" (Beaujour 1995: 40). In Nabokov's later novels, and especially *Ada*, these linguistic practices have positive connotations:

> *Ada* displays the complexity of the ways in which cultivated polyglots can communicate with each other using the full resources of several languages. Many of the novel's riches and much of its humor are hidden from the monolingual reader, who does not have access to the personal polyglot idiolect, sometimes referred to as "Nabokese," which overarches or underlies the three other languages at the author's command, and which is the outgrowth of the interplay between them [ibid.: 41].

In *Ada*, the inventors and users of the linguistic games construct their own reality as infinitely richer and subtler than the world accessible only to those who use one language, and their use of private and semi-private languages undermines the power of public language and culture articulated through and supported by this language.

Godard's approach to language is more democratic than Nabokov's. He invites to his linguistic games not only sophisticated polyglots, but also those who do not understand or understand them only partially. Such partial access to language is in his view a stimulus to linguistic creativity. We see it in *Le Gai savoir* (1968), whose "action" is limited to two characters studying words, images and their connections. Yet, soon they — and we, the viewers — discover that the greatest pleasure consists of enjoying the accidental connections of freed signifiers.

Inevitably, taking into account Nabokov's and Godard's affinity for linguistic games, the issue of translation is prominent in their works. Both are keen to explore not only what is lost, but also what is gained by transferring meanings from one language to another. For example, Nabokov in a conversation with Penelope Gilliatt, among the diatribes directed at Russian writers of the Soviet era, especially Boris Pasternak, says that "Pasternak himself has been very much *helped* by translation. Sometimes when you translate a *cliché*— you know, a cloud has a silver lining — it can sound like Milton because it is in another language" (Gilliatt 1980b: 246). In the same interview Nabokov mentions minor French poets and Racine, who in the translation into Russian by Pushkin became "breathtaking" (ibid.: 247). Godard, to an even greater extent, revels in the opportunities resulting from inexact, imperfect or even bad translation. Onscreen it is put most clearly by Jerzy in *Passion*, who says to his German lover Hanna when she complains that she does not understand him: "If you do not understand something, take advantage of that." The advantage consists of the possibility of creating something new: valuable expressions and meanings rising from the ruins of those which became exhausted. To an extent, this advantage is explored in *Le Gai savoir*. Offscreen, Godard once famously said, "American people like to say, 'What do you mean exactly?' I would answer: 'I mean, but not exactly'" (Godard, quoted in Smith 1996: 186). The not-exact-meaning produced during translation is, in his view, an important (perhaps *the* most important) condition of creativity, both for the artist and for the consumer of art.

The sign of Nabokov's and Godard's belief in the creative potential of translation is their propensity to create inexact copies through imitation or translation. Nabokov translated his Russian poetry and prose into English, and his English works into Russian. The clearest sign of the transformations of the respective versions are their different titles. His Russian novel *Kamera obskura* in English became *Laughter in the Dark*; *Conclusive Evidence* on the way from English to Russian changed into *Drugie berega*, and retranslated into English into *Speak, Memory*. If we stretch the idea of creating a new version of old works further, we can even regard *Look at the Harlequins!* as a new, abbreviated version of Nabokov's biography combined with motifs from all the novels he wrote during his lifetime. Similar transformations can be detected in the translations of the works of other authors: *Alice in Wonderland* became *Ania v strane chudes*, while *Colas Breugnon* became *Nikolka Persik*. In relation to the first book Julian Connolly wrote that "while Nabokov's work can loosely be called a 'translation' (*perevod*), it should perhaps be more properly called an 'adaptation' or 'transposition' (*perelozhenie*)" (Connolly 1995: 19). For Nabokov, such distinctions became of crucial importance during his work on the translation into English of Pushkin's *Evgeny Onegin*, which he completed in 1964. During this period, as I mentioned in my introduction, he created his theory of "literal translation" as "producing with absolute exactitude the whole text, and nothing but the text" (OIE: 134).

Godard has also produced what can be regarded as multiple versions of his original works. From the 1970s, he even began making, along with the proper films, "scenarios" to these films — for example, *Scénario de Sauve qui peut (la vie)* (1979) or *Scénario du film Passion* (1982); the first being shot before the feature film as a sort of audiovisual scenario, and the latter afterwards (as a metacritical reflection). They can thus be compared to Nabokov's forewords and commentaries to his works. Godard, to an even greater extent than Nabokov, also acts as an adapter of the works of other artists. The 1980s, beginning with *Passion*, (the narrative of which revolves around recreating the works of old masters) and continuing, through *Prénom Carmen, Je vous salue Marie* (*Hail Mary*, 1983), *Detective* (1984), *Soigne ta droite* (*Keep Your Right Up*, 1987) and *King Lear* (1987), can be described as his period of adaptation. This reliance on works already created prompted Harun Farocki to say that for Jerzy, who in *Passion* acts as Godard's alter ego, "art means creating texts which are in a dialogue with earlier texts" (Silverman and Farocki 1998: 171). This does not preclude creating new works but points to the fact that an artist like Godard (with his experience, knowledge and living in the postmodern times) carries too heavy a burden of intertextuality to attempt to discard it or pretend that it does not exist. Yet, one cannot imagine Godard advocating "literal translation" or believing in such a possibility. For him, even repeating the same words in the same language amounts to creating something new. Hence, in their approach to translation, the Nabokov of his *Onegin* period and Godard are poles apart. In my opinion, however, one author's obsessive search for fidelity to an original text and the other's blank skepticism about the possibility of resurrecting the original in a different language or medium testify to their shared concern about the status of a work of art as being always at risk of escaping its creator and mutating into something unexpected.

The use of many ethnic languages and styles of speaking without pronouncing an unconditional loyalty to any of them, as conveyed by Nabokov's saying, "My head says English, my heart, Russian, my ear, French" (SO: 49), begs the question of what happens in the minds of these artists before their content is communicated in a verbal language. Elizabeth Klosty Beaujour, drawing on Nabokov's statement, published in *Strong Opinions*, claims that

> Nabokov's polyglottism functioned in symbiosis with other, essentially non-linguistic, systems of cognition. For example, he has claimed, as bilinguals frequently do, that although he writes in several languages, he does not think in any of them but rather in *images*. His conviction that he thinks in images and that "now and then a Russian

or English phrase will form with the foam of the brainwave" correlates with studies which suggest that bilinguals process even *language* input at some common semantic level "below" or "beyond" the language specific [Beaujour 1995: 42].

Godard never claimed that he thinks in images, as opposed to words, but as I will argue in the later part of this chapter, for him thinking does not consist of formulating verbal statements, but connecting "mental units," which can be words, ideas, images or fragments of music — everything which can appear in the human mind (see, for example, Smith 1996). Only after making this connection can one verbalize it or convey it in a different way (for example, by making a picture or a graph). The director frequently expresses an ambition to dispense with words altogether by creating visual "scenarios," or even the whole language, which would combine discursive and non-discursive elements. For example, in *Scénario de Sauve qui peut (la vie)* he says that he would like to write "horizontally and vertically," and write in a similar way to that of Japanese people. Godard is also renowned for having only vague ideas of what he wants to do in his films prior to shooting them; they crystallize when he starts to "see" his films.

Nabokov scholars are divided about whether he uses language to mirror and comment on the world (real world and "otherworld"), or as a way to create a different reality. In light of the versatility of his works and styles applied in them, I propose that Nabokov uses language for all these purposes; he is both a realist and a constructivist, and a master in both capacities. In a similar vein, Alan Williams identifies two approaches towards language in Godard's films, which he names Bazinian and Eisenstenian (Williams 1982). As both a realist and a constructivist, Godard has no equals in his generation, or perhaps in the whole century or so of cinema's existence. Both Nabokov and Godard are widely praised for being among the greatest masters of language in the twentieth century. Both are also sometimes loathed for being among its greatest manipulators.

## *Approaches to History and Theory of One's Discipline*

Nabokov and Godard are linked also by their interest in the history and theory of their respective disciplines. Such interest is not unique among writers and filmmakers, especially those active after the Second World War, which can be explained by two interconnected factors. One is a huge increase in the number of artists working in academia, where they found a more stable source of income; the second is the blurring of the division between culture and science, and, hence, between practicing art and theorizing it. Among the first to capture this phenomenon was Susan Sontag, who, in her influential essay "One culture and the new sensibility" from 1965, identified some crucial features of postmodern art. Sontag claims that the boundary between the two cultures, literary-artistic and scientific, is melting because "art is becoming increasingly the terrain of specialists," and that "the most interesting works of contemporary art are full of references to the history of the medium" (Sontag 1994b: 295). Her essay finishes with the listing of a number of artists, whose work illustrates the new sensibility; meaningfully, Godard is among them.

Both Nabokov and Godard fit well the category of artists who were also teachers and researchers, and whose output perfectly illustrates the blurring of the division between the two cultures listed by Sontag: literary-artistic and scientific. Nabokov spent almost twenty years of his life teaching courses in Russian and European literature in Wellesley College and Cornell University in the 1940s and 1950s, which led to the publication of two volumes, *Lectures on Russian Literature* and *Lectures on Literature*, and a number of other literary studies. Godard's career as a university lecturer was limited to a short and rather unsuccessful episode in the late 1980s and early 1990s, when Jack Lang, France's socialist minister of culture, recruited him as a guest professor in La Fémis (Fondation Européenne des Métiers de l'Image et du Son — the European Foundation for Image and Sound Trades) (Brody 2008: 545–48). However, if we take into account the numerous guest lectures he gave at university campuses and film festivals, and in other semi-educational circumstances, then we can regard him as one of the most committed educators among filmmakers. He also produced a number of historical studies in the form of written articles and using the medium of film. Two of his visual histories of cinema, *Deux Fois cinquante ans de cinéma français* (1995) and *Histoire(s) du cinéma* (1988–98) can be regarded as the equivalent of Nabokov's *Lectures on Russian Literature* and *Lectures on Literature*, because the first concerns Godard's "native" French cinema and the second world cinema.

Their histories can be viewed as extensions of histories they wrote in their novels and fictional films. Nabokov's novels are full of discussions of the works of other authors, and one of them, *The Gift*, includes a biography of the writer, philosopher and politician Nikolay Chernyshevski, which also, through the critical evaluation of Chernyshevski's achievements, offers Nabokov's own views on the purpose of literature. Godard's films are full of comments on the work of other filmmakers, such as Jean Renoir, Roberto Rossellini, Otto Preminger and François Truffaut. From the early part of his career to the present day, Godard is consistent in claiming that making films and writing about them belong to the same continuum of making cinema. For example, in an interview given in the 1990s he says, "I don't make a distinction between directing and criticism. When I began to look at pictures, that was already part of moviemaking. If I go to see that last Hal Hartley picture, that's part of making a movie, too. There is no difference" (Smith 1998: 180).

Nabokov and Godard also point to the (quasi) scientific process of creating and consuming cinema and literature. Nabokov states, "The boundary line between the two [a work of fiction and a work of science] is not as clear as is generally believed" (LL: 3); "A good formula to test the quality of a novel is, in the long run, a merging of the precision of poetry and the intuition of science" (ibid.: 6); "The best temperament for a reader to have, or to develop, is a combination of the artistic and the scientific one" (ibid.: 4–5); and "In high art and pure science detail is everything" (SO: 168). In a similar vein, Godard describes his films as "complex in a scientific sense" (Sterritt 1998: 176), and claims that "motion pictures were invented to look, tell, and study things. They were mainly a scientific tool ... for seeing life in a different way (ibid.: 176). No wonder then, through such pronouncements both authors advocate a more scientific art, but they also see art as fundamentally mimetic.

In their (proper) studies of the histories of their fields, both authors privilege the achievements of earlier periods over those in which they live. Nabokov in *Lectures on Literature* focuses on a small numbers of modernists; Godard in *Histoire(s) du cinéma*, although discussing a vast number of directors and works, favors what can be regarded as the cinematic equivalent of literary modernism, paying special attention to the work of Alfred Hitchcock (Rancière 2007). He praises him, among other things, for his vivid evocation of details: the glass of milk or the key — so memorable that the rest is forgotten, but the details stay in the viewer's mind. This attention to detail evokes Nabokov's focus on detail in his analyses of his favorite authors, his own prose and his literary theory.

Another common trait is the broad geographical spread of their interest. Among literary masters of the twentieth century Nabokov includes Andrei Bely, whose novel *Petersburg* (1916) stands alongside such unquestionable masterpieces as Joyce's *Ulysses* and *Remembrance of Things Past* by Proust. Godard, on the other hand, in his *Histoire(s)* pays much attention to the cinema of Russian cinematic formalists, especially Sergei Eisenstein, and almost obsessively returns to the film by Polish director Andrzej Munk, *Pasażerka* (*Passenger*, 1963). Yet, one has to acknowledge the difference between Nabokov and Godard as historians. The former is hostile towards any attempts to situate his favorite authors and works within any recognized paradigms. Godard, on the other hand, pays much attention to cinematic movements, such as German Expressionism, Italian Neorealism and the French New Wave. He maintains that the most conducive environment for producing cinematic masterpieces is one in which filmmakers are united around a joint project and cinema acts as the main means of social communication (which, since the proliferation of television, is no longer the case). This difference of attitude towards movements can be attributed partly to the fact that Nabokov was an ardent individualist, while Godard is more community-minded, and partly by their employing different media — literature being created by individual authors, cinema being the product of collective work.

In their historical, as well as fictional, works, Nabokov and Godard also reveal a similar approach to the mechanism of producing and consuming art, describing artistic experience in terms of revelation or epiphany. They see art's main function as making unexpected and illuminating connections between distant objects. Nabokov writes in *Speak, Memory*:

> Vivian Bloodmark [Nabokov], a philosophical friend of mine, in later years, used to say that while the scientist sees everything that happens in one point of space, the poet feels everything that happens in one point of time. Lost in thought, he taps his knee with his wandlike pencil, and at the same instant a car (New York license plate) passes along the road, a child bangs the screen door of a neighboring porch, an old man yawns in a misty Turkestan orchard, a granule of cinder-gray sand is rolled by the wind of Venus, a Doctor Jacques Hirsch in Grenoble puts on his reading glasses, and trillions of other such trifles occur — all forming an instantaneous and transparent organism of events, of which the poet (sitting in a lawn chair, at Ithaca, N.Y.) is the nucleus [SM: 169].

And in the following passage the writer uses the term "cosmic synchronization" and adds that already in the beginning of his writing he discovered that "a person hoping to become a poet must have the capacity of thinking of several things at a time." He confesses that when discussing with the village school master his father's sudden journey to town,

> I registered simultaneously and with equal clarity not only his wilting flowers, his flowing tie and the blackheads on the fleshy volutes of his nostrils, but also the dull little voice of a cuckoo coming from afar, and the flash of a Queen of Spain settling on the road, and the remembered impression of the pictures (enlarged agricultural pests and bearded Russian writers) ... and all the while I was richly, serenely aware of my own manifold awareness [ibid.: 170].

Compare that with Godard's theory of cinema as "montage," conveyed, for example, in this passage:

> If you say that around 1540 Copernicus introduced the idea that the Sun no longer revolved around the Earth, and if you say that a few years later Versalius published *De humani corporis fabrica*, which shows the inside of the human body, the skeleton and écorchés, well, then, you have Copernicus in one book and Vesalius in another.... And then four hundred years later you have François Jacob who says: "The same year, Copernicus and Vesalius..." Well, Jacob isn't doing biology anymore, he's doing cinema. And that's what history really is [Godard, quoted in Wright 2000: 56].

These words suggest that media other than cinema on occasion are also able to bring distant images, ideas or objects together, but cinema is privileged in this respect because not only can it achieve this without special effort, thanks to employing the technique of editing, but it allows the viewer to see the connections rather than only imagining them or grasping them intellectually. Godard also states explicitly that cinema's ability to see and show the connections between things furnishes it with great responsibility towards humanity. Cinema, in his view, is able to warn people against approaching disasters, such as wars and genocide. On occasion, it has played this role; an example is German Expressionism, which, following Siegfried Kracauer (Kracauer 2004), Godard perceives as a movement predicting and warning against the perils of Hitler rule.

We cannot find comparable statements by Nabokov. On the contrary, the author of *Bend Sinister* strongly opposes socially-engaged literature, exemplified by writers such as Zola, Sartre, Pasternak or Gorki, and in literature put "enchanters" above "teachers" (namely, propagandists, moralists and prophets) (LL: 5–6). However, in his literary practice he often acts in the way which Godard attributes to the great montage artists of the twentieth century: showing connections which were obscure to those who bore their witness. Serving example is his description of Franz in *King, Queen, Knave* as a proto-Nazi (see Chapter 3), or, more importantly, his finding similarities between Nazism, Russian communism and American popular culture in *Bend Sinister*.

## Aesthetics

Perceiving literature and cinema as a form of montage impinges on the aesthetic values of art that the respective authors privilege in their own work and, by extension, in that of others writers and film directors. One such value in Nabokov's works Leona Toker defines as "refinement" and I will simply describe as "originality:"

> The principle of *refinement* is phrased negatively in Nabokov's on-record remarks: it consists in the exclusion of common, heavy-duty, ready-made tired forms of language and thought — except for parodic purposes.... The common is kept away from Nabokov's authorial prose not because his aristocratic claims but because of it is a dead-wood encumbrance on the flow of consciousness modeled by his style. For the same reason it is often represented in the speech and behavior of the characters who are the butt of Nabokov's satire [Toker 2005: 233].

Godard, like Nabokov, also believes that the duty of the artist is to tell the viewer something s/he does not know in a manner which has not been explored and avoid repeating the obvious, as conveyed in the fragment of an interview which I used as a motto for this chapter: "Pictures are made to make seen the unseen. Afterward you can drop it and go on again. It's like tourists who go into an unknown country." The accent put on refinement explains Godard's antipathy towards most of contemporary cinema, which he finds riddled with clichés, and his diatribes against television, which he regards both as the creator and enforcer of commonplaces and an obstacle to the development of the intellectual faculties of its audience. "Television discovers nothing," he says (Sterritt 1998: 177; see also Witt 1999).

Toker also describes Nabokov as an advocate, both in his practice and theory, of literature's saturation, which she defines as

> the richness of the semiotic and symbolic loads of meaning economically signaled by lexical choices, collocations, and recurrences. What remains unsaid frequently impinges on the shape of what is said in the text ("the little I can express would not have been expressed, had I not known more"), so that a slight lexical change can alter the whole ethical or aesthetic construct of a passage — this, no doubt, was one of the reasons for Nabokov's and his family's insistence on controlling, as much as polyglotically possible, the work of his translators [Toker 2005: 233–4].

The same insistence on saying/showing what is necessary — and no more or less — we find in Godard's utterances. Take, for example, this passage: "I don't like what I call empty shots, that are there just for screenwriting reasons.... I can't imagine how a lot of moviemakers are doing shots just to explain something in the story. No painter would ever paint an image ... for such a reason" (Godard, quoted in Rosenbaum 1998: 105–106).

Being an art of "cosmic synchronization" and "montage," great literature and great cinema, including that produced by Nabokov and Godard themselves, puts an immense obligation on the consumer of art. Nabokov begins his *Lectures on Literature* with an essay titled "Good Readers and Good Writers," in which he warns against unreflective reading of books — for example, by identifying with their main characters at the expense of overlooking their complex structures. The good reader, in Nabokov's eyes, is a re-reader who reads the book many times until s/he is able to see it in its wholeness — in the way the viewer sees a painting and is able to admire it as a separate world (LL: 3). Vladimir Alexandrov develops this concept by claiming that Nabokov uses a special narrative tactic that puts the burden on the reader either to accumulate the components of a given series or to discover the one detail that acts as a "key" for it; when this is achieved, the significance of the entire preceding concealed chain or network is retroactively illuminated. To describe this mechanism of coding and encoding of Nabokov's work, Alexandrov uses the term "hermeneutic imperative" (Alexandrov 1991: 7–14). The word "imperative" suggests that the good reader has no choice or right to divert from the author's intentions, read the book against the grain, or build his/her own world on the foundations s/he finds in the book. S/he has to follow the writer — in the same way the solver of a chess problem has to follow its composer.

The principle of saturation is also at the core of Godard's aesthetics, as conveyed by his resolve to say much by saying little, inviting ambiguity, and his frequent rebuking of the audience when they accuse him of making his films too difficult or incomprehensible. For example, when challenged by the claim "But people go to see your movies to see a movie," Godard replies:

> I want to change it. I don't want people to come to see my movies the way they go to see other movies. This has to be changed. It's the most important thing we can do. I said it yesterday and the day before. It's not only making movies — that's why I think it's important that moviemaking be learned in universities. Maybe that way it will change." "You mean you are trying to change the audience?" "Well, I'm trying to change the world. Yes" (Youngblood 1998: 49).

Yet, unlike Nabokov, Godard is not an advocate of a "correct reading'; he rather prefers multiple readings, and although he is happy when viewers watch his films many times, he also welcomes those who watch them only once and only get part of the message or even find one the author did not intend.

The reasons which render the works of both artists difficult are also the reasons which led to numerous volumes explaining them. Nabokov studies and Godard studies function almost as sub-disciplines of literary and film studies. While in literary studies such a phenomenon is not uncommon, in film studies Godard's position is unique; there are no other filmmakers, perhaps with the exception of Hitchcock, who would attract so much serious scholarship in the form of publications and academic conferences.

## *Politics, Ethics and Metaphysics*

In my opinion, Godard's and Nabokov's political views reveal a large degree of similarity. For many readers it might come as a surprise because Nabokov was hostile to politically and socially engaged literature, while Godard's reputation is that of a politically committed filmmaker. Moreover, in his private life Nabokov revealed what can be described as conservative or right wing views; he was in favor of the American bombing of Vietnam and against students' strikes in the 1960s, as revealed by this statement: "I deplore the attitude of foolish or dishonest people who ridiculously equate Stalin with McCarthy, Auschwitz with the atom bomb, and the ruthless imperialism of the U.S.S.R. with the earnest and unselfish assistance extended by the U.S.A. to nations in distress" (SO: 50). Godard, by contrast, condemned America on and off-screen for the same actions that Nabokov congratulated, most importantly for its "assistance to nations in distress."

Although Nabokov would have described himself as politically disengaged and Godard as highly engaged, if we look closer at what they mean by such labels, we find that they have much in common. For Godard, being committed means first and foremost speaking in one's name rather than on behalf of a group of people. As early as 1962 he said in an interview, in response to a suggestion about the lack of political commitment among French New Wave directors:

> When the Nouvelle Vague started, several films included scenes of wild parties, and everybody pounced on them to label the Nouvelle Vague as interested only in wild parties. But it was really mere chance.... In any case the word "commitment" is mostly used wrongly, generally by people on the Left. One is not committed just because one makes films about the working class or about social questions; one is committed in so far as one is responsible for what one does. In the early days I felt less responsible because I was not fully aware, but now ... yes, I am committed in that I grow more and more conscious of what I am doing and my responsibility for it [Milne 1998: 4].

A decade later, when Godard became renowned or loathed for his involvement in political filmmaking, in a television interview following the production of *Tout va bien*, he repeated that for him political filmmaking means talking in his own name and taking full responsibility for the outcome of his work. Not only that, but he advocated the superiority of this film as a political statement over *Coup for coup* (1972) by fellow left-leaning director Marin Karmitz, which, like Godard's work, concerns an unauthorized strike in a factory. Godard claimed that Karmitz made his film on behalf of the workers, while he made his in his own name.[5] And again, some years later, when his political period appeared to be over, he said that making political films means for him simply making personal films (Godard, quoted in MacBean 1986: 11).

Political individualism concurs with their ontological views, namely their perception of reality as subjective. Nabokov, in this oft-quoted passage from *Strong Opinions*, says:

> Reality is a very subjective affair. I can only define it as a kind of gradual accumulation of information; and as specialization. If we take a lily, for instance, or any kind of natural object, a lily is more real to a naturalist than it is to an ordinary person. But it is still more real to a botanist. And yet another stage of reality is reached with that botanist who is a specialist in lilies. You can get nearer and nearer, so to speak, to reality; but you never get near enough because reality is an infinite succession of steps, levels of perception, false bottoms, and hence unquenchable, unattainable [SO: 10–11].

Compare that statement with this utterance by Godard: "A century ago, scientists believed the atom was the ultimate matter. Then they discovered that in one atom there are many things, and in one of those there are many more things, and so forth" (Godard, quoted in Sterritt 1998: 176).

Not surprisingly, in light of their perception of reality as subjective, both authors see the world as fragmented and coreless. As Leona Toker observes:

> Whereas most of Nabokov's modernist contemporaries deplored what they saw as the fragmentation of the modern world, in his pre–World War II fiction Nabokov presented the deliberate fragmentation of experience in positive terms, as a measure against totalitarian assault on individual experience.... If the world is in fragments, this is where it ought to be: the stage set of *Invitation* eventually collapses and disintegrates in a way that, in 1934, prophetically foreshadows the long-awaited collapses of the totalitarian regimes which the novel evokes. The very notion of the "world" is totalizing; Nabokov responds to it by asking "whose world?" [Toker 2005: 243].

While I agree with Toker's diagnosis of Nabokov's early works, I do not think it captures accurately some of his later works, such as *Lolita*. In particular, Humbert's inability to see Lolita as a whole person independent of his perceptions, or indeed to see anything in this way, can be partly explained by the fragmentation of his life, marked by the premature deaths of his mother and first love, and later by his emigration.

Even if we agree that Nabokov's attitude toward fragmentation is positive, it is not reflected in the form of his works. His novels and short stories come across as very finished and polished wholes, and the writer was horrified by the possibility of having his unfinished works published. He even objected to giving unprepared interviews, which by its very nature is an unpolished genre, and edited them before reprinting in *Strong Opinions*. The publishing of his last, unfinished novel, *The Original of Laura* (2009), caused considerable controversy largely because of its author's opposition to fragmented art.

Although Godard shares Nabokov's perception of the world as fragmented, his attitude toward this phenomenon appears to have changed over the years. While in his New Wave films he was more positive about the world in fragments, in his later works, made in the 1970s and later, he rather mourns than welcomes it. Especially films such as *Sauve qui peut (la vie)* and *Detective*, which show people whose life is in pieces due to divorce, not having a proper home or being torn between different projects, are the best examples of his opposition to fragmented experiences. On the other hand, unlike Nabokov, Godard's films come across as mimicking this modernist fragmentation, as works in progress, or even as essentially broken. One reason that his early works attracted critical attention was his provocative rejection of the smooth style of his predecessors, contemptuously labeled "cinema du papa," by introducing such means as jump cuts, juxtaposing different film genres virtually in one sequence, or abruptly abandoning characters in whom the viewer has emotionally invested.

Finally, both authors convey a belief in an "otherworld": a place beyond "this" world, and impossible to grasp and describe by rational means. Nabokov admitted to not believing in a personal God and refused to construe his transcendent realm as it tends to be presented in official religions (as heaven or hell one is thrown into after death). One difference between his construction and that of religions is his conviction or intuition that the otherworld is, in a sense, in this world; it is its hidden dimension, which at certain moments — "epiphanies" — becomes visible. In *Speak, Memory* he mentions "leakings and drafts" from the otherworld to the quotidian reality, which a well trained artist or even a consumer of art is able to capture. Consequently, Vladimir Alexandrov attributes to Nabokov "a faith in the apparent existence of a transcendent, non-material, timeless, and beneficent ordering and ordered realm of being that seems to provide for personal immortality, and that affects everything that exists in the mundane world" (Alexandrov 1991: 5). Such an idea is supported by analyses of specific works — for example, Gennady Barabtarlo's discussion of *The Enchanter*, in which he identifies a ghostly intervention of the mother to protect her daughter against the pedophile (Barabtarlo 1993: 51–69); and, less convincingly for me, Vladimir Alexandrov's attribution of such a ghostly presence to Charlotte Haze in *Lolita* (Alexandrov 1991: 179–81).

In his works, Nabokov often inscribes an author who mimics the workings of God. In the Introduction to *Bend Sinister* he even explains that by introducing an author who releases the hero from his misery, he hints at "an anthropomorphic deity impersonated by me" (BS: 11). John Burt Foster claims that in this device "self-reflexivity dovetails ingeniously with ontology to produce a sense of revelation that mimics the way an elusive deity might manifest itself in the world" (Foster 1995: 26).

Leona Toker connects Nabokov's concept of an otherworld, which, in a somewhat contradictory fashion, coexists with his claim that he is "an indivisible monist," with Bergson's philosophy, which might have influenced the writer's vision:

> If one is to make a case for the possibility of subsuming the two-world cosmogony within a monistic vision, one must take into account the twist that also occurs in Bergson's system: inert matter is at certain points transmuted into creative consciousness. Whether this happens at some stage of collective evolution or through the workings of genuine individual memory which Bergson regards as a point of intersection between matter and mind, the result is that the subject and the object become one. The consciousness of the transformation of the duality of the physical and the spiritual into a continuum may be regarded as the metaphysical background of the self-reflexive Möbius-strip narrative structures in most of Nabokov's major novels [Toker 1995: 369].

Although Godard does not talk about an otherworld as such, he talks about cinema's duty to see and show the invisible, as in his previously quoted statement, "Pictures are made to make seen the unseen," and his comment from *Scénario du film Passion* (1982) that "The work to be done is seeing, seeing the invisible become visible and describing it." In common with Nabokov, in some of his works Godard also mimics the work of God by inscribing himself in the text; most famously, in *Je vous salue Marie* he offers us a vision of Marie which could be available only to God.

Godard's belief in the existence of the transcended realm is also conveyed by the motifs of sky and other natural objects, which in his later films gain autonomy, unlike in most movies by other directors, where they are merely a background to human actions. The camera in these films often, in a way unmotivated by the narrative or even contrary to the logic of the storytelling, turns to the sky as if to seek there a divine presence. This happens, naturally, in his films from the "cosmic" period — *Passion, Prénom Carmen* and *Je vous salue Marie* — as well as in *Nouvelle Vague*. Discussing *Nouvelle Vague*, Kaja Silverman and Harun Farocki draw attention to the fact that even when something dramatic happens to the (human) characters in the film, the camera tends to focus on nature — for example, a tree, which is "a kind of a heathen god. Or better: *Nouvelle Vague* treats nature as if it were animated by the spirits of the dead" (Silverman and Farocki 1998: 201). A sign of Godard's intimation of the otherworld is also his obsession with light. He is known for using reluctantly artificial light in his films and his insistence on capturing the perfect light on camera. In *Passion*, this obsession is passed onto the director Jerzy, who acts as Godard's surrogate. He wants a perfect light but cannot get it, and eventually abandons his cinematic project (consisting of reproducing masterpieces of art as *tableaux vivants*). According to Silverman and Farocki, "The subtitle of Jerzy's film could be *À la recherche de la lumière perdue*" (ibid.: 175). Although I agree that "light is his impossible lost object," in my opinion, Jerzy cannot find it not because a contemporary artist cannot recreate or recover in the studio the illumination which was available to Rembrandt and El Greco, as the authors of the quoted study claim. Rather, being a callous and selfish man, Jerzy cannot see the world in the way the divine power sees it and which, perhaps, Rembrandt and El Greco, being more spiritual artists, managed to capture. Not without reason is the word "grace" frequently mentioned in the film. Not only Jerzy, but other characters in *Passion* also search for light, as if aware that without it their life would be devoid of significance. Conversely, they almost radiate when they move out of the dark or faceless interiors and come close to nature, to plants and flowers, even if this nature needs human intervention to flourish (for example, in a greenhouse, where we can observe such a transformation in Jerzy's lover, Hanna).[6]

Nabokov also talks about life in terms of energy, of light, as in this sentence:

"The cradle rocks above the abyss, and common sense tells us that our existence is but a brief crack of light between two eternities of darkness" (SM: 19). However, as was mentioned, Nabokov, against common sense, later in life started to believe in the possibility of prolonging this light.

## Conclusions

In conclusion, I want to reiterate that there are many links between Godard and Nabokov, despite the fact that there is a generational gap between them and they use different media. Some of these parallels result simply from them being great artists. Others pertain to the fact that, despite the difference in age, they belong to the same age of modernism and postmodernism. Others might be explained by their belonging, ultimately, to the Western world. Some, however, especially the idea of great poetry and cinema as a "cosmic synchronization" and "montage," the way they inscribe themselves in their work and convey their faith in the "otherworld," make them unique in their respective categories and render their similarity captivating.

# Appendix
## Films Discussed in the Book

### Adaptations of Nabokov

#### LOLITA

UK, USA, 1962; *Direction:* Stanley Kubrick; *Screenplay:* Vladimir Nabokov, based on his novel *Lolita; Cinematography:* Oswald Morris; *Editing:* Anthony Harvey; *Music:* Nelson Riddle; *Sound:* Len Shilton, H. L. Bird; *Producer:* James B. Harris; *Production company:* MGM; *Running time:* 152 min.; Black and white; *Cast:* James Mason (Humbert Humbert), Sue Lyon (Lolita), Shelley Winters (Charlotte Haze), Peter Sellers (Clare Quilty), Jerry Stovin (John Farlow), Diana Decker (Jean Farlow).

#### LAUGHTER IN THE DARK

France, UK, 1969; *Direction:* Tony Richardson; *Screenplay:* Edward Bond, based on the novel *Laughter in the Dark* by Vladimir Nabokov; *Cinematography:* Dick Bush; *Editing:* Charles Rees; *Music:* Raymond Leppard; *Sound:* Gerry Humphreys; *Producers:* Neil Hartley, Elliott Kastner; *Production companies:* Les Films Marceau, Winkast Film Productions, Woodfall Film Productions; *Running time:* 104 min.; Color; *Cast:* Nicol Williamson (Sir Edward More), Anna Karina (Margot), Jean-Claude Drouot (Hervé), Peter Bowles (Paul), Siân Phillips (Lady Pamela More), Kate O'Toole (Amelia More).

#### KING, QUEEN, KNAVE

West Germany, USA, 1972; *Direction:* Jerzy Skolimowski; *Screenplay:* David Shaw, David Seltzer, based on the novel *Korol', Dama, Valet / King, Queen, Knave* by Vladimir Nabokov; *Cinematography:* Charly Steinberger; *Editing:* Melvin Shapiro; *Music:* Stanley Myers; *Sound:* Kersten Ullrich, Hans-Joachim

Richter; *Producer:* Lutz Hengst; *Production companies:* Maran-Film (Munich), Wolper Pictures (Los Angeles); *Running time:* 92 min.; Color; *Cast:* Gina Lollobrigida (Martha Dreyer), David Niven (Charles Dreyer), John Moulder-Brown (Frank Dreyer), Mario Adorf (Professor Ritter), Barbara Valentin (optician).

## *DESPAIR* (*DESPAIR—EINE REISE INS LICHT*)

West Germany, France, 1978; *Direction:* Rainer Werner Fassbinder; *Screenplay:* Tom Stoppard, based on the novel *Despair* by Vladimir Nabokov; *Cinematography:* Michael Ballhaus; *Editing:* Rainer Werner Fassbinder, Juliane Lorenz; *Music:* Peer Raben; *Sound:* Jim Willis, Milan Bor; *Producers:* Lutz Hengst, Peter Märthescheimer, Edward R. Pressman; *Production company:* Bavaria Atelier; *Running time:* 119 min.; Color; *Cast:* Dirk Bogarde (Hermann Hermann), Andréa Ferréol (Lydia Hermann), Klaus Löwitsch (Felix Weber), Volker Spengler (Ardalion), Bernhard Wicki (Orlovius).

## *MADEMOISELLE O*

France, Russia, 1994; *Direction:* Jérôme Foulon; *Screenplay:* Jérôme Foulon, Sandra Joxe, based on the short story "Mademoiselle O" by Vladimir Nabokov; *Cinematography:* Valeri Martnov; *Editing:* Frédéric Viger; *Music:* Isaac Schwarts; *Sound:* André Rigaut; *Producer:* Michelle Cagnard; *Production company:* France 2 (FR2); *Running time:* 90 min.; Color; *Cast:* Maîté Nahyr (Mademoiselle O), Anton Minachkine (Volodia), Grichka Khaoustov (Sergei), Elena Safonova (Volodia's Mother), Alexandre Arbatt (Volodia's Father), Vernon Dobtcheff (Uncle Ruka), Serguei Berkhterev (Lenski).

## *LOLITA*

UK, USA, 1997; *Direction:* Adrian Lyne; *Screenplay:* Stephen Schiff, based on the novel *Lolita* by Vladimir Nabokov; *Cinematography:* Howard Atherton; *Editing:* David Brenner, Julie Monroe; *Music:* Ennio Morricone; *Sound:* Willy Allen; *Producer:* Mario Kassar, Joël B. Michaels; *Production company:* Guild, Lolita Productions; *Running time:* 137 min.; Color; *Cast:* Jeremy Irons (Humbert Humbert), Dominique Swain (Lolita), Melanie Griffith (Charlotte Haze), Frank Langella (Clare Quilty), Ben Silverstone (young Humbert Humbert).

## *LURJUS* (*AN AFFAIR OF HONOR*)

Estonia, 1999; *Direction:* Valentin Kuik; *Screenplay:* Valentin Kuik, based on the short story "An Affair of Honor" by Vladimir Nabokov; *Cinematography:*

Arko Okk; *Editing:* Sirje Haagel; *Music:* Olav Ehala; *Sound:* Tina Andreas; *Producer:* Valentin Kuik; *Production company:* Onfilm; *Running time:* 76 min.; Color; *Cast:* Taavi Eelmaa (Henrik Timmer), Elina Reinold (Evelin Timmer), Andres Puustusmaa (Berg), Arvo Kukumägi and Vello Janson (the Seconds), Ene Järvis (Henrik's boss).

### THE LUZHIN DEFENCE

UK, USA, France, Italy, Hungary, 2000; *Direction:* Marleen Gorris; *Screenplay:* Peter Berry, based on the novel *The Luzhin Defense* by Vladimir Nabokov; *Cinematography:* Bernard Lutic; *Editing:* Michiel Reichwein; *Music:* Alexandre Desplat; *Sound:* Richard Fettes; *Producers:* Caroline Wood, Stephen Evans, Louis Becker, Philippe Guez; *Production companies:* Renaissance Films and Clear Blue Sky; *Running time:* 109 min.; Color; *Cast:* John Turturro (Aleksandr Luzhin), Emily Watson (Natalia Kharkov), Geraldine James (Natalia's Mother), Stuart Wilson (Valentinov), Christopher Thompson (Jean de Stassard), Fabio Sartor (Turati), Alexander Hunting (Young Aleksandr), Orla Brady (Aleksandr's Aunt), Mark Tandy (Aleksandr's Father), Kelly Hunter (Aleksandr's Mother).

## *Intertextual Connections*

### TRIPLE AGENT

France, Italy, Spain, Greece, Russia, 2003; *Direction:* Eric Rohmer; *Screenplay:* Eric Rohmer; *Cinematography:* Diane Baratier; *Editing:* Mary Stephen; *Music:* Dmitri Shostakovich; *Sound:* Pascal Ribier; *Producers:* Françoise Etchegaray, Jean-Michel Rey, Philippe Liégeois; *Production companies:* REZO productions, C.E.R./France 2 Cinéma.; *Running time:* 115 min.; Color; *Cast:* Katerina Didaskalou (Arsinoé Voronin), Serge Renko (Fiodor Voronin), Amanda Langlet (Janine), Emmanuel Salinger (André), Cyrielle Clair (Maguy), Grigori Manoukov (Boris), Dimitri Rafalsky (General Dobrinsky), Jeanne Rambur (Dani).

# Chapter Notes

## Introduction

1. Bidding for the rights to this novel began at the then magical sum of $1,000,000 (Boyd 1991: 532).

2. It is difficult to provide an exact number of adaptations, because not all adaptations are "official." This refers especially to short films and video productions, whose visibility is much less than full-length feature films. Moreover, Nabokov himself refers to some television adaptations of his books that I was unable to identify.

3. Mireya Aragay's Introduction to the volume she edited presents and discusses with praiseworthy thoroughness and lucidity the changes which occurred in the adaptation studies from the 1920s to the beginning of the 21st century.

## Chapter 1

1. Almost all authors writing about *Lolita* mention its "pre-texts." They are discussed most extensively by Carl R. Proffer in *Keys to Lolita*, published in 1968, and in Alfred Appel's *The Annotated Lolita*, published for the first time in 1971. The list includes Nabokov's *The Gift* and *The Enchanter*, the works of Edgar Allan Poe, Dante, Petrarch, James Fenimore Cooper, Dostoevsky's *Crime and Punishment*, Joyce's *Ulysses*, Proust's *Remembrance of Things Past* and Mérimée's *Carmen*.

2. Gabriel Josipovici's reading of *Lolita* strikes as even more bizarre than Appel's. He writes: "Beside Humbert's sudden surges of tenderness, his constant ability to put himself in her place, Lolita's total lack of imagination is horrifying. She is quite unable to imagine his state of mind, and thinks of him only as a dirty old man. But she is not wholly to blame. The weight of Humbert's hatred and sarcasm falls not on her but on the country which has nurtured her, and especially on its system of education" (Josipovici 1971: 208).

3. Currently many readings of *Lolita* (including this one) are meta-readings, consisting of identifying the competing and evolving interpretations. This is an approach taken, among other authors, by Ellen Pifer (Pifer 1995; 2005).

4. However, in common usage the "nymphet" post–Nabokov has signified a teenager who possesses an obvious sexual allure. Richard Corliss observes that "the tabloids attach the name of Nabokov's girleen to any teenager involved in a sex scandal" (Amy Fisher: the Long Island Lolita). Filmmakers in search of uncopyrighted trademark paste it on schlock in the softcore (*Emmanuelle e Lolita*), hardcore (*Lolita 2000*), and fiction-film (*Black Lolita*) genres (see Corliss 1998: 35). Similar arguments are presented by a number of critics quoted in the essay "Lolita Unclothed" (see Paglia 1995).

5. There are many more similarities between Humbert's nympholepsy and Nabokov's lepidoptery, as thoroughly examined by Diana Butler (Butler 1960). However, the cruelty and selfishness of each passion strikes me as most important. Accordingly, I regard Nabokov's passion for butterflies, or, more precisely, the way he fulfilled this passion, as his least appealing character trait.

6. Humbert's attitude to the opposite sex as disposable and always short of the ideal evokes the Lacanian *objet a* (object little *a*). For Lacan, the severance of the child from its mother's body during development causes a gap. Unable to attain this precious object again in its fullness, he is thus condemned to

continuously search for its substitutes, with which he tries vainly to plug the gap at the very center of his being (Grosz 1990: 74–77). Humbert perfectly fits the image of a man who yearns for his mother because she died when he was only three "in a freak accident (picnic, lightning)" (Lo: 12); and as a child he fell in love with Annabel, who also perished before he could quench his desire for her. Lacanian reading of Nabokov is offered by Maurice Couturier in *Nabokov ou la cruauté du désir: lecture psychanalytique* (Couturier 2004).

7. On the other hand, her character points forward in time, bearing a resemblance to self-satisfied and self-obsessed rich philistines, epitomized by Cher Horowitz in Amy Heckerling's *Clueless* (1995), regarded as a Hollywood variation on Jane Austen's *Emma*. Cher, like Lolita, is unable to see in "high art" anything more than a version of "low art"; she assesses the value of a play by Shakespeare by its adaptation, seen on television, not the other way round.

8. Existentialism shares with absurdism its outlook on life, so it is not surprising that Humbert is regarded as a specialist in existentialism.

9. However, in this case it is worth distinguishing between early and late Kubrick, since in his later years the director also became a recluse.

10. In late 1959 the Nabokovs moved to Europe and, apart from short visits, never again lived in America (Boyd 1991: 388).

11. This feature, together with her restlessness and mobility, brings her even closer to the nymphet in Nabokov's *The Enchanter* than to the original *Lolita*.

12. In this respect Humber in Lyne's film follows in the footsteps of another of Nabokov's lovers, as depicted in film: Sir More in Tony Richardson's *Laughter in the Dark* (discussed in Chapter 2).

13. My reading of Polanski's *Tess* is not shared by all critics. Jane Marcus wrote a review of Polanski's film entitled "A Tess for Child Molesters." Her argument is largely based on the claim that Polanski's film provides visual pleasure for men interested in women like Tess (Marcus 1981). This might be the case. However, if we accept Marcus argument, then we have to agree that any film explicitly dealing with illicit sex gives pleasure to those yearning for such sex, even if its narrative offers its condemnation.

## Chapter 2

1. This is true of Toker's entire book, which very successfully, in my opinion, combines the discussion of Nabokov's technique with presenting his humanistic interests.

2. The conviction that we see only what we want to see is also conveyed by Marcel Proust in *Remembrance of Things Past*, and Nabokov comments on it in his *Lectures on Literature* (LL: 217). Proustian motifs in *Kamera obskura* are discussed at length by John Burt Foster, Jr. (Foster 1993b: 73–90).

3. Nabokov's interest in and respect for married love is reflected in his *Lectures on Russian Literature* and *Lectures on Literature*, especially the chapters devoted to *Anna Karenina* and *Madame Bovary* (LRL: 144–54; LL: 125–177).

4. This is one reason why *Lolita* is potentially a more attractive novel for adapting to the screen than *Laughter in the Dark*. As Kubrick noted, in modern times it is difficult to find a love story which shocks society (Kubrick, quoted in Walker 1972: 28).

5. In *Vivre sa vie*, for example, she is shot during her exchange between her old and new pimp.

6. Richardson's behavior in his private life suggests that he did not regard infidelity as a mortal sin. For example, while making *Mademoiselle* and *The Sailor from Gibraltar*, he carried on a passionate affair with Jeanne Moreau, despite being married to Vanessa Redgrave. He died of AIDS.

7. In the short section devoted to the screen version of *Laughter in the Dark*, Appel moves swiftly from Richardson's film to cinematic influences in Nabokov's *Ada*, demonstrating that for Nabokov scholars the cinematic influences in Nabokov's prose is an important issue, while Nabokov's influence on cinema (of other authors) hardly matters (Appel 1974: 135).

8. A good indicator of its neglect is the fact that the main book on Richardson published in English, *The Cinema of Tony Richardson: Essays and Interviews* (Welsh and Tibbetts 1999) virtually ignores *Laughter in the Dark*.

## Chapter 3

1. In this respect, my reading of the novel differs from Toker, who regards Franz's moral numbness and life passivity as progressing with the same speed and reinforcing each other (Toker 1989: 47–66, especially 50). In my

opinion, however, his moral numbing eventually allows him to become more active and consider being disloyal towards Martha.

2. The motif of dolls also brings to mind the films by Kira Muratova, where dolls tend to be "plastic, naked, alone and unloved" (Taubman 2005: 38).

3. Skolimowski's antipathy towards Martha was accompanied by his deep dislike of the actress playing the role, Gina Lollobrigida. In the interview which I conducted with him, he claimed that during shooting she behaved like a diva and attempted to dominate him, and even to wreck the whole film; while he, after initially succumbing to her growing demands, eventually stood up to her and forced her to accept his superiority. Symbolically, the confrontation took place during the shooting of the crucial event of Martha's drowning.

## Chapter 4

1. For example, in *The Gift* the narrator, Fyodor, mentions "the Russian conviction that the German is in small numbers vulgar and in large numbers unbearably vulgar" (Gift: 79). Although he admits that such an opinion is unworthy of an artist, he cannot help that it always comes to him when walking the streets of Berlin or travelling by tramcar.

2. Hermann is the name of the great love of Vladimir Nabokov's homosexual brother, Sergei. This Hermann was also an industrialist, but he did not kill Sergei, although their affair played an indirect part in Sergei's demise during the Second World War (Grossman 2000).

## Chapter 5

1. J. E. Rivers has a different hypothesis regarding the name of Nabokov's heroine. He maintains that "O" in her name stands for "zero" or "void." He supports this hypothesis by quoting Mademoiselle, who says, "I'm just poor nothing" (Rivers 2000: 110). Maurice Couturier, on the contrary, maintains that "O" more likely stands for "everything," even perfection (Couturier1993: 49–50). The charm of this story lies in its invitation to such multiple and even competing readings.

2. On the other hand, cinema knows many cases of "self-colonization," although typically they occur in countries which perceive themselves as culturally inferior and strive to achieve a higher cultural status. Many examples of this phenomenon are provided by Eastern European films made during communist times.

## Chapter 6

1. Shortly after *An Affair of Honor* was completed, I encountered rumors about Aleksei Balabanov's attempts to film *Laughter in the Dark* and *Mary*, but neither of the films materialized.

2. Marina Turkevich Naumann also notes a similarity between *An Affair of Honor* and *King, Queen, Knave*, but she does not explore it, only mentioning that both works concern a love triangle (Turkevich Naumann 1978: 126). She also notes the importance of the water theme in *An Affair of Honor* and links it to other works by Nabokov, but not *King, Queen, Knave* (ibid.: 129–30).

3. As I mentioned in Chapter 3, the lack of precise background was also noted by Andrew Field in relation to *King, Queen, Knave*. According to Field, it testifies to emigrants' inability to see their surroundings (Field 1967: 158).

4. This information was provided by Valentin Kuik himself. I am grateful to Eva Näripea for contacting the director on my behalf and finding all the essential details about his film, as well as explaining to me some of its "Estonian" aspects.

5. Andrus Puustusmaa, who plays Berg, went to Russia a few years later and started there his new career as a director. His debut in Russia, a film entitled *1814* (2007), is a story about young Pushkin and his circle of friends at the Tsarskoselsky Liceum.

## Chapter 7

1. Luzhin shares his interest with characters such as, Godunov-Cherdyntsev in *The Gift*, who invents chess problems, and John Shade and Kinbote in *Pale Fire*, who are both ardent chess players.

2. Belén Vidal discusses Gorris' *The Luzhin Defence* along with such literary adaptations in the form of romance and costume films as *Mansfield Park* (1999) by Patricia Rozema and *The Governess* (1998) by Sandra Goldbacher (Vidal 2005).

## Chapter 8

1. However, in other stories and novels the author makes the conscious attempt to efface

the details of the physical surroundings. Some examples were discussed in this book — for instance, *King, Queen, Knave* and *Laughter in the Dark*.

2. *The Conspirators* by Goeffrey Bailey is the most detailed and comprehensive account of the Skoblin affair.

3. My discussion of the parallels between Rohmer and Nabokov's works can be compared to Maria Tortajada's investigation of Rohmer's films as linked to "libertinage" of Laclos and Crebillon Fils (Tortejada 2004).

## *Chapter 9*

1. The closest distance between them was a hundred pages in a book of interviews with artists published by Penelope Gilliatt in 1980 (Gilliat 1980a and 1980b: 109–38; 239–49). Godard's name is also evoked several times in Appel's *Nabokov's Dark Cinema*, but without really drawing comparisons between these two artists. On one occasion Appel writes, for example, that Kubrick is unlike Godard (Appel 1974: 251).

2. However, as Will Norman aptly argues, this very desire betrays a distinctive political viewpoint (Norman 2009).

3. Yet, Lolita's getting married immediately after freeing herself from her pedophile oppressor, and her expecting a child at a young age, still points to her overall oppression.

4. However, perhaps such a scenario was also anticipated by Nabokov by making the adult Lolita ask Humbert for money.

5. The interview is available on YouTube, *http://www.youtube.com/watch?v=mKrtdKfiv8k*.

6. A somewhat different but persuasive interpretation of the motifs of the "sacred" and light in the work of Godard is offered by Vicki Callahan (Callahan 2007).

# Works Cited

## Works by Vladimir Nabokov

*Ada or Ardor*. London: Penguin, 1969 (2000).
"An Affair of Honor," in *A Russian Beauty and Other Stories*. London: Penguin, 1927 (1975), pp. 83–111.
"The Assistant Producer," in *Collected Stories*. London: Penguin, 1943 (2001), pp. 546–59.
*Bend Sinister*. London: Penguin, 1947 (1981).
*Dear Bunny, Dear Volodya. The Nabokov-Wilson Letters 1940–1971, Revised and Expanded Edition*. Edited, annotated, and with an introductory essay by Simon Karlinsky. Berkeley: University of California Press, 2001.
*Despair*. London: Penguin, 1966 (2000).
*The Enchanter*. London: Picador, 1986.
*The Gift*. London: Penguin, 2001.
*King, Queen, Knave*. London: Panther, 1970.
*Laughter in the Dark*. London: Penguin, 1938 (1993).
*Lectures on Don Quixote* (1983). Edited by Fredson Bowers. San Diego: Harcourt Brace Jovanovich, 1983.
*Lectures on Literature*. San Diego: Harvest, 1980 (1982).
*Lectures on Russian Literature*. New York and London: Harcourt Brace Jovanovich, 1981.
*Lolita*. London: Weidenfeld and Nicolson, 1955 (1959).
*Lolita: A Screenplay*. New York: Vintage, 1974 (1997).
*The Luzhin Defense*. London: Penguin, 1964 (2000).
*The Original of Laura: A Novel in Fragments*. London: Penguin, 2009.
*Pale Fire*. London: Penguin, 1962 (2000).
"Problems of Translation: 'Onegin' in English," *Partisan Review*, 22 (1955), pp. 486–512.
*Speak, Memory: An Autobiography Revisited*. London: Penguin, 1967 (1999).
*Strong Opinions*. New York: Vintage, 1990.

## Secondary Sources

Adair, Gilbert (1984). "Prenom Carmen (First Name Carmen)," *Monthly Film Bulletin*, 601 (February 1984), pp. 31–2.
Alexandrov, Vladimir E. *Nabokov's Otherworld*. Princeton: Princeton University Press, 1991.
_____. (1995). "*The Defense*," in Vladimir E. Alexandrov (ed.), *The Garland Companion to Vladimir Nabokov*. New York & London: Garland, 1995, pp. 75–88.
Amis, Martin. "Lolita Reconsidered," *Atlantic*, September 1992, pp. 109–20.
Andrew, Dudley (1992). "Adaptation," in Gerald Mast et al. (eds.), *Film Theory and Criticism, Fourth Edition*. Oxford: Oxford University Press, 1992, pp. 420–8.
Appel, Alfred, Jr. *The Annotated Lolita*. London: Penguin, 1971 (1995).
_____. *Nabokov's Dark Cinema*. New York: Oxford University Press, 1974.
Arendt, Hannah. *The Origins of Totalitarianism*. London: Allen & Unwin, 1951 (1961).
Bader, Julia. *Crystal Land: Artifice in Nabokov's English Novels*. Berkeley: University of California Press, 1972.
Bailey, Geoffrey. *The Conspirators*. London: Victor Gollancz, 1961.
Bainbridge, Caroline. "Screening *Parler Femme*: *Silences of the Palace*, *Antonia's Line* and *Faithless*," in her *A Feminine Cinematics: Luce Irigaray, Women and Film*. Houndmills, Basingstoke: Palgrave Macmillan, 2008, pp. 99–124.
Bakhtin, Mikhail. *Rabelais and His World*, trans. Hélène Iswolsky. Bloomington: Indiana University Press, 1941 (1984).
Barabtarlo, Gennady. *Aerial View: Essays on Nabokov's Art and Metaphysics*. New York: Peter Lang, 1993.
Bauman, Zygmunt. *Intimations of Postmodernity*. London: Routledge, 1992.

_____. *Life in Fragments: Essays in Postmodern Morality*. Oxford: Blackwell, 1995.

Beaujour, Elizabeth Klosty. "Bilingualism," in Vladimir E. Alexandrov (ed.), *The Garland Companion to Vladimir Nabokov*. New York & London: Garland, 1995, pp. 37–43.

Blackwelder, Bob. "Marleen Gorris — Interview," *Contactmusic.com*, http://www.contactmusic.com/new/home.nsf/interviewee/mgorris, 2001, accessed 12/01/2009.

Blackwell, Stephen B. "Nabokov's Fugitive Sense," in Will Norman and Duncan White (eds.), *Transitional Nabokov*. Oxford: Peter Lang, 2009, pp. 15–29.

Bourdieu, Pierre. "The Forms of Capital," in J. E. Richardson (ed.), *Handbook of Theory of Research for the Sociology of Education*, trans. Richard Nice. Westport, CT: Greenwood Press, 1986, pp. 241–58.

Bovkis, A. "The Magical World of the Ultimate Matriarch," *Cineaction*, 43 (1997), pp. 50–7.

Bowlby, Rachel. "*Lolita* and the Poetry of Advertising," in Ellen Pifer (ed.), *Lolita: A Casebook*. Oxford: Oxford University Press, 2003, pp. 155–79.

Boyd, Brian. *Vladimir Nabokov: The Russian Years*. Princeton: Princeton University Press, 1990.

_____. *Vladimir Nabokov: The American Years*. Princeton: Princeton University Press, 1991.

_____. "Nabokov as storyteller," in Julian W. Connolly (ed.), *The Cambridge Companion to Nabokov*. Cambridge: Cambridge University Press, 2005, pp. 31–48.

_____. "Literature, Pattern, *Lolita*: Or Art, Literature, Science," in Will Norman and Duncan White (eds.), *Transitional Nabokov*. Oxford: Peter Lang, 2009, pp. 31–53.

Brand, Dana. "The Interaction of Aestheticism and American Consumer Culture in Nabokov's *Lolita*," *Modern Language Studies*, 2 (1987), pp. 14–21.

Brodsky, Anna. "Nabokov's *Lolita* and the Postwar Émigré Consciousness," in Dominica Radulescu (ed.), *Realms of Exile: Nomadism, Diasporas, and Eastern European Voices*. Lanham, MD: Lexington Books, 2002, pp. 49–66.

Brody, Richard. *Everything Is Cinema: The Working Life of Jean-Luc Godard*. London: Faber and Faber, 2008.

Buhks, Nora. "The Novel-Waltz (on the Structure of *King, Queen, Knave*)," *Zembla*, 1987, http://www.libraries.psu.edu/nabokov/buhksl, accessed 3/03/2007.

Burdick, Dolores M. "'The Line down the Middle': Politics and Sexuality in Fassbinder's *Despair*," in Eugene J. Crook (ed.), *Fearful Symmetry: Doubles and Doubling in Literature and Film*. Tallahassee: University Press of Florida, 1982, pp. 138–48.

Burns, Dan. "Pistols and Cherry Pies: *Lolita* from Page to Screen," *Literature Film Quarterly*, 4 (1984), pp. 245–50.

Butler, Alison. *Women's Cinema: The Contested Screen*. London: Wallflower, 2002.

Butler, Diana. "Lolita Lepidoptera," *New World Writing*, 16 (1960), pp. 58–84.

Callahan, Vicki. "'Gravity and Grace': On the 'Sacred' and the Cinematic Vision in the Films of Jean-Luc Godard," in Michael Temple, James S. Williams and Michael Witt (eds.), *For Ever Godard*. London: Black Dog, 2007, pp. 188–99.

Cerisuelo, Marc. *Jean-Luc Godard*. Paris: Éditions des quatres-vents, 1989.

Chamberlin, Carloss James. "Emigrating to Madness: *Despair (Eine Reise ins Licht)*," *Senses of Cinema*, http://www.sensesofcinema.com/contents/cteq/03/27/despair.html, 2008, accessed 15/04/2008.

Chatman, Seymour. *Story and Discourse: Narrative Structure in Fiction and Film*. Ithaca and London: Cornell University Press, 1978.

Ciancio, Ralph A. "Nabokov's Painted Parchments," in Lisa Zunshine (ed.), *Nabokov at the Limits*. New York & London: Garland, 1999, pp. 235–69.

Clancy, Laurie. *The Novels of Vladimir Nabokov*. London: Macmillan, 1984.

Collins, Emily. "'A Luminous Web': Nabokov's Magical Objects," in Will Norman and Duncan White (eds.), *Transitional Nabokov*. Oxford: Peter Lang, 2009, pp. 185–204.

Connolly, Julian W. "*King, Queen, Knave*," in Vladimir E. Alexandrov (ed.), *The Garland Companion to Vladimir Nabokov*. New York & London: Garland, 1995a, pp. 203–14.

_____. "*Laughter in the Dark*," in Vladimir E. Alexandrov (ed.), *The Garland Companion to Vladimir Nabokov*. New York & London: Garland, 1995b, pp. 214–26.

_____. "*Ania v strane chudes*," in Vladimir E. Alexandrov (ed.), *The Garland Companion to Vladimir Nabokov*. New York & London: Garland, 1995c, pp. 18–25.

Corliss, Richard. *Lolita*. London: BFI, 1994.

_____. "From Lyon to Lyne," *Film Comment*, 5 (1998), pp. 34–8.

Corrigan, Timothy. *A Cinema Without Walls:*

*Movies and Culture After Vietnam*. London: Routledge, 1991.

Cott, Jonathan. "Godard: Born-Again Filmmaker," in David Sterritt (ed.), *Jean-Luc Godard: Interviews*. Jackson: University Press of Mississippi, 1980 (1998), pp. 91–9.

Couturier, Maurice. "The Distinguished Writer vs. the Child," *Cycnos*, 10 (1993), pp. 47–54.

——. *Nabokov ou la cruauté du désir: lecture psychanalytique*. Seyssel: Champ Vallon, 2004.

Crisp, C. G. *Eric Rohmer: Realist and Moralist*. Bloomington and Indianapolis: Indiana University Press, 1988.

Croce, Arlene. "*Lolita*," *Sight and Sound*, Autumn 1962, pp. 191–92.

Daney, Serge. "Godard Makes [Hi]stories: Interview with Serge Daney," in Raymond Bellour and Mary Lea Bandy (eds.), *Jean Luc Godard Son + Image*. New York: The Museum of Modern Art, 1992, pp. 159–67.

Davidson, James A. "Some Thoughts on Alfred Hitchcock and Vladimir Nabokov," *Images*, 3 (1987), http://www.imagesjournal.com/issue03/features/hitchnabl.htmDabDavidson, accessed 25/06/2009.

Debord, Guy. *The Society of Spectacle*, translated into English by Nicholson-Smith. New York: Zone Books, 1967 (1994).

De la Durantaye, Leland. *Style Is Matter: The Moral Art of Vladimir Nabokov*. Ithaca: Cornell University Press, 2007.

——. "Artistic Selection: Science and Art in Vladimir Nabokov," in Will Norman and Duncan White (eds.), *Transitional Nabokov*. Oxford: Peter Lang, 2009, pp. 55–66.

De Montvalon, Jean Baptiste. "Tournage Mademoiselle O, de Jérôme Foulon: Nuit blanche sur le Neva," *Le Monde*, 13/06 (1993).

Devlin, Rachel. *Relative Intimacy: Fathers, Adolescent Daughters, and Postwar American Culture*. Chapel Hill and London: The University of North Carolina Press, 2005.

Dick, Leslie. "*Lolita*," *Sight and Sound*, 5 (1998), pp. 51–2.

Dolinin, Alexander. "The Caning of Modernist Profaners: Parody in *Despair*," *Zembla*, 2008, http://www.libraries.psu.edu/nabokov/dolil.htm, accessed 12/04/08.

Donoghue, Denis. "Denis Donoghue in *Listener*," in Normal Page (ed.), *Nabokov: The Critical Heritage*. London: Routledge & Kegan Paul, 1982, p. 204.

Eco, Umberto. "*Casablanca*: Cult Movies and Intertextual Collage," in David Lodge (ed.), *Modern Criticism and Theory*. London: Longman, 1988, pp. 446–55.

Edmunds, Jeff. "Look at Valdemar! (A Beautified Corpse Revived)," *Nabokov Studies* (Los Angeles), 2 (1995), pp. 153–171.

Elley, Derek. "*Triple Agent*," *Variety*, 15/02, 2004, http://www.variety.com/review/VE1117923114.html?categoryid=31&cs=1&p=0, accessed 15/06/2009.

Elliott, Kamilla. *Rethinking the Novel/Film Debate*. Cambridge: Cambridge University Press, 2003.

——. "Novels, Films, and the Word/Image Wars," in Robert Stam and Alessandra Raengo (eds.), *A Companion to Literature and Film*. Oxford: Blackwell, 2004, pp. 1–22.

Elsaesser, Thomas. *Fassbinder's Germany: History, Identity, Subject*. Amsterdam: Amsterdam University Press, 1996.

Esslin, Martin. *The Theatre of the Absurd*. Harmondsworth, Middlesex: Penguin Books, 1968.

Etkind, Alexander. "Internal Colonization and Russian Cultural History," *Ulbandus. the Slavic Review of Columbia University*, 7 (2003), pp. 17–25.

Fanger, Donald. "Nabokov and Gogol," in Vladimir E. Alexandrov (ed.), *The Garland Companion to Vladimir Nabokov*. New York and London: Garland, 1995, pp. 420–28.

Field, Andrew. *Nabokov: His Life in Art*. London: Hodder and Stoughton, 1967.

——. *VN: The Life and Art of Vladimir Nabokov*. London: Futura, 1988.

Foster, Hal. *Compulsive Beauty*. Cambridge: Massachusetts Institute of Technology Press, 1993.

Foster, John Burt, Jr. "An Archeology of 'Mademoiselle O': Narrative Between Art and Memory," in Charles Nicol and Gennady Barabtarlo (eds.), *A Small Alpine Form: Studies in Nabokov's Short Fiction*. New York: Garland, 1993a, pp. 111–35.

——. *Nabokov's Art of Memory and European Modernism*. Princeton: Princeton University Press, 1993b.

——. "*Bend Sinister*," in Vladimir E. Alexandrov (ed.), *The Garland Companion to Vladimir Nabokov*. New York and London: Garland, 1995, pp. 25–36.

——. "Nabokov and Modernism," in Julian W. Connolly (ed.), *The Cambridge Companion to Nabokov*. Cambridge: Cambridge University Press, 2005, pp. 85–100.

Foster, Ludmila A. "Nabokov in Russian Emigre Criticism," in Carl R. Proffer (ed.), *A Book of Things About Vladimir Nabokov*. Ann Arbor, MI: Ardis, 1974, pp. 42–53.

French, Philip (2000). "Grandmaster Crash," *The Guardian*, 10/09, http://www.guardian.co.uk/film/2000/sep/10/chess.philipfrench, accessed 25/08/2008.

Gezari, Janet. "Chess and Chess Problems," in Vladimir E. Alexandrov (ed.), *The Garland Companion to Vladimir Nabokov*. New York and London: Garland, 1995, pp. 44–54.

Gilliatt, Penelope. "The Urgent Whisper: Jean-Luc Godard," in her *Three-Quarter Face*. London: Secker and Warburg, 1980a, pp. 109–38.

———. "Nabokov," in her *Three-Quarter Face*. London: Secker and Warburg, 1980b, pp. 239–49.

Gow, Gordon. "*Laughter in the Dark*," *Films and Filming*, November 1969, p. 40.

Grayson, Jane. *Nabokov Translated: A Comparison of Nabokov's Russian and English Prose*. Oxford: Oxford University Press, 1977.

Green, Geoffrey. "Visions of a Perfect Past: Nabokov, Autobiography, Biography and Fiction," *Nabokov Studies*, 3 (1996), pp. 89–100.

Grossman, Lev. "The Gay Nabokov," *Salon*, 2000, http://archive.salon.com/books/feature/2000/05/17/nabokov/index.html, accessed 15/04/08.

Grosz, Elizabeth. *Jacques Lacan: A Feminist Introduction*. London: Routledge, 1990.

Haegert, John. "Artist in Exile: The Americanization of Humbert Humbert," in Ellen Pifer (ed.), *Lolita: A Casebook*. Oxford: Oxford University Press, 2003, pp. 137–53.

Hall, Sheldon. "Tony Richardson," in Robert Murphy (ed.), *Directors in British and Irish Cinema: A Reference Companion*. London: BFI, 2006, pp. 511–13.

Hampshire, Stuart. "Stuart Hampshire in *New Statesman*," in Normal Page (ed.), *Nabokov: The Critical Heritage*. London: Routledge and Kegan Paul, 1982, pp. 159–62.

Hamrit, Jacqueline. "French Echoes in 'Mademoiselle O,'" *Zembla*, http://www.libraries.psu.edu/nabokov/hamrit.htm, accessed 25/10/2009.

Harcourt, Peter. "Le Nouveau Godard: An Exploration of *Sauve qui peut (la vie)*," *Film Quarterly*, Winter 1981/2, pp. 17–27.

Hentzi, Gary. "American Beauty," *Film Quarterly*, 2 (2001), pp. 46–50.

Jackson, Kevin. "*American Beauty*," *Sight and Sound*, 2 (2000), p. 40.

Jahn, Hubertus F. *Patriotic Culture in Russia during World War I*. Ithaca and London: Cornell University Press, 1995.

James, Nick. "Humbert's Humbert," *Sight and Sound*, 5 (1998), pp. 21–3.

Jameson, Fredric. *Postmodernism, or, the Cultural Logic of Late Capitalism*. London: Verso, 1991.

Jeffries, Stuart (2004). "Agent Provocateur," *The Guardian*, 26/10 (2004), http://www.guardian.co.uk/world/2004/oct/26/france.film, accessed 12/06/2009.

Jenkins, Greg. *Stanley Kubrick and the Art of Adaptation*: Jefferson, NC: McFarland, 1997.

Johnson, Barton D. "Contrasting Phonoaesthetics, or, Why Nabokov Gave Up Translating Poetry as Poetry," in Carl R. Proffer (ed.), *A Book of Things About Vladimir Nabokov*. Ann Arbor, MI: Ardis, 1974, pp. 28–41.

———. "Nabokov and the Sixties," in David H. J. Larmour (ed.), *Discourse and Ideology in Nabokov's Prose*. London: Routledge, 2002, pp. 139–49.

Johnson, Roy. "Nabokov Tutorials: 50 Studies of *The Collected Stories*," 2001, http://www.mantex.co.uk/ou/a319/nab-042.htm, accessed 14/06/01.

Josipovici, Gabriel. "*Lolita*: Parody and the Pursuit of Beauty," in his *The World and the Book: A Study of Modern Fiction*. Bristol: Macmillan, 1971, pp. 201–20.

Kael, Pauline. "*Lolita*," in her *I Lost It at the Movies*. Boston: Little, Brown, 1965, pp. 203–209.

———. "The Uprooted Artist," in her *Reeling: Film Writing 1972–1975*. London: Marion Boyars, 1992, pp. 356–61.

Karshan, Thomas. "Nabokov's Transition from Game Towards Free Play," in Will Norman and Duncan White (eds.), *Transitional Nabokov*. Oxford: Peter Lang, 2009, pp. 245–64.

Kauffman, Linda. "Framing *Lolita*: Is There a Woman in the Text?" in Patricia Yaeger and Beth Kowaleski-Wallace (eds.), *Refiguring the Father: New Feminist Reading of Patriarchy*. Carbondale and Edwardsville: Southern Illinois Press, 1989, pp. 131–52.

Kenny, Glenn. "Jean-Pierre Melville Is Vladimir Nabokov in Jean-Luc Godard's *Breathless*!!!" *In the Company of Glenn: The online hangout of Premiere film critic Glenn Kenny*, 08/10 (2007), accessed 5/07/2009.

Kent. "*Laughter in the Dark*," *Variety*, 14/05 (1969), p. 6.

Khodasevich Vladislav. "Luzhin Defense," trans. from Russian by Jeff Edmunds, *Zembla*, 1997, *http://www.libraries.psu.edu/nabokov/khodas2.htm*, accessed 25/07/2008.

Kimney, John. "The Three Voices of Nabokov's *Despair*," *Russian Language Journal*, 34 (119), 1980, pp. 101–108.

Kitchin, Valeri. "Nabokov in the Tradition of Jules Verne" (Набоков в традициях Жюля Верна), film.ru, 2000, http://www.film.ru/article.asp?ID=1508A, accessed 28/07/2008.

Kittler, Friedrich A. *Discourse Networks 1800/1900*, trans. from German by Michael Metteer. Stanford: Stanford University Press, 1990.

Kopper, John M. "Correspondence," in Vladimir E. Alexandrov (ed.), *The Garland Companion to Vladimir Nabokov*. New York and London: Garland, 1995, pp. 54–67.

Koszarski, Richard. "Words and Movies: Stanley Kubrick," in his *Hollywood Directors 1941–1976*. Oxford: Oxford University Press, 1977.

Krabbé, Tim. "Nabokov as a Feminist," *Open Chess Diary*, Entry 22/03 (2001), *http://www.xs4all.nl/~timkr/chess2/diary_6.htm*, accessed 222/08/2008.

Kracauer, Siegfried. *From Caligari to Hitler: A Psychological History of the German Film*. Princeton: Princeton University Press, 1947 (2004).

Leitch, Thomas. "The Adapter as Auteur: Hitchcock, Kubrick, Disney," in Mireya Aragay (ed.), *Books in Motion: Adaptation, Intertextuality, Authorship*. Amsterdam: Rodopi, 2005, pp. 107–24.

Levine, Robert T. "'My Ultraviolet Darling': The Loss of Lolita's Childhood," *Modern Fiction Studies*, 3 (1979), pp. 471–79.

LoBrutto, Vincent. *Stanley Kubrick: A Biography*. London: Faber and Faber, 1997.

Long, Michael. *Marvell, Nabokov: Childhood and Arcadia*. Oxford: Clarendon Press, 1984.

MacBean, James Roy. "*Sauve qui peut/la vie* (*Every Man for Himself*): An Open Letter to Godard," *Jump Cut: A Review of Contemporary Media*, 31 (1986), pp. 8–12.

MacCabe, Colin. *Godard: A Portrait of the Artist at 70*. London: Bloomsbury, 2003.

Macnab, Geoffrey. "*The Luzhin Defence*," *Sight and Sound*, 10 (2000), p. 50.

Maddox, Lucy. *Nabokov's Novels in English*. London: Croom Helm, 1983.

Maimik, Andres. "Kolme teraga habemenuga [Tripple-bladed razor]," *Sirp*, March 12 (1999), http://www.sirp.ee/archive/1999/12.03.99/Film/film1-1.html, accessed 30/07/2008.

Marcus, Jane. "A Tess for Child Molesters," *Jump/Cut*, 26 (1981), p. 3.

Mazierska, Ewa. *Roman Polanski: The Cinema of a Cultural Traveller*. London: I. B. Tauris, 2007.

———. *Jerzy Skolimowski: The Cinema of a Noncomformist*. Oxford: Berghahn, 2010.

Mazierska, Ewa, and Laura Rascaroli. *From Moscow to Madrid: Postmodern Cities, European Cinema*. London: I. B. Tauris, 2003.

McKinney, Devin. "*Lolita*," *Film Quarterly*, 3 (1999), pp. 48–52.

Metz, Christian. "Story/Discourse: Notes on Two Kinds of Voyeurism," in Bill Nichols (ed.), *Movies and Methods*. Berkeley: University of California Press, 1985, pp. 543–49.

Meyer, Priscilla. "Nabokov's Short Fiction," in Julian W. Connolly (ed.), *The Cambridge Companion to Nabokov*. Cambridge: Cambridge University Press, 2005, pp. 119–34.

Milne, Tom. "Jean Luc Godard and *Vivre sa vie*," in David Sterritt (ed.), *Jean-Luc Godard: Interviews*. Jackson: University Press of Mississippi, 1962 (1998), pp. 3–8.

———. "*King, Queen, Knave*," *Monthly Film Bulletin*, 12 (1973), p. 250.

Mizruchi, Susan. "*Lolita* in History," *American Literature*, 3 (2003), pp. 629–652.

Moore, Tony. "Seeing Through Humbert: Focusing on the Feminist Sympathy in *Lolita*," in David H. J. Larmour (ed.), *Discourse and Ideology in Nabokov's Prose*. London: Routledge, 2002, pp. 91–110.

Morrissey, Kim. *Poems for Men Who Dream of Lolita*. Regina: Coteau Books, 1992.

Mosk. "*King, Queen, Knave*," *Variety*, 24/05 (1972), p. 26.

Moynahan, Julian. *Vladimir Nabokov*. Minneapolis: University of Minnesota Press, 1971a.

———. "*Lolita* and Related Memories," in Alfred Appel, Jr., and Charles Newman (eds.), *Nabokov: Criticism, Reminiscences, Translations and Tributes*. London: Weidenfeld and Nicolson, 1971b, pp. 247–52.

Murphy, Robert. *Sixties British Cinema*. London: BFI, 1992.

———. "Strange Days: British Cinema in the Late 1960s," in Robert Murphy (ed.), *The British Cinema Book, 3rd Edition*. London: BFI, 2009, pp. 321–32.

Nabokov, Dmitri. "The *Lolita* Legacy: Life with Nabokov's Art," *The Nabokovian*, 37 (1996), pp. 8–29.

Nafisi, Azar. *Reading Lolita in Tehran: A Memoir in Books*. New York: Random House, 2003.

Narboni, Jean, and Tom Milne (eds.). *Godard on Godard*, trans. from French by Tom Milne. London: Secker and Warburg, 1972.

Naremore, James. *On Kubrick*: London: BFI, 2007.

Näripea, Eva. "Medieval Socialist Realism: Representations of Tallinn Old Town in Soviet Estonian Feature Films, 1969–1972," *Koht ja paik /Place and Location: Studies in Environmental Aesthetics and Semiotics*, 4 (2004), Tartu: Estonian Literary Museum, pp. 121–43.

———. "Spojrzenie turysty jako strategiczne narz dzie przedstawienia architektonicznego: starówka talli ska a sowiecki marketing turystyczny w latach sze dziesi tych i siedemdziesi tych XX wieku [Tourist Gaze as a Strategic Device of Architectural Representation: Tallinn Old Town and Soviet Tourism Marketing in the 1960s and 1970s]," *Panoptikum: Film, Media, Sztuka*, 8 (2009), Gdansk: Gdansk University, pp. 108–16.

Neumann, Iver B. *Uses of the Other: "The East" in European Identity Formation*. Manchester: Manchester University Press, 1999.

Nicol, Charles. "Finding the 'Assistant Producer,'" in Charles Nicol and Gennady Barabtarlo (eds.), *A Small Alpine Form: Studies in Nabokov's Short Fiction*. New York: Garland, 1993, pp. 155–65.

Noguiera, Rui. *Melville on Melville*. London: Secker and Warburg, 1971.

Norman, Will. "Is *Ada* World Literature? The Swiss Nabokov and the Postnational Novel," unpublished paper given at the Fourth International Nabokov Conference, St. Petersburg State University, 25 June, 2009.

Orlov, Alexander. *The March of Time: Reminiscences*. London: St. Ermin's Press, 2004.

Paglia, Camille. "Lolita Unclothed," in her *Vamps & Tramps*. London: Viking, 1995.

Pauly, Rebecca M. "Impossible Dreams: *Mademoiselle* (1966) and *The Sailor from Gibraltar* (1967)," in James M. Welsh and John C. Tibbetts (eds), *The Cinema of Tony Richardson: Essays and Interviews*. New York: State University of New York Press, 1999, pp. 141–60.

Pifer, Ellen. *Nabokov and the Novel*. Cambridge, MA: Harvard University Press, 1980.

———. "*Lolita*," in Vladimir E. Alexandrov (ed.), *The Garland Companion to Vladimir Nabokov*. New York and London: Garland, 1995, pp. 305–21.

———. "Nabokov's Novel Offspring: Lolita and Her Kin," in Ellen Pifer (ed.), *Lolita: A Casebook*. Oxford: Oxford University Press, 2003, pp. 83–109.

———. "The *Lolita* Phenomenon from Paris to Tehran," in Julian W. Connolly (ed.), *The Cambridge Companion to Nabokov*. Cambridge: Cambridge University Press, 2005, pp. 185–99.

Poole, Steven. "The Nabokov Gambit," *The Guardian*, 25/08 (2000), p. 8.

Proffer, Carl R. *Keys to Lolita*. Bloomington: Indiana University Press, 1968a.

———. "From *Otchaianie* to *Despair*," *Slavic Review* (New York), 27 (1968b), pp. 258–67.

Pushkin, Alexander. "'The Shot,'" in his *The Queen of Spades and Other Stories*, trans. from the Russian by T. Keane. New York: Dover, 1994, pp. 43–53.

Radgowski, Michał. "Miłe wakacyjne rozrywki," *Polityka*, 30 (1973), p. 18.

Rampton, David. *Vladimir Nabokov: A Critical Study of the Novels*. Cambridge: Cambridge University Press, 1984.

Rancière, Jacques. "Godard, Hitchcock, and the Cinematographic Image," in Michael Temple, James S. Williams and Michael Witt (eds.), *For Ever Godard*. London: Black Dog, 2007, pp. 214–31.

Rennert, Hal F. "Literary Revenge: Nabokov's 'Mademoiselle O' and Kleist's 'Die Marquise von O,'" *Germano-Slavika*, 4 (1984), pp. 331–37.

Richardson, Tony. *Long Distance Runner: A Memoir*. London: Faber and Faber, 1993.

Rivers, J. E. "Alone in the Void: 'Mademoiselle O,'" in Steven G. Kellman and Irving Malin (eds.), *Torpid Smoke: The Stories of Vladimir Nabokov*. Amsterdam: Rodopi, 2000, pp. 85–131.

Robinson, David. "Fassbinder after *Despair*," *Sight and Sound*, 4 (1977), pp. 216–17.

Rohmer, Eric. "The Old and the New: Rohmer in Interview with Jean-Claude Biette, Jacques Bontemps, Jean-Louis Comolli (extracts)," in Jim Hillier (ed.), *Cahiers du Cinéma, Vol. 2*. London: Routledge and Kegan Paul, 1986, pp. 84–94.

Rondi, Gian Luigi. "'Madness and Terrorism':

Conversations with Gian Luigi Rondi about *Despair* and *The Third Generation*," in Michael Töteberg and Leo A. Lensing (eds.), *Rainer Werner Fassbinder. the Anarchy of Imagination: Interviews, Essays, Notes*. Baltimore and London: The Johns Hopkins University Press, 1978/79 (1992), pp. 124–27.

Rorty, Richard. "The Barber of Kasbeam," in his *Contingency, Irony, and Solidarity*. Cambridge: Cambridge University Press, 1989, pp. 141–68.

Rosenbaum, Jonathan. "Godard in the Nineties: An Interview, Argument and Scrapbook," *Film Comment*, 5 (Sept.-Oct.), 1998, pp. 52–60.

———. "Bringing Godard Back Home," in David Sterritt (ed.), *Jean-Luc Godard: Interviews*. Jackson: University Press of Mississippi, 1980 (1998), pp. 100–106.

Rosenfeld, Claire. "*Despair* and the Lust for Immortality," in L. S. Dembo (ed.), *Nabokov: The Man and His Work*. Madison: University of Wisconsin Press, 1967, pp. 66–84.

Ruppert, Peter. "Fassbinder's *Despair*: Hermann Hermann through the Looking Glass," *Post-Script: Essay in Film and the Humanities*, 2 (1984), pp. 48–64.

Said, Edward W. "Orientalism Reconsidered," *Cultural Critique*, Fall 1985, pp. 89–107.

———. *Orientalism*. London: Penguin, 1978 (2003).

Saniewski, Wiesław. "Najgorszy film Skolimowskiego," *Wiadomośa*, 24 (1973), p. 12.

Sarris, Andrew. "Movie Journal," *The Village Voice*, July 5, 1962, pp. 7 and 11.

Schilling, Derek. *Eric Rohmer*. Manchester: Manchester University Press, 2007.

Schrader, Paul. "*Laughter in the Dark*," *Film Quarterly*, 3 (1970), pp. 45–48.

Scott, A. O. "*The Luzhin Defence* (2000)," *The New York Times*, 20/04 (2001), http://movies.nytimes.com/movie/review?res=9901E1DD153BF933A15757C0A9679C8B63, accessed 30/08/2008.

Sharpe, Tony. *Vladimir Nabokov*. London: Edward Arnold, 1991.

Sheen, Erica. "Introduction," in Robert Giddings and Erica Sheen (eds.), *The Classic Novel: From Page to Screen*. Manchester: Manchester University Press, 2000, pp. 1–13.

Shohat, Ella. "Gender and Culture of Empire: Toward a Feminist Ethnography of the Cinema," in Matthew Bernstein and Gaylyn Studlar (eds.), *Visions of the East: Orientalism in Film*. London: I. B. Tauris, 1997, pp. 19–66.

Short, Robert (1997). "Magritte and the Cinema," in Silvano Levy (ed.), *Surrealism: Surrealist Visuality*. Edinburgh: Keele University Press, 1997, pp. 95–108.

Shrayer, Maxim D. "Mapping Narrative Space in Nabokov's Short Fiction," *Slavonic and East European Review*, 4 (1997), pp. 624–41.

Silverman, Kaja, and Harun Farocki. *Speaking About Godard*. New York: New York University Press, 1998.

Smith, Alison (2007). "The Auteur as Star: Jean-Luc Godard," in John Gaffney and Diana Holmes (eds.), *Stardom in Postwar France*. Oxford: Berghahn, 2007, pp. 126–51.

Smith, Gavin. "Jean-Luc Godard," in David Sterritt (ed.), *Jean-Luc Godard: Interviews*. Jackson: University Press of Mississippi, 1996 (1998), pp. 179–93.

Sontag, Susan. "Notes on Camp," in her *Against Interpretation*. London: Vintage, 1965 (1994), pp. 275–92.

———. "One Culture and the New Sensibility," in her *Against Interpretation*. London: Vintage, 1965 (1994), pp. 293–304.

Stam, Robert (2000). "Beyond Fidelity: The Dialogics of Adaptation," in James Naremore (ed.), *Film Adaptation*. London: The Athlone Press, 2000, pp. 54–76.

———. *Literature Through Film: Realism, Magic, and the Art of Adaptation*. Oxford: Blackwell, 2005.

———. "Film and Narration: Two Versions of *Lolita*," in R. Barton Palmer (ed.), *Twentieth-Century American Fiction on Screen*. Cambridge: Cambridge University Press, 2007, pp. 106–26.

Steegmuller, Francis. *Cocteau: A Biography, Second Edition*. Boston: Godine, 1986.

Sterritt, David. "Ideas, Not Plots, Inspire Jean-Luc Godard," in David Sterritt (ed.), *Jean-Luc Godard: Interviews*. Jackson: University Press of Mississippi, 1994 (1998), pp. 175–78.

Stone, Alan A. "Selling (Out) Nabokov," *Boston Review*, October/November 1998, http://bostonreview.net/BR23.5/Stone.html, accessed 17/11/2009.

———. "No Defence," *Boston Review*, Summer 2001, http://bostonreview.net/BR26.3/stone.html, accessed 18/01/2009.

Straumann, Barbara. *Figurations of Exile in Hitchcock and Nabokov*. Edinburgh: Edinburgh University Press, 2008.
Strick, Philip. "*Laughter in the Dark*," *Monthly Film Bulletin*, September 1969, pp. 188–9.
Stringer-Hye, Suellen. "An Interview with Stephen Schiff," *Zembla*, 1996, http://www.libraries.psu.edu/nabokov/foriles.htm, accessed 16/01/2009.
———. "Vladimir Nabokov and Popular Culture," in David H. J. Larmour (ed.), *Discourse and Ideology in Nabokov's Prose*. London: Routledge, 2002, pp. 150–9.
Stuart, Dabney. "*Laughter in the Dark*: Dimensions of Parody," in Alfred Appel, Jr., and Charles Newman (eds.), *Nabokov: Criticism, Reminiscences, Translations and Tributes*. London: Weidenfeld and Nicolson, 1971, pp. 72–95.
———. *Nabokov: The Dimensions of Parody*. Baton Rouge and London: Louisiana State University Press, 1978.
Taubman, Jane. *Kira Muratova*. London: I. B. Tauris, 2005.
Thompson, Kristin. "Godard's Unknown Country: *Sauve qui peut (la vie)*," in her *Breaking the Glass Armor: Neoformalist Film Analysis*. Princeton: Princeton University Press, 1988, pp. 263–88.
Thomsen, Christian Braad. "Five Interviews with Fassbinder," in Tony Rayns (ed.), *Fassbinder*. London: BFI, 1980.
———. *Fassbinder: The Life and Work of a Provocative Genius*. London: Faber and Faber, 1997.
Toffler, Alvin. *The Third Wave*. London: Collins, 1980.
Toker, Leona. *Nabokov: The Mystery of Literary Structures*. Ithaca, NY: Cornell University Press, 1989.
———. "Nabokov and Bergson," in Vladimir E. Alexandrov (ed.), *The Garland Companion to Vladimir Nabokov*. New York and London: Garland, 1995, pp. 367–73.
———. "Nabokov's Worldview," in Julian W. Connolly (ed.), *The Cambridge Companion to Nabokov*. Cambridge: Cambridge University Press, 2005, pp. 232–47.
Tortajada, Maria. "From Libertinage to Eric Rohmer: Transcending 'Adaptation,'" in Robert Stam and Alessandra Raengo (eds.), *A Companion to Literature and Film*. Oxford: Blackwell, 2004, pp. 343–57.
Tracz, Tamara. "*Triple Agent*: Portrait of the Unknowable Other, Reflection of the Unknowable Self," *Senses of Cinema*, 2005, http://archive.sensesofcinema.com/contents/05/34/triple_agent.html, accessed 18/07/2009.
Trilling, Lionel. "The Last Lover: Vladimir Nabokov's *Lolita*," *Encounter*, October 1958, pp. 9–19.
Troubetzkoy, Wladimir. "Vladimir Nabokov's *Despair*: The Reader as 'April's Fool,'" *Cycnos*, 2 (1995), pp. 55–62.
Truffaut, François. *Hitchcock, Revised Edition*. New York: Simon and Schuster, 1985.
Turkevich Naumann, Marina. *Blue Evenings in Berlin: Nabokov's Short Stories of the 1920s*. New York: New York University Press, 1978.
Tuumalu, Tiit. "Valentin Kuik kirjutab filme, vahel j uab m ni ekraanile ka [Valentin Kuik Writes Films, and Sometimes Some of Them Make Their Way to the Screen: An Interview with Valentin Kuik]," *Postimees*, October 6, 2005, http://www.postimees.ee/061005/esileht/kultuur/179230.php, accessed 30/07/2008.
Unwin, Tim. "Place, Territory, and National Identity in Estonia," in Guntram H. Herb and David H. Kaplan (eds.), *Nested Identities: Nationalism, Territory, and Scale*. Lanham, MD: Rowman and Littlefield, 1999, pp. 151–73.
Updike, John. "John Updike in *New Republic*," in Normal Page (ed.), *Nabokov: The Critical Heritage*. London: Routledge and Kegan Paul, 1982, pp. 154–8.
———. "Afterword" to Vladimir Nabokov, *The Luzhin Defense*. London: Penguin, 2000, pp. 257–66.
Uszyński, Jerzy. "Ousiderzy są zmęczeni?" *Kino*, 11 (1989), pp. 4–7.
———. "Jerzy Skolimowski o sobie: Całe życie jak na dłoni," *Film na świecie*, 379 (1990), pp. 3–47.
Vidal, Belén. "Playing in a Minor Key: The Literary Past Through the Feminist Imagination," in Mireia Aragay (ed.), *Books in Motion: Adaptation, Intertextuality, Authorship*. Amsterdam: Rodopi, 2005, pp. 263–85.
Vincendeau, Ginette. "Painting from Nature," *Sight and Sound*, November 2004, 38–9.
Von Kleist, Heinrich (2004). "The Marquise of O–," in his *The Marquise of O– and Other Stories*. London: Penguin, 2004, pp. 68–113.
Wagner, Geoffrey. *The Novel and Cinema*. London: Tantivy Press, 1975.
Walker, Alexander. *The Celluloid Sacrifice: Aspects of Sex in the Movies*. London: Michael Joseph, 1966.

_____. *Stanley Kubrick Directs*. London: Abacus, 1972.
Watson, Wallace. "The Bitter Tears of RWF," *Sight and Sound*, 3 (1992), pp. 24–9.
Waugh, Patricia. *Feminine Fictions: Revisiting the Postmodern*. London: Routledge, 1989.
Weil, Simone. *Gravity and Grace*, trans. from French by Emma Craufurd. London: Routledge, 1972.
Welsh, James M., and John C. Tibbetts (eds.). *The Cinema of Tony Richardson: Essays and Interviews*. New York: State University of New York Press, 1999.
Williams, Alan. "Godard's Use of Sound," *Camera Obscura: A Journal of Feminism and Film Theory*, 8-9-10 (1982), pp. 193–208.
_____. "*Pierrot* in Context(s)," in David Wills (ed.), *Jean-Luc Godard's Pierrot le fou*. Cambridge: Cambridge University Press, 2000, pp. 43–63.
Winn, Marie. *Children Without Childhood*. New York: Pantheon, 1983.
Witt, Michael. "The Death(s) of Cinema According to Godard," *Screen*, 3 (Autumn 1999), pp. 331–46.
_____. "Qu'était-ce le cinema, Jean-Luc Godard: An Analysis of the Cinema(s) at Work in and Around Godard's *Histoire(s) du Cinéma*," in Elizabeth Ezra and Susan Harris (eds.), *France in Focus: Cinema and National Identity*. Oxford: Berg, 2000, pp. 23–41.

Wood, Michael (1994). *The Magician's Doubts: Nabokov and the Risks of Fiction*. London: Chatto and Windus, 1994.
Woolf, Virginia. *Mrs. Dalloway*. London: Penguin, 1925 (1996).
Wrathal, John. "*A Summer's Tale/Conte d'ete*," *Sight and Sound*, October 1996, pp. 53–54.
Wright, Alan. "Elizabeth Taylor at Auschwitz: JLG and the Real Object of Montage," in Michael Temple and James S. Williams (eds.), *The Cinema Alone: Essays on the Work of Jean-Luc Godard, 1985–2000*. Amsterdam: Amsterdam University Press, 2000, pp. 51–60.
Wyllie, Barbara. *Nabokov at the Movies*. Jefferson, NC: McFarland, 2003.
_____. "Nabokov and Cinema," in Julian W. Connolly (ed.), *The Cambridge Companion to Nabokov*. Cambridge: Cambridge University Press, 2005, pp. 215–31.
Yakir, Dan. "Polestar," *Film Comment*, November-December 1982, pp. 28–32.
Youngblood, Gene. "Jean-Luc Godard: No Difference Between Life and Cinema," in David Sterritt (ed.), *Jean-Luc Godard: Interviews*. Jackson: University Press of Mississippi, 1968 (1998), pp. 9–49.
Zunshine, Lisa (ed.). *Nabokov at the Limits*. New York and Garland: Garland, 1999.

# Index

À bout de souffle (*Breathless*) 31, 186–187
*Ada or Ardor* 1, 2, 126, 185, 195, 216, 219
Adair, Gilbert 192, 219
*An Affair of Honor* 4, 88, 125–142, 159, 162–163, 212, 217, 219
*Age of Consent* 65
Albee, Edward 14
Albinoni, Tomaso 82
Alexandrov, Vladimir E. 143, 203, 207, 219
*Alice in Wonderland* 196
*All the Right Noises* 65
Allen, Woody 21
Almodóvar, Pedro 54
*American Beauty* 45–46
Amis, Martin 16–17, 219
*L'Amour l'après-midi* (*Love in the Afternoon*) 173–174
*Les Amours d'Astrée et de Céladon* (*Romance of Astrea and Celadon*) 171–172
Andrew, Dudley 4, 219
*L'Anglaise et le duc* (*The Lady and the Duke*) 171
*Angst essen Seele auf* (*Fear Eats the Soul*) 92
*Ania v strane chudes* 196
*Anna Karenina* 114, 168, 181, 216
*L'Année dernière à Marienbad* (*Last Year in Marienbad*) 103
*The Annotated Lolita* 17, 215, 219
*Antonia* (*Antonia's Line*) 148, 158
*Antonia's Line* (*Antonia*) 148, 158
Antonioni, Michelangelo 57, 63, 103
Appel, Alfred, Jr. 4, 16–18, 21, 25–26, 30, 33, 47, 51–52, 54, 68, 89, 169–170, 215–216, 218–219
Aragay, Mireya 6, 215
Arendt, Hannah 171, 219
Artaud, Antonin 101
Ashby, Hal 30
Asher, Jane 65
"The Assistant Producer" 163, 165–180, 219
Austen, Jane 5, 147, 216
*Autumn Ball* (*Sügisball*) 132
*The Aviator's Wife* (*La Femme de l'aviateur*) 173

Bader, Julia 15, 219

Bailey, Geoffrey 167, 169, 171, 218–219
Bainbridge, Caroline 148, 219
Bakhtin, Mikhail 6, 108, 219
Balabanov, Aleksei 69, 217
*Bande à part* 188
Barabtarlo, Gennady 207, 219
Bardot, Brigitte 188–189
*Bariera* (*Barrier*) 76
*Barrier* (*Bariera*) 76
Barry, John 14
*Barry Lyndon* 24
Barthes, Roland 6
*Das Bastardzeichen* (*Bend Sinister*) (film) 91, 195, 202
Bataille, Georges 80
Baudrillard, Jean 21
Bauman, Zygmunt 80, 219–220
Beaujour, Elizabeth Klosty 193–195, 197–198, 220
Beethoven, Ludwig van 54
*Being There* 30
Bellmer, Hans 79–80
Belmondo, Jean-Paul 187–188
Bely, Andrei 200
*Bend Sinister* (book) 91, 195, 202, 207, 219
Bergman, Ingmar 103
Bergson, Henri 207
Berry, Peter 147, 212
Bertolucci, Bernardo 41
Blackwelder, Bob 147, 157, 220
Blackwell, Stephen S. 10–11, 186, 220
*Bleak House* 181
*Blowup* 57, 63–64
Bogarde, Dirk 92, 98, 102, 212
Bond, Edward 57, 63, 211
Borowczyk, Walerian 34
Borowski, Tadeusz 17
Bourdieu, Pierre 110, 115, 220
Bovkis, A. 148, 220
Bowlby, Rachel 17, 220
Boyd, Brian 15, 18, 20, 105, 118, 166, 169–171, 185–186, 215–216, 220
*Bram Stoker's Dracula* 37
Brand, Dana 16, 20, 191, 220
Brass, Tinto 34

229

*Breaking the Waves* 152
*Breathless* (*À bout de souffle*) 31, 186–187
Breton, André 80
*British Sounds* 194
Brodsky, Anna 16, 220
Brody, Richard 199, 220
*The Brothers Karamazov* 87–88
Buhks, Nora 72, 83, 220
Burdick, Dolores M. 96, 102–103, 220
Burns, Dan 35, 220
Burton, Richard 27
Butler, Alison 147, 220
Butler, Diana 19–20, 215, 220

Callahan, Vicki 218, 220
*Camera Obscura* 51
Cammell, Donald 103
Campion, Jane 147
*Carmen* 3, 192, 215
*Casablanca* 35
Cavani, Liliana 98
Cerisuelo, Marc 185, 220
Chamberlin, Carloss James 89, 220
Chatman, Seymour 4, 220
Chekhov, Anton 126, 141
Chernyshevski, Nikolay 199
Chiancio, Ralph A. 72, 123, 220
*La Chinoise* 22
Chopin, Frédéric 82
*Citizen Kane* 30
Clair, Cyrielle 173, 213
Clancy, Laurie 73, 220
Clarke, Kenneth 58
Clayton, Jack 19
Clayton, Sue 147
*A Clockwork Orange* 24, 37
*Closely Observed Trains* (*Ostře sledované vlaky*) 138
*Clueless* 216
Cocteau, Jean 1
Coen brothers 42
*Colas Breugnon* 196
*La Collectionneuse* (*The Collector*) 175
*The Collector* (*La Collectionneuse*) 175
Collins, Emily 16–17, 155, 191, 220
*Conclusive Evidence* 104, 196
Connolly, Julian W. 11, 54, 59, 70–71, 73, 85, 196, 220
*The Conspirators* 171, 218–219
*Contempt* (*Le Mépris*) 188–189
Cooper, James Fenimore 215
Corliss, Richard 4, 23, 25–26, 31, 36–38, 45, 215, 220
Corneille, Pierre 110
Cott, Jonathan 181, 221
*Coup for coup* 205
Couturier, Maurice 216–217, 221
*Crime and Punishment* 88, 215
Crisp, C.G. 164, 221
Croce, Arlene 33, 221
Curtiz, Michael 31, 35

*Damage* 41
Daney, Serge 182, 221
Dante 215
*Dar* (*The Gift*) 89, 134, 199, 215, 217
*Darling* 62
Davidson, James A. 3, 181, 221
*Dead Souls* 88, 132, 181
*Dear Bunny, Dear Volodia: The Nabokov-Wilson Letters* 11, 54, 219
*Death in Venice* (*Morte a Venezia*) 98, 103, 160
Debord, Guy 80–81, 221
*Deep End* 65, 75–76, 83
*The Defense* 104
De la Durantaye, Leland 16, 143, 186, 221
De Montvalon, Jean Baptiste 120, 221
*Il deserto rosso* (*Red Desert*) 103
*Despair* 1, 13, 18, 24, 55, 57, 66, 87–103, 112, 170, 175, 212, 219
*Detective* (*Détective*) 190–192, 197, 206
*Détective* (*Detective*) 190–192, 197, 206
*Deux Fois cinquante ans de cinéma français* 199
Devlin, Rachel 16–17, 221
Dick, Leslie 44, 221
Dickens, Charles 5
Didaskalou, Katerina 173, 213
*Un Dimanche à la campagne* (*A Sunday in the Country*) 123
*Dr. Strangelove; or, How I Learned to Stop Worrying and Love the Bomb* 24, 30
Dolinin, Alexander 87–88, 221
*Don Quixote* 181
Donner, Richard 65, 75
Donoghue, Denis 74, 221
Dostoevski, Fyodor 87–88, 215
*The Double* 88
*The Draughtsman's Contract* 66
Dreyer, Carl Theodor 189
Drouot, Jean-Claude 60–61, 63, 211
*Drugie berega* (*Other Shores*) 104, 196
Duras, Marguerite 56

"Easter Rain" 105
*Easy Rider* 31
Eco, Umberto 35, 221
Edmunds, Jeff 72, 78, 221
Edwards, Blake 30
Eelmaa, Taavi, 131–132, 136, 139, 212
*Effi Briest* 92
Egoyan, Atom 54
*8½* 103
*Einladung zur Enthauptung* (*Invitation to a Beheading*) (film) 91
Einsenstein, Sergei 177, 200
El Greco 208
Elley, Derek 179, 221
Elliott, Kamilla 6, 8, 221
Elsaesser, Thomas 89, 93, 96–98, 102–103, 221
*Elvira Madigan* 42
*Emma* 216
*The Enchanter* 29, 41, 190, 207, 215–216, 219

Esslin, Martin 72, 221
Etkind, Alexander 110, 221
*Eugene Onegin* (*Evgeny Onegin*) 9, 10, 88, 126, 196
*Evgeny Onegin* (*Eugene Onegin*) 9, 10, 88, 126, 196
*Eyes Wide Shut* 24

Fanger, Donald 133, 221
Farocki, Harun 197, 208, 225
Fassbinder, Rainer Werner 24, 57, 66, 87–103, 212
*Fatal Attraction* 37
*Fear Eats the Soul* (*Angst essen Seele auf*) 92
Fellini, Federico 21, 103
*La Femme de l'aviateur* (*The Aviator's Wife*) 173
Ferréol, Andréa 92, 97, 212
Field, Andrew 70, 87, 110, 166, 169–170, 217, 221
Finney, Albert 28
"First Love" 104
Fitzgerald, F. Scott 170
*Five Easy Pieces* 31
*Flashdance* 36
Flick, Horst 91
*For Ever Mozart* 183
Forster, E.M. 5
Foster, Hal 80, 221
Foster, John Burt, Jr. 91, 102, 105, 111, 182, 207, 216, 221
Foster, Ludmila A. 73, 221
Foucault, Michel 6, 182
Foulon, Jérôme 104–124, 125, 131, 212
Fox, James 57
Fox, Robin 57
French, Philip 160, 162, 222
*The French Lieutenant's Woman* 38
Freud, Sigmund 148
*Full Metal Jacket* 24

*Le Gai savoir* 195–196
Genet, Jean 56, 93
Gezari, Janet 143, 158, 186, 222
Gide, André 183
*The Gift* (*Dar*) 89, 134, 199, 215, 217, 219
Gilliatt, Penelope 196, 218, 222
Godard, Jean-Luc 3, 7, 22, 31, 47, 54, 60, 62, 81, 103, 181–209, 218
Gogol, Nikolai 71, 132–133, 141
Golan, Menahem 65
Goldbacher, Sandra 217
Goldschmidt, John 113
Gombrich, E.H. 3, 4, 12
"Good Readers and Good Writers" 9, 178, 203
Goodman, Nelson 3, 4, 12
*Goon Show* 33
Gorki, Maxim 202
Gorris, Marleen 143–162, 212
*The Governess* 217

Gow, Gordon 68, 222
*Gravity and Grace* 87
Grayson, Jane 11, 194, 222
Green, Geoffrey 10, 222
Greenaway, Peter 65
Gris, Juan 176
Grossman, Lev 112, 217, 222
Grosz, Elizabeth 216, 222
*Guernica* 176
*Guinevere* 45–46

Haegert, John 26, 39, 222
*Hail Mary* (*Je vous salue Marie*) 197, 208
Hall, Peter 65
Hall, Sheldon 56, 222
Hampshire, Stuart 146, 222,
Hamrit, Jacqueline 110, 222
*Hands Up!* (*Ręce do góry*) 74
Harcourt, Peter 190, 222
Hardy, Thomas 47–48
Harris, James B. 23–24, 26, 211
Hartley, Hal 200
Heckerling, Amy 216
Hengst, Lutz 91
Hentzi, Gary 45, 222
*A Hero of Our Time* 126
*Hilary and Jackie* 158
*Hiroshima mon amour* 31
*Histoire(s) du cinéma* 199, 200
Hitchcock, Alfred 2–3, 23, 26, 83, 150, 171, 179, 181–182, 200, 204
Hitler, Adolf 91, 202
Hockney, David 64
Holbein, Hans 58
Homer 188
Hopper, Dennis 31

*Identification Marks: None* (*Rysopis*) 79, 84
*Indecent Proposal* 36
*The Innocents* 12
*Invitation to a Beheading* 167–168
Irigaray, Luce 148
Irons, Jeremy 36, 38–41
Ivory, James 157

Jackson, Kevin 45, 222
Jahn, Hubertus F. 165–166, 169, 222
James, Henry 19
James, Nick 36, 222
Jameson, Fredric 21, 80, 222
Jannings, Emil 170
*Je vous salue Marie* (*Hail Mary*) 197, 208
Jeffries, Stuart 163, 179, 222
Jenkins, Greg 4, 24, 26, 222
Johnson Barton D. 1, 32, 222
Johnson, Roy 127, 170, 222
Josipovici, Gabriel 16, 215, 222
Joxe, Sandra 114, 212
Joyce, James 29, 182, 200, 215
*Joys of the Middle Age* (*Keskea rõõmud*) 129
*Jules et Jim* 56

# 232　　Index

Kael, Pauline 29–30, 32–33, 222
*Kamera obskura* 51, 196, 216
Karina, Anna 59–63, 188, 211
Karlinsky, Simon 219
Karmitz, Marin 205
Karshan, Thomas 11, 144, 222
Kauffman, Linda 16–17, 222
Keeler, Christine 64
*Keep Your Right Up* (*Soigne ta droite*) 197
Kelly, Grace 26, 38
Kenny, Glenn 186, 222
Kent, 68, 223
Kerouac, Jack 31
*Keskea rõõmud* (*Joys of the Middle Age*) 129
Khodasevich, Vladislav 143, 223
Kimney, John 90–91, 100
*King Lear* 3, 194, 197
*King, Queen, Knave* 2, 4, 22, 24, 55, 67, 70–86, 91, 101, 127, 131, 134, 146, 168, 202, 211, 217–219
Kinski, Nastassja 48
Kitchin, Valeri 160, 223
Kittler, Friedrich A. 19, 223
Koszarski, Richard 24, 223
Krabbé, Tim 160, 162, 223
Kracauer, Siegfried 102, 202, 223
Kubrick, Stanley 3, 9, 12, 13, 21, 23–38, 40–46, 49–50, 56, 59, 66, 162, 181, 188, 211, 216, 218
Kugel, Aleksandr 166
Kuik, Valentin 4, 125–142, 159, 162–163, 212, 217

Lacan, Jacques 148, 215
*The Lady and the Duke* (*L'Anglaise et le duc*) 171, 178
Lang, Fritz 79, 188
Lang, Jack 199
Langella, Ben 42
*The Last Command* 170
*The Last Tycoon* 170
*Last Year in Marienbad* (*L'Année dernière à Marienbad*) 103
*Laughter in the Dark* 2, 4, 9, 11, 16, 51–69, 71–72, 74, 82, 101, 157, 170, 193, 196, 211, 216–219
*Laura* 31
*Lectures on Don Quixote* 181, 219
*Lectures on Literature* 9, 10, 164, 178, 185, 199–203, 216, 219
*Lectures on Russian Literature* 168, 199, 216, 219
Leitch, Thomas 2–3, 23–24, 223
Lenin, Vladimir 182
Leppard, Raymond 65
Lermontov, Mikhail 126, 141
Lerner, Alan Jay 14
Levine, Robert T. 16, 223
Lichfield, Lord 58
LoBrutto, Vincent 3, 34, 223
*Lolita* 1–5, 7, 9, 11, 13–52, 54–55, 66, 69, 79, 82, 87, 100, 113, 159, 161, 167–168, 175, 181, 186–192, 206–207, 211, 216, 218–219
*Lolita: A Screenplay* 21–23, 32
Lollobrigida, Gina 76–78, 84–85, 212, 217
*The Loneliness of the Long Distance Runner* 56–57, 61
Long, Michael 15, 145, 223
*Look at the Harlequins!* 196
*Look Back in Anger* 56
*Look Homeward Angel* 99
Losey, Joseph 98, 103
*Love in the Afternoon* (*L'Amour l'après-midi*) 173–174
*The Loved One* 67–68
Lukash, Ivan 166
*Lurich* 129
Lurich, Georg 129
*Lurjus* (*An Affair of Honor*) 4, 88, 125–142, 159, 162, 212–213, 217
*The Luzhin Defence* 143–162, 213, 217
*The Luzhin Defense* 134, 143–162, 213, 219
Lynch, David 31, 46–47
Lyne, Adrian 13, 23, 30, 36–46, 49–50, 69, 161, 212, 216
Lyon, Sue 25–27, 34, 211

*Ma Nuit chez Maud* (*My Night with Maud*) 173, 179
MacBean, James Roy 205, 223
MacCabe, Colin 183, 223
Mackenzie, John 65
Macnab, Geoffrey 157, 223
*Madame Bovary* 9, 181, 216
Maddox, Lucy 18, 223
*Mademoiselle* 56, 67, 216
*Mademoiselle O* 104–124, 125, 131, 159, 168, 212
Magritte, René 4
Maimik, Andres 130, 223
Malle, Louis 41
Mamet, David 14
Mann, Thomas 98
*Mansfield Park* 217
Marcus, Jane 216, 223
*La Marquise d'O...* (*The Marquise of O...*) 174
*The Marquise of O...* (*La Marquise d'O...*) 174
"The Marquise of O" (*Die Marquise von O*) 106, 111
"Die Marquise von O" (*The Marquise of O*) 106, 111
*Mary* (*Maschenka*) 113, 134, 217
*Mary Shelley's Frankenstein* 37
*Maschenka* (*Mary*) 113, 134, 217
Mason, James 25, 27–28, 31, 36, 38, 40–41, 182, 211
Maugham, William Somerset 160
Mazierska, Ewa 6, 134, 223
McCarthy, Joseph 204
McKinney Devin 36, 42, 223
Meier, Armin 93
Melville, Jean-Pierre 186

Mendes, Sam 4
*Las Meninas* 192
Menzel, Jiří 138
*Le Mépris* (*Contempt*) 188–189
Merchant, Ismail 157
Mérimée, Prosper 215
*Metropolis* 79
Metz, Christian 52, 223
Meyer, Priscilla 125, 223
Miauton, Cécile 105
*Mildred Pierce* 31
Milne, Tom 78, 86, 188, 205, 223–224
Miller, Evgenii 165, 171, 175, 178
Minachkine, Anton 123, 212
*Mr. Klein* 103
Mizruchi, Susan 16, 223
*Moby Dick* 26
Moll, Giorgia 189
Monroe, Marilyn 27
Monteverdi, Claudio 65
*Moonlighting* 41
Moore, Henry 57
Moore, Tony 15, 223
More, Thomas 57
Moreau, Jeanne 56, 216
Morricone, Ennio 42, 212
Morrisey, Kim 13, 18, 159, 223
*Morte a Venezia* (*Death in Venice*) 98, 103, 160
Mosk 86, 223
Moulder-Brown, Joh 76–77, 84–85, 212
Moynahan, Julian 2, 16, 54, 223
*Mrs. Dalloway* 148–149, 151, 154, 157, 160
Munk, Andrzej 17, 200
Muratova, Kira 217
Murphy, Robert 56, 65, 223
Müür, Jüri 130
*My Night with Maud* (*Ma Nuit chez Maud*) 173, 179

Nabokov, Dmitri 69, 128, 158, 224
Nabokov, Elena 110, 114–118, 121
Nabokov, Sergei 112–121, 217
Nabokov, Véra 158
Nafisi, Azar, 13, 224
Nahyr, Maïté 116, 212
Narboni, Jean 188, 224
Naremore, James 4, 26, 29, 33, 44, 224
Näripea, Eva 132, 135, 217, 224
Neumann, Iver B., 106, 224
Nicol, Charles 169–171, 224
*The Night Porter* (*Il portiere di notte*) 98
Nikolai I 165
*Nikolka Persik* 196
*9½ Weeks* 36–37
Niven, David 76–78, 212
Nogueira, Rui 186, 224
Norman, Will 10, 185, 218, 220–222, 224
*The Nose* 71
*Notes from the Underground* 88
*Nouvelle Vague* 183, 208
Nyman, Michael 66

*Odd Man Out* 31
*Odyssey* 188
O'Hara, Gerry 65
Olivier, Laurence 27
*The Omen* 75
*On the Road* 31
*One Brief Summer* 65
"Orache" 126
*The Original of Laura: A Novel in Fragments* 206, 219
*The Origins of Totalitarianism* 171
Orlov, Alexander, 165–166, 169, 224
*Ostře sledované vlaky* (*Closely Observed Trains*) 138
*Otchayanie* (*Despair*) (book) 87
*Other Shores* (*Drugie berega*) 104, 196
Õunpuu, Veiko 132
*The Oval Portrait* 189

Paglia, Camille 18, 20, 42, 215, 224
Palance, Jack 189
*Pale Fire* 87, 167, 217, 219
Parain, Brice 189
*Pasazerka* (*Passenger*) 17, 200
Pasolini, Pier Paolo 176
*Passenger* (*Pasazerka*) 17, 200
*Passion* 185, 193, 196–197, 208
*La Passion de Jeanne d'Arc* (*The Passion of Joan of Arc*) 189
*The Passion of Joan of Arc* (*La Passion de Jeanne d'Arc*) 189
Pasternak, Boris 196, 202
*Pauline à la plage* (*Pauline at the Beach*) 175
*Pauline at the Beach* (*Pauline à la plage*) 175
Pauly, Rebecca M. 56, 224
Pera, Pia 18–19
*Performance* 64–65, 103
*Persona* 103
Peter the Great 112
*Petersburg* 200
Petrarch 215
"Philistines and Philistinism" 168
Phillips, Siân 59, 211
Picasso, Pablo 176–177
*Pierrot le fou* 22, 62, 188–189, 192, 194
Pifer, Ellen 13–14, 16, 30, 89, 215, 224
*Pink Panther* 30
Pinter, Harold 14, 19
Plevitskaya, Nadezhda 165–167, 169, 171–172, 175, 180
Plevitsky, Edmond 166
Poe, Edgar Allan 22, 28, 31, 188–189, 192, 215
*Poems for Men Who Dream of Lolita* 18, 159
Polanski, Roman 6, 47–49, 216
*Il portiere di notte* (*The Night Porter*) 98
*A Portrait of the Artist as a Young Man* 28
Potter, Sally 147
Powell, Michael 65
Preminger, Otto 31, 199
*Prénom Carmen* 185, 190, 192, 197, 208
*The Prince and the Showgirl* 27

"Problems of Translation: 'Onegin' in English" 10, 219
Proffer, Carl R. 16, 52, 99–100, 215, 224
Profumo, John 64
Proust, Marcel 10, 112, 116, 200, 215–216
*Psycho* 83
*Püha Tõnu kiusamine* (*The Temptation of St. Tony*) 132
Pushkin, Alexander 126, 141, 196, 217, 224
Puustusmaa, Andrus 136, 212, 217
*Pygmalion* 27–28

*Querelle* 93

Rachmaninoff, Sergei 166
Racine, Jean 109–110, 196
Radgowski, Michał 86, 224
Rafelson, Bob 31
Rampton, David 14, 54, 126, 224
Rancière, Jacques 200
Rascaroli, Laura 134, 223
*Reading Lolita in Tehran* 13
*The Real Life of Sebastian Knight* 104
*Rear Window* 38, 150
*Red Desert* (*Il Deserto rosso*) 103
Redgrave, Vanessa 216
Reed, Carol 31
*Reigi õpetaja* (*Reigi's Teacher*) 130
*Reigi's Teacher* (*Reigi õpetaja*) 130
Reinold, Elina 131, 137, 212
Reisz, Karel 38
Rembrandt 208
*The Remembrance of Things Past* 112, 200, 215–216
Renko, Serge 213
Rennert, Hal F. 106–107, 111, 224
Renoir, Jean 199
Renoir, Pierre-Auguste 188
Resnais, Alan 31, 103
*Ręce do góry* (*Hands Up!*) 74
Richardson, Tony 9, 51, 56–69, 71, 75, 82, 147, 157, 211, 216, 224
Riddle, Nelson 31, 211
Rivers, J.E. 104–105, 108, 109, 111, 117, 217, 224
Robinson, David 91, 224
Roeg, Nicolas 103
Rohmer, Eric 7, 163–180, 213, 218, 224
*Roman* 49
*Romance of Astrea and Celadon* (*Les Amours d'Astrée et de Céladon*) 171–172
Rondi, Gian Luigi 92, 224
*A Room with a View* 157
Rorty, Richard 186, 225
Rosenbaum, Jonathan 184, 203, 225
Rosenfeld, Claire 88, 90, 98, 225
Rossellini, Roberto 199
Rozema, Patricia 147, 217
Ruppert, Peter 93–95, 101–102, 225
*Rysopis* (*Identification Marks: None*) 79, 84

Said, Edward 106–107, 225

*The Sailor from Gibraltar* 56, 216
Saniewski, Wiesław 86, 225
Sarris, Andrew 33, 225
Sartre, Jean-Paul 202
*Sauve qui peut (la vie)* 186, 190–191, 194, 198, 206
*Scénario de Sauve qui peut (la vie)* 186, 197
*Scénario du film Passion* 197, 208
"Scenes from the Life of a Double Monster" 88
Schiff, Stephen 30, 36–37, 43, 212
Schilling, Derek 164, 172, 178–179, 225
Schlesinger, John 62
Schlöndorff, Volker 41
Schrader, Paul 68, 225
Scott, A.O. 160, 225
Scott, Ridley 36
Scott, Tony 36
Seberg, Jean 187
Sellers, Peter 30, 32, 43, 211
Seltzer, David 75, 211
*The Servant* 98
Shakespeare, William 5, 99, 216
Shaliapin, Fëdor 166
Sharpe, Tony 15, 19, 21, 225
Shaw, Bernard 27–28
Shaw, David 75, 211
Sheen, Erica 6, 225
*The Shining* 24
Shohat, Ella 107, 225
Short, Robert 4, 225
*The Shot* 126, 138
Shrayer, Maxim D. 163–164, 225
"Signs and Symbols" 144
Silverman, Kaja 197, 208, 225
*Single Combat* 126
Skoblin, Nikolai 165–167, 171–172, 178, 180
Skolimowski, Jerzy 4, 6, 22, 24, 41, 65, 67, 70–86, 91, 147, 211, 217
Smith, Alison 185, 225
Smith, Gavin 184, 196, 198, 200, 225
*Soigne ta droite* (*Keep Your Right Up*) 197
Sontag, Susan 98, 199, 225
*Spartacus* 24, 30
*Speak, Memory: An Autobiography Revisited* 72, 104, 106–108, 111–114, 117–120, 122, 183, 196, 201, 207, 209, 219
Stalin, Joseph 177, 204
Stam, Robert 4, 5, 14, 19, 21, 28, 31–32, 42, 44–45, 225
*Stealing Beauty* 41
Steegmuller, Francis 1, 225
Sterritt, David 200, 203, 206, 225
Stewart, James 150
Stone, Alan A. 36, 44–45, 161, 225
Stoppard, Tom 91, 102, 212
Straumann, Barbara 3, 181, 226
Strick, Philip 58, 60, 62, 67–68, 226
Stringer-Hye, Suellen 3, 30–31, 37, 43, 181, 226
*Strong Opinions* 1, 9, 11, 18, 20, 43, 67, 89, 164–165, 182–184, 187, 191, 197, 200, 204–206, 219

Stuart, Dabney 4, 51–52, 226
Sturges, Preston 32
*Sügisball (Autumn Ball)* 132
*A Sunday in the Country (Un Dimanche à la campagne)* 123
*Suspicion* 179
Swain, Dominique 37–39, 44
*Swann in Love* 41
*Swann's Way* 10
Syberberg, Hans-Jürgen 91

Taubman, Jane 217, 226
Tavernier, Bertrand 123
*Tess* 47–49, 216
Thompson, Kristin 186, 226
Thomsen, Christian Braad 91–93, 226
*Three into Two Won't Go* 65
Tibbetts, John C. 216, 227
Toffler, Alvin 80, 226
Toker, Leona 52, 54, 71–72, 74, 144–146, 162, 202–203, 206–207, 216, 226
Tolstoy, Lev 62, 114, 168
*Tom Jones* 56
Tortajada, Maria 218, 226
*Tout va bien* 205
Tracz, Tamara 179, 226
Trilling, Lionel 16, 37, 226
*Triple Agent* 7, 163–180, 213
Troubetzkoy, Wladimir 91, 100, 226
Truffaut, François 3, 56, 184, 199, 226
Tucker, Anan, 158
Turkevich Naumann, Marina 127–128, 217, 226
*The Turn of the Screw* 19
Turturro, John 152, 156, 158–160, 213
Tuumalu, Tiit 128, 226
*2001: A Space Odyssey* 37
*Twin Peaks* 46–47
*Twin Peaks: Fire Walk with Me* 46–47
*Twinky* 65

Ulfsak, Lembit 129
*Ulysses* 163, 200, 215
Unwin, Tim 133, 226
Updike, John 145–146, 152–153, 226
Uszyński, Jerzy 74–75, 86, 226

Valéry, Paul 183
van Gogh, Vincent 101
Velázquez, Diego 192

*Veronica Voss* 102
Vertov, Dziga 177
Vesely, Hubert 91
Vidal, Belén 147, 162, 217, 226
Vincendeau, Ginette 172, 177, 226
Visconti, Luchino 98, 103, 160
*Vivre sa vie* 62, 188, 216
von Kleist, Heinrich 106–107, 120, 174, 183, 226
von Sternberg, Josef 170
von Trier, Lars 158

Wagner, Geoffrey 7, 226
Walker, Alexander 25–26, 216, 226
*Walkover (Walkower)* 84
*Walkower (Walkover)* 84
Watson, Emily 150, 156, 158–160, 213
Watson, Wallace 93, 227
Waugh, Evelyn 160
Waugh, Patricia 149, 227
Weil, Simone 87, 227
Wells, Audrey 45
Welsh, James M. 216, 227
*What's Good for the Goose* 65
White, Duncan 10, 220–222
Wicki, Bernhard 92, 212
Widerberg, Bo 42
Williams, Alan 194, 198, 227
Williamson, Nicol 58–59, 61, 63, 211
Willingham, Calder 24
Wilson, Edmund 54
Wilson, Stuart 156, 213
Winn, Marie 37, 227
Winters, Shelley 211
Wisdom, Norman 65
Witt, Michael 103, 203, 227
Wolfe, Thomas 99
Wood, Michael 113, 184, 194, 227
Woolf, Virginia 148–149, 227
Wrathal, John 164, 227
Wright, Alan 201, 227
Wyllie, Barbara 4, 227

Yakir, Dan 74, 227
Youngblood, Gene 204

Zola, Émile 202
Zunshine, Lisa 5, 227
Zürn, Unica 101

www.ingramcontent.com/pod-product-compliance
Lightning Source LLC
Chambersburg PA
CBHW051220300426
44116CB00006B/649